THE HEART & SOUL OF EFT and Beyond…

Phillip Mountrose and Jane Mountrose

Holistic Communications
Arroyo Grande, California

Published by: Holistic Communications
                  P.O. Box 279
                  Arroyo Grande, CA 93421-0279 USA
                  E-mail: joy@gettingthru.org

For information about special discounts for bulk purchases, please contact the publisher.

ISBN: 0-9700289-6-2

Mountrose, Phillip.
The heart & soul of EFT and Beyond: a soulful exploration of the emotional freedom techniques and holistic healing / Phillip Mountrose and Jane Mountrose – 1st ed.
p. cm
Includes biographical references and index.
ISBN 0-9700289-6-2
1. Self-actualization (Psychology). 2. Mind and body. 3. Emotions.
I. Mountrose, Jane. II. Title.
2006

Acknowledgments

This book is about achieving genuine emotional freedom. We have been fortunate to meet many wonderful and talented people who have contributed to our understanding. They have helped us in innumerable ways as we have moved forward on our own journeys of self-discovery, and in the development of the techniques we use in our work helping others.

A book on EFT would not be complete without thanking Gary Craig and Adrienne Fowlie for developing the Emotional Freedom Techniques and making them so readily available to others. Through his website (www.emofree.com) and e-mail forum, Gary Craig continues to provide invaluable updates on the use of these techniques.

We also want to thank the eleven EFT experts who contributed to this volume for their efforts, and the many professional and lay people who are developing EFT and related energy techniques around the world.

In addition, we thank Sharon Williamson for her input in the writing of this book. Also, we would like to add our appreciation to all the people who, through classes and personal consultations, have provided examples for this book and helped us to refine our use of the techniques. They have provided encouragement and invaluable support.

Publisher's Disclaimer

The Emotional Freedom Techniques (EFT), Spiritual Kinesiology (SK), the Getting Thru Techniques (GTT), and the other methods described in this book have helped many people to make positive changes in their lives, but there is no guarantee they will work for you. We do not recommend substituting these techniques for the professional services of a doctor, psychologist or psychiatrist. Please consult your medical health professionals regarding their use.

EFT, SK, and GTT are self-help and self-healing techniques, and you are in control of their use. As such, you have sole responsibility when you use them. If you do not wish to be bound by this disclaimer, you may return this book with proof of purchase to the publisher for a full refund.

Table of Contents

FOREWORD BY PHILIP H. FRIEDMAN, PH.D. xi

INTRODUCTION 1

PART 1
THE ESSENCE OF EFT

CHAPTER ONE 7
The Evolution of EFT

    THE EVOLUTION OF EFT 9
    EFT RESEARCH 12
    THE JOURNEY OF SELF-DISCOVERY 14
    TAKING CONTROL OF YOUR LIFE 15

CHAPTER TWO 19
EFT as a Holistic Healing Tool

    A HOLISTIC APPROACH 20
    THE REALMS OF HOLISTIC HEALING 22
    THE FOUR PARTS OF THIS BOOK 24
    MORE RESOURCES 28

CHAPTER THREE 31
The EFT Tapping Sequences

    EXAMPLE: HELPING HER FOR HER OWN GOOD! 32
    GETTING STARTED 33

THE SHORT SEQUENCE.. 34
THE FLOOR–TO-CEILING EYE ROLL 46
THE COMPLETE SEQUENCE.. 47
EXPERIMENTING WITH THE TAPPING SEQUENCES.................... 54

CHAPTER FOUR 55
Supercharging Your Results

10 SIMPLE TIPS.. 56
WHEN EFT IS NOT WORKING, THE MAGIC QUESTION 64
THE HEALTHY EXPRESSION OF EMOTIONS............................... 65
ENHANCING YOUR RESULTS.. 67
TAPPING IN POSITIVE EMOTIONS.. 68
LOOKING INTO THE FUTURE.. 73
INTEGRATING A MORE SOULFUL PERSPECTIVE ON LIFE 76
TAPPING COMBINED WITH REFRAMING 81
CONCLUSION.. 82

PART 2
EXPLORING THE MYSTERIOUS DEPTHS OF THE MIND

CHAPTER FIVE 85
Psychological Reversal and Kinesiology

USING KINESIOLOGY WITH EFT 86
THE NATURE OF PSYCHOLOGICAL REVERSAL 86
OVERCOMING PSYCHOLOGICAL REVERSAL............................... 88
PERSONALIZING THE TEST STATEMENTS.................................. 89
GETTING STARTED WITH KINESIOLOGY.................................... 96
ARM TESTING WITH TWO PEOPLE 97
SELF TESTING 100
INTERPRETING YOUR RESULTS..101
TIPS FOR SUCCESS AND ACCURACY..102
UNDERSTANDING INCONSISTENT RESULTS WITH MUSCLE
TESTING...106

MASSIVE PSYCHOLOGICAL REVERSAL 109
CONCLUSION 113

CHAPTER SIX 115
A Holistic Approach to PR

THE NATURE OF HOLISTIC HEALING 116
THE HOLISTIC MAP 118
THE FOUR KEY QUESTIONS 119
SOUL CENTERING AND GROUNDING 125
THE SK REFRAMING AND ANCHORING (R&A) PROCESS 131
EYE MOVEMENTS 138
IMPLEMENTING THE HOLISTIC MODEL 141

CHAPTER SEVEN 143
Reaching Further into the Heart and Mind

THE DIAMOND APPROACH 144
CONNECTING WITH YOUR HEARTFELT JOY AND EXCITEMENT 149
TWO COMMON FEARS 151
FORGIVENESS 153
APPRECIATING YOURSELF AND YOUR POSSIBILITIES 164

PART 3
SPECIAL CHALLENGES, SPECIAL OPPORTUNITIES

CHAPTER EIGHT 169
Correcting Neurological Disorganization

WHAT IS NEUROLOGICAL DISORGANIZATION? 170
CORRECTING NEUROLOGICAL DISORGANIZATION 171

CHAPTER NINE 177
Exploring Energy Toxins

OUR INCREASINGLY TOXIC WORLD 178

LEARNING FROM OUR BODIES 181
WAYS TO ADDRESS ENERGY TOXINS.............................182
ENERGY TOXINS AND KINESIOLOGY 184
USING ENERGY TECHNIQUES ON TOXINS 193

CHAPTER TEN.. 197
Optimizing Your Effectiveness

COMPARTMENTALIZING 198
THE SEVEN DEFENSE PATTERNS...........................202
OTHER SOUL QUALITIES...207
CONCLUSION..208

CHAPTER ELEVEN 209
Stepping into the Future

LEAVING THE PAST BEHIND.....................................209
SETTING YOUR COURSE 211
FUTURE PACING...211

PART 4
THE EFT EXPERTS

CHAPTER TWELVE 217
Meet the EFT Experts

USING EFT CREATIVELY by Patricia Carrington 219
REACHING YOUR GOALS WITH EFT by Carol Look 223
WHY I USE AND TEACH EFT by Alexander R. Lees..................228
EFT AND HYPNOTHERAPY by Marilyn Gordon 231
EFT AND SUBSTANCE SENSITIVITIES by Sandra Radomski........234
EFT AND PEAK PERFORMANCE by Steve Wells.....................237
EFT FOR TRAUMA AND PHYSICAL PAIN by Loretta Sparks 241
EFT FOR PHYSICAL ISSUES by Betty Moore-Hafter 245
FRIENDSHIP IN RELATIONSHIP by David Lake 250

EVERYDAY EFT by Carol Tuttle..256
PRESSURE POINT THERAPY (PPT) by Philip H. Friedman 260

AFTERWORD.. 269
Following Up and Following Thru
A COMPLETE BEGINNER...270
FOLLOWING YOUR HEARTFELT JOY 271

APPENDIX A.. 273
Fostering Therapeutic Relationships

APPENDIX B 277
Glossary

APPENDIX C.. 283
Resources

INDEX.. 291

ABOUT THE AUTHORS

AWAKENINGS INSTITUTE: OFFERINGS AND E-NEWS

x

Foreword

The field of emotional and spiritual healing and growth is in the process of shifting away from psychodynamic, cognitive, emotional, mental, behavioral and pharmacological methods toward energetic and spiritual approaches. In addition, the field has been moving toward an integrative approach that includes the best of the earlier approaches with the newer more innovative, though at times, controversial approaches.

All fields of knowledge evolve and grow. As that growth and change develops there are certain people who are at the forefront of the innovative changes taking place. These innovators have the capacity to contribute to and enhance the changes impacting the field and integrate them effectively with prior knowledge. Moreover, the changes taking place in the field of emotional and spiritual healing draw upon knowledge and methodologies from Eastern, Middle Eastern and Western philosophies and techniques. From this perspective, it is an exciting time to be alive, as many people from diverse backgrounds are contributing to these pioneering changes.

Phillip and Jane Mountrose, the authors, of this book, have been pioneers, innovators and integrators for many years, now having contributed a number of excellent books, DVDs/videos and audios to this growing field of energy and spiritual healing and change. I have been privileged to read, watch or listen to many of these innovative products and been amazed at times at how prolific they have become. I have been both delighted to observe their own professional growth along the way and very appreciative of their willingness to be of service to both their clients and their colleagues.

The Heart and Soul of EFT and Beyond is the latest of their many contributions and builds on their earlier book *Getting Thru to Your Emotions with EFT*. It explores not only the basics of EFT but also the many more sophisticated aspects of EFT that usually are reserved for more advanced courses in energy healing. In a sense it is a kind of encyclopedia of knowledge in EFT and energy and spiritual healing though written in an easy-to-understand manner. In addition it seamlessly integrates their Getting Thru (GT) techniques with the EFT techniques in a way that could be called the heart and soul of energy healing itself, or perhaps even the heart and soul of energy and spiritual healing. The range of information conveyed in this book is very impressive as the reader will quickly discover after reading a few chapters. Moreover, the tables and diagrams alone convey in an easy-to-grasp manner many wonderful ideas, methods or approaches.

A novel feature of this book is the invited contributions and suggestions by many of the leaders in the field of energy healing in general and EFT in particular. One of those contributions is my own article called "Emotional Freedom Techniques (EFT), Pressure Point Techniques (PPT) and the Path of Light." Although Phillip and Jane Mountrose don't explicitly use the term "the path of light" as I have, there is no doubt that their work in general and this book in particular guides the reader gently along the path of light to the essence of their

Being. Any book or book that helps people reduce emotional distress, gain emotional freedom, uplift their spirits and gently leads them along the path of light to their essence is more than noteworthy, it is exceptional. In this sense, *The Heart and Soul of EFT and Beyond* can be described as exceptional as is the work of Phillip and Jane Mountrose in general.

Philip II. Friedman, Ph.D.
Director: Foundation for Well-Being
P.O. Box 627
Plymouth Meeting, PA 19462

Introduction

It's been five years since we completed our book *Getting Thru to Your Emotions with EFT*. At the time of its publication, we were bubbling with enthusiasm about the effectiveness, ease, and speed of EFT. With the wealth of experience we have gained in recent years, our enthusiasm has grown and EFT has withstood the test of time.

These years have taken us on a wonderful journey of exploration and sharing. We have learned more about ourselves and helped thousands of people to tap into their hidden potential with EFT, the Getting Thru Techniques we wrote about in our earlier book, and the Spiritual Kinesiology methods we use with them, which are described in our book *Getting Thru to Your Soul*.

We now know much more about how to apply these powerful techniques effectively. With a focus on helping others to live more vibrant, soulful, joyful, purposeful, and loving lives, we have experienced increasing success with all of these methods. We have also developed ways to supercharge EFT by enhancing the positive, soulful qualities that emerge organically as the clouds of limitation disperse.

Other experts in the field have also been emerging and evolving, honing their skills, developing new additions, and focusing on specific applications for EFT. In this book, along with providing detailed instructions on the use of EFT and a number of related techniques, we add a wealth of knowledge gathered by ourselves and some of EFT's foremost experts, who have generously added their contributions. Readers who are new to EFT can now benefit from the collective accumulation of hundreds of years of experience and those who already know EFT can add to their skills.

THE GT (GETTING THRU) APPROACH

Along with exploring EFT, we have continued to develop a soul-based approach that features the Getting Thru Techniques. This "Getting Thru" (GT) Approach accelerates personal and spiritual development. We have also developed Spiritual Kinesiology (SK), another powerful system that dovetails well with EFT. In addition to providing more ways to use kinesiology, which is included with EFT, the SK methods include another fast and easy clearing technique that works quickly and effectively, like EFT. You will find a description of this method, called Reframing and Anchoring (R&A) in Chapter Six of this book. Both EFT and R&A have their strong points, so we use them interchangeably, along with the Getting Thru Techniques.

The GT Approach is built upon four cornerstones we use personally and with others:

1. **Enlist our inner resources for optimal growth.** These resources connect us with the soul's guidance, which allows us to make positive changes, align ourselves with our purpose, and create vibrantly joyful lives.

2. **Identify the nature of our purpose in all aspects of life.** We explore how to recognize different aspects of our essential nature, develop our strengths while overcoming limitations, and realize our dreams.

3. **Clear obstacles and blockages that stand in our way.** Using easy, fast, and effective methods that include EFT and Spiritual Kinesiology, we can release energetic blockages that stand between ourselves and our goals, and reach a higher level of awareness. Learning these techniques empowers us all to make tremendous progress on our own.

4. **Take action.** The most important part of making positive changes in awareness is to incorporate these changes into our everyday lives. Choosing to take action includes setting goals and implementing them. We discuss goal-setting in detail in our audio True Purpose Program entitled *Awaken to Your True Purpose.*

With this soulful approach in mind, we are incorporating these four cornerstones into our presentation of EFT in this book. We hope it will help you to awaken to your true purpose, release the obstacles and blockages that stand in your way, and create the life of your dreams.

Part 1

THE ESSENCE
OF EFT

CHAPTER ONE

The Evolution of EFT

The power of imagination
makes us infinite.

- JOHN MUIR

Would you like to learn how to heal a whole host of maladies with a technique that is fast, effective, easy to use, available any time and any place – and free of cost once you have learned how to do it?

Well, these all describe EFT. Even after exploring these methods for some years now, it still amazes us how simple EFT is to use with a vast array of common emotions, including stress, anger, depression, fears and phobias, painful memories, self-doubt, guilt, grief, confusion, and more. It is also an effective tool for improving health, relieving pain, overcoming insomnia, reducing cravings for substances like chocolate and cigarettes, and creating vibrant well-being. It can even help increase your effectiveness by improving performance, relationships, and public speaking skills. Though it is not intended as a substitute for required professional medical treatment, EFT has also been shown to help with physical conditions.

Adding to these credentials, EFT is rapid and gentle. What more could you possibly want from a healing method that just about everyone can learn in a short period of time and use to make dramatic positive changes in their lives?

We consider the time and money we have spent learning EFT and the other methods we use to be a great investment in our futures and our qualities of life. Over the years, it has exceeded our expectations. It has also opened new doors in what Gary Craig, its originator, calls the Healing High-Rise, an infinitely tall structure that allows us to rise to unimagined heights. These and other healing methods that are being developed are placing us on the threshold of a new era, an age of self-realization. With such methods, every one of us has the opportunity to attain wholeness and achieve the love, joy, and freedom we deeply desire.

At this pivotal time, it is no surprise that approaches like EFT are emerging, creating tremendous possibilities for anyone seeking expansion and growth. Here is how Craig described the development of EFT in our book *Getting Thru to Your Emotions with EFT*:

> In 1991, I had the opportunity to study a meridian-based healing system under the tutelage of Dr. Roger Callahan. By 1995, I transformed and simplified those remarkable procedures into a form that just about anyone can use. I call it Emotional Freedom Techniques (EFT for short). ... Some are understandably skeptical of the validity of these procedures. Such doubts always accompany new breakthroughs and innovations. But the proof is in the dramatic results, and, not surprisingly, many therapists are drawn to the speed and effectiveness of EFT.
>
> EFT is simple, relatively painless, quick, and can be self-administered. Further, it can provide relief for an extraordinary range of problems. After years of developing these techniques, my jaw still drops at the many

"one-minute wonders" people experience, sometimes eliminating what were severe problems that had been around for decades. But even when the cases are more complex, it often takes only a few sessions for the client to gain relief. It is rare for a problem to take weeks or months with EFT.

Though it may sound too good to be true, as it did to us and many others who have become EFT converts, this book contains everything you need to find out for yourself.

THE EVOLUTION OF EFT

EFT is clearly an integral part of the future of healing. A decade after its public debut in 1995, thousands of people worldwide now use these methods and we still regard this as EFT's infancy, because it, along with a number of other related methods, is still evolving.

As mentioned, EFT is an offshoot of a series of meridian-based techniques developed by Dr. Roger Callahan, which he calls TFT (Thought Field Therapy). TFT involves tapping on a specific series of points on the body to release painful emotions and more. Gary Craig, an engineer who studied with Dr. Callahan, experimented with these techniques, simplified them, and presented his version as the Emotional Freedom Techniques (EFT). EFT is firmly rooted in this creative experimental approach, and this process is continuing as professionals in related fields use Gary Craig's methods, combine them with other modalities, and discover approaches that add to their effectiveness.

These EFT experts come from a number of different medical, psychological, and complementary fields, including physicians, psychologists, hypnotherapists, family therapists, holistic healers, and more. They specialize in a broad range of specific applications of these methods, including reducing pain, managing weight, improving performance, dealing with allergies, and accelerating spiritual development. Each adds his or her specific expertise to this evolving field and contributes to creating a brighter future for us all. EFT expert and hypnotherapist Marilyn Gordon describes it this way:

> I marvel at how so many people have created their own forms of EFT. It's a fluid kind of modality, and it allows for creative interpretation. ... Clients and practitioners of all persuasions and in all walks of life can find ways to doing the tapping techniques that create results in anything they do.

Playing a part of the remarkable evolution of EFT is exciting and inspiring, with results that often transcend words. Our approach is holistic, focused on accessing the healing power of the soul and creating a joyful, loving, purposeful life. We have had success on all levels, addressing physical, emotional, mental, and spiritual issues. Releasing blockages at any and all levels unites us more with our souls and our true purpose, and improves our quality of life.

To present what we perceive as the heart and soul of EFT, this book describes all of the basic techniques Gary Craig developed. Building on its creative legacy, we go beyond Gary Craig's approach, offering variations and complementary methods we have added to our EFT toolbox. And, to provide a broad range of EFT's possibilities, you also have the benefit of advice from eleven other recognized experts in the field:

- **Patricia Carrington**, a contributing editor to Gary Craig's EFT Email List and author of *How to Create Positive Choices in Energy Psychology*

- **Carol Look**, a Psychotherapist specializing in addictions, contributing editor to Gary Craig's EFT Email List and author of *Attracting Abundance with EFT*

- **Alexander R. Lees**, a Registered Clinical Counselor with a Doctorate in Clinical Hypnotherapy and author of *Emotional Freedom Techniques – What Is It and How Does It Work?*

- **Marilyn Gordon**, a Certified Hypnotherapist, teacher, speaker, healer, and author of *Extraordinary Healing*

- **Sandra Radomski**, a certified Social Worker, Psychotherapist, and Naturopathic Doctor specializing in allergy work, and author of *Allergy Antidotes*

- **Steve Wells**, a Psychologist, professional speaker and peak performance consultant who teaches and consults worldwide with elite athletes and corporate personnel

- **Loretta Sparks**, Director of the Center for Energy Psychotherapy and TAAP Training Institute and licensed Marriage and Family Therapist

- **Betty Moore-Hafter**, trained in hypnotherapy and related healing arts and author of *Tapping Your Amazing Potential with EFT*

- **David Lake**, a Medical Practitioner and Psychotherapist with extensive experience in helping people with post-traumatic stress and with relationships

- **Carol Tuttle**, an Energy Psychologist and Certified Master Level Rapid Eye Therapist, speaker, and author of *Remembering Wholeness*

- **Phillip H. Friedman**, a Clinical Psychologist Psychotherapist, Director of the Foundation for Well-Being, and author of *The Integrative Healing Manual* and *Creating Well-Being*

Each of these experts has also gone beyond EFT's origins, adding valuable contributions to the field. As EFT has supercharged our Holistic Healing practice, many of these experts describe how EFT has helped them personally and in their work. Carol Look says, "When I discovered EFT, my entire private practice changed for the better. While I was trained as a traditional Social Worker, using EFT for anxiety, addictions, and overall blocks to success made a huge difference in my life as well as the lives of my clients."

EFT RESEARCH

Science is beginning to confirm the effectiveness of these methods. Here are some of the highlights to date:

- Using EFT daily with children who had epileptic seizures, Canadian researcher Dr. Paul Swingle showed that it significantly reduced their seizures. In the study, the parents used EFT, "tapping" on their children every time they suspected a seizure might occur. Something remarkable happened. The EEG, or brain scans, of the children showed a significant positive change after two weeks of this simple "tapping" therapy.

- Another study by Dr. Swingle and Lee Pulos, Ph.D., showed marked improvements in the brain waves of auto accident victims suffering from post traumatic stress disorder. Three months after learning to "tap" with EFT, these subjects also experienced significant reductions in symptoms like panic attacks, traumatic flashbacks, and nightmares.

- Australian EFT practitioner and psychologist Steve Wells performed a study with people who had a fear of small animals or insects like spiders. The subjects were given a single thirty-minute treatment of "tapping" with EFT. They showed a significant reduction in their fear response. Six to nine months later that reduction in fear was still present. From his psychology clinic in Inglewood, Western Australia, Wells said:

> If you told me ten years ago I'd be teaching people to tap on meridian points to treat psychological problems, I would have said you're crazy. It really does sound like new age mumbo jumbo. But now EFT is rapidly gaining a wealth of scientific and especially clinical evidence.

Perhaps the greatest vindication for EFT is the growing list of highly credentialed psychologists, counselors and medical professionals employing EFT with their patients. You simply wouldn't keep using something that seems so strange unless it worked."

This first peer-reviewed research study on the effectiveness of EFT was published in the September 2003 issue of the prestigious *Journal of Clinical Psychology*. The complete study is now available. Wells et al concluded: "The findings are largely consistent with the hypothesis that EFT can reduce phobias of small animals in a single treatment session...."

* Dr. Joseph Mercola, a natural physician, states in his e-newsletter (www.mercola.com):

> There is no greater enemy to your physical health than a negative self-image or high stress... In my clinical practice, I have tried a variety of methods, and have been exposed to many more (both traditional and alternative) through my medical background, but none have come close to the success rate I have experienced with EFT.

Dr. Mercola used to routinely prescribe anti-depressants for his patients. Now he hardly ever does, since he uses EFT to successfully treat patients to remove the core of the problem rather than masking the symptoms with drugs.

In coming years, we expect many more confirmations of the effectiveness of these methods. We also understand the reluctance of established medical professionals to embrace them at this early stage. It is common for traditional medicine to defend the status quo and resist new developments. As Schopenhauer once observed: "All truth goes through three stages: First it is ridiculed. Then it is violently opposed. Finally it is accepted as self evident."

In the meantime, EFT is attracting growing numbers of users and advocates — both professional and lay people — because it works. EFT will endure because of the results people receive from it, regardless of how new and different it may seem now. As time passes, EFT will gain increasing acceptance by individuals, institutions, and the media.

THE JOURNEY OF SELF-DISCOVERY

This book can take you on an adventure of self-discovery. It is like a treasure chest filled with priceless tools that you can explore and adapt to meet your needs. As mentioned, the essence of EFT and other state-of-the-art energy healing techniques invites you to experiment with the methods and discover what works best for you. We encourage you to use this approach with the many methods presented in this book. You will find a wide range of options and uses for EFT, some of which may draw your attention more than others. You may also know other methods you would like to use along with EFT.

These resources are the creative part of entering the healing high-rise and participating in the future of healing. You can benefit from the experience of those who have gone before you and, if you feel bold, you can add your own inventions to EFT's future.

As with anything new, the key to success with these methods is practice. The basic techniques are easy to learn, but there are some subtleties that can affect your results. The Holistic Process found in Chapter Six and some of the enhancements techniques go deeper. They may take more time to master, particularly for those who are new to self-exploration.

If you are new to EFT, we suggest reading over the whole book while you start practicing the first one or two techniques. Practice each technique until you feel comfortable enough to move on to the next. This will allow you to develop competence and eliminate some troubling emotions along the way. Once you have mastered the basic techniques, you may also feel more drawn to exploring some of the more advanced options over others. This is fine; we provide a variety of approaches, so you can find the ones that feel right to you. Let your heartfelt joy and excitement be your guides.

If you feel a need for support, you can also contact us or one of the EFT experts mentioned in this book for assistance with your learning or with addressing specific challenges. As with other healing modalities, you may also find EFT to be more effective when done with another person. If possible, we recommend sharing your learning experience with a person or group of people who are open-minded, supportive, and ready to move forward in their lives. When a group of people with the common goal of healing come together in a loving and nurturing environment, the results are magnified many times. You can help one another to master the methods and learn more about yourselves by including a variety of perspectives.

TAKING CONTROL OF YOUR LIFE

Before starting to use the techniques, we want to let you know that you are in control. Like coaches, we are available to teach you some effective methods for helping yourself. You are free to progress in your own way and at your own pace. We are not licensed psychologists or medical health professionals. We are ordained Ministers of Holistic Healing, serving others as spiritual counselors and teachers. Our focus is on helping normal people with normal problems to make dramatic improvements in their lives.

The purpose of this book is to help you to deal with the kinds of challenges normal people face in the course of their lives, and to heal them holistically. We do not recommend substituting these techniques for the services of doctors, psychologists, and psychiatrists. In any areas where their professional services are needed, we recommend having their permission before using any of these techniques.

Fortunately, these methods are practically risk-free. Gary Craig reported in his *EFT Training Manual* that after using the techniques for six years with hundreds of people, he observed no material side effects. EFT does not involve the use of needles, chemicals, or invasive surgical procedures. It includes gentle tapping in specific places on the body, humming, counting, and rotating your eyes. Dr. Callahan, whose TFT (Thought Field Therapy) processes are similar, has performed his techniques on thousands of people. He reported no side effects except the rare occasion when people bruised themselves from tapping too hard. This, of course, is unnecessary.

Although experts in the field have observed no significant side effects, a few people have had reactions. Craig mentions these examples in his *EFT Training Manual.*

- Craig reported that several ladies told him that they felt mildly nauseated after doing the tapping. In all cases, the nausea went away after a short time.

- Craig reported using EFT in a restaurant with a woman who had been abused sexually as a child. As he began to guide her in the use of EFT, her memories of the abuse became increasingly intense. Since they were in a public place, he became concerned and decided to stop working with her. No problem occurred after that.

- A friend of Craig's, working with a large group of people with fibromyalgia, reported that a few of them became weak in the knees while doing EFT and had to sit down. Gary has not had this experience himself.

- A professional therapist called in Craig to help a very disturbed lady with EFT. The EFT tapping techniques relaxed her to such a degree that she fell into a deep sleep. The therapist woke her up an hour later, but apparently the woman was still sleepy on the way home and got into an auto accident. Craig suggested that common sense is needed in such cases.

Craig also took a survey of 250 therapists, asking them to respond with any serious reactions by their clients using EFT and Dr. Callahan's TFT techniques. Out of 10,000 uses, they reported 20 incidences. Most of the reactions were reported by seriously disturbed patients.

We cite these examples to let you know that it is highly unlikely that you will experience a negative reaction from these techniques. Nonetheless, as Gary Craig says,

> That does not mean you won't have a problem. You or someone you help with EFT may be an exception. As I'm sure you can appreciate, Adrienne [Fowlie] and I will not assume responsibility in this regard. The responsibility for your emotional and physical well-being must rest with you.

We likewise pass the responsibility for the use of the techniques in this book to you.

We conclude with the following statements, which also come directly from Craig. We pass them on as our agreement with you, our readers regarding the use of EFT and the other methods described in this book.

- You are required to take complete responsibility for your own emotional and/or physical well-being....

- You are also required to instruct others whom you help with EFT (and the other methods described in this book) to take complete responsibility for their emotional and /or physical well-being.

- You must agree to hold harmless Gary Craig, Adrienne Fowlie, Phillip Mountrose, Jane Mountrose, and anyone involved with EFT from any claims made by anyone whom you seek to help with EFT (and related methods).

- Where professional medical treatment is indicated, we urge you to use these techniques under the supervision of a qualified psychologist or physician. Don't use these techniques to try to solve a problem where your common sense would tell you it is not appropriate.

If you are not able to agree with these statements, please do not read further and do not use the techniques in his book. If you are ready to proceed, it's time to put things in a holistic context, so you can learn to use EFT for healing on all levels.

CHAPTER TWO

EFT as a Holistic Healing Tool

The aim of life is to live,
and to live means to be aware,
joyously, serenely, divinely aware.

- HENRY MILLER

"Why am I here?" and "What do I want to do with my life?" During the three decades that we have been exploring personal and spiritual growth, these questions have motivated us and now seem to be foremost in the minds of the clients and students we assist in our holistic healing practice. For people in general, these heartfelt questions are at the essence of being human. And, if we are open to them, the synchronous flow of life and the challenges we face take us on a journey of self-discovery that elevates us to new levels of meaning of life and the unique parts we are here to play.

In our own explorations and helping students and clients, it has become abundantly clear that each of us is here for a reason, with lessons to learn and a uniquely wonderful purpose to fulfill. As we step forward on our journeys, we face challenges that help us to learn about ourselves and grow as individuals. In our own lives, we have found that though the lessons can be difficult, they serve a positive purpose. Once we grasp them and release the associated emotional charges, limiting beliefs, and judgments toward ourselves and others, our consciousness expands. We then feel more connected with our selves, our sense of wholeness, and our reason for being.

From a spiritual perspective, our problems are opportunities to increase our understanding of the deeper meaning of life and the soul's higher purpose. The combination of EFT and the other methods presented in this book can help you to move rapidly along on this journey by releasing your fears, unresolved emotions, and all types of limitations, so you can experience a life filled with joy, love and freedom to fulfill your heart's true desires.

A HOLISTIC APPROACH

On the journey to self-discovery, we have opened to different forms of healing and become increasingly aware of how everything is connected. Though it may not be immediately apparent, any emotional disturbance also has a mental, spiritual, and sometimes even a physical component. Complete healing includes clearing the blockages on all four levels and expands our understanding of ourselves. True healing is holistic. It considers all of the parts of the whole and deals with the source of the problem, rather than relieving the symptoms.

Through our explorations of Holistic Hypnotherapy, we have also confirmed again and again that the origin of the negative thoughts and emotions that plague us is the unconscious mind. You could compare the unconscious mind to a complex group of computer programs that are running in the background of our consciousness. Though we are not aware of them, these programs are determining our responses in many situations in which we find ourselves.

In relation to the unconscious mind, most of us operate on automatic, allowing the programs to run without attention. This is convenient, but it does not always produce the results we desire. Left unobserved, the unconscious mind responds in the best way it can based on the input it has received from our repeated thoughts, our families, peers, business associates, and society as a whole.

A woman who was told as a child that she was clumsy may repress her desire to dance or play tennis. Similarly, a boy who was frequently told to be a man and hide his feelings may not be able to express his heartfelt desires.

Many of us also have suffered from the limiting consequences of criticism, having been blamed for perceived shortcomings far more than we have been encouraged to develop our strengths and realize our heartfelt desires. Rather than learning that we have infinite potential to live a vibrant, fulfilling, joyful, and loving life, our unconscious minds may have become clouded in limitation and fear.

Fortunately, all of this can change and with EFT, it can change relatively easily. With a holistic approach, we look at the physical, emotional, mental, and spiritual components of each issue, and seek healing at each level. From the perspective of this reality, the physical level seems the most real to us, because we can touch it and feel it, but this is not actually the case. Through experience, we have found that the physical level is more of a reflection of what is happening emotionally, mentally, and spiritually. The deepest level of healing actually occurs at the spiritual level and the most powerful resource you can access through the unconscious mind is the True Self or Soul, which is the spiritual part of your nature.

Holistically, we are spiritual beings with physical bodies, minds, and emotions. Through the unconscious, we can tap into the soul, which different people may also refer to as the creative intelligence, spiritual essence, inner guide, or higher wisdom. The soul knows the answers to all of our questions about the meaning of life, who we really are, what we need to learn from the experiences we are having, how to overcome our challenges, and the nature of our true purpose. With its vast perspective, the soul is not fooled by what other people say about us, or by what we say about ourselves.

This is why taking a holistic approach is so important. Everything that is happening in our lives physically, emotionally, mentally, and spiritually provides valuable clues about who we are and why we are here. When we are able to connect with the soul, we can find out what we need to learn from our experiences to make transformational changes.

THE REALMS OF HOLISTIC HEALING

With EFT, we are moving into the realms of holistic and energetic healing, touching our emotions, thoughts, and feelings about ourselves. For many people, these may be new concepts that raise some doubt and apprehension.

The theory behind what makes EFT work is that it releases blockages in the energy meridians that run through the human body. In Chinese medicine, the meridian system is the interface between the energy system and the physical body. Where there are blockages in the energy system, there are corresponding disruptions in flow of energy through the meridian system. These blockages are, in turn, reflected in the unconscious patterns (thoughts and emotions) in the mind and in the functioning of the physical body.

Fortunately, you do not have to know anything about the meridian system to use EFT effectively. You do not even have to agree with these concepts for the techniques to work. We are just providing an overview to give you a general idea of what is happening when you use EFT. The meridians are channels that transmit energy upward and downward through the body.

Each is associated with an organ system, so they have names like the stomach meridian and the lung meridian. Each one is also associated with specific emotional patterns. For example, the kidney meridian is associated with fear and the liver meridian is associated with anger.

Together, the meridians form a unified system. The end of one meridian is the beginning of the next one, so energy flows continuously through the system. The 361 acupuncture points are all located along these energy channels and through the acupuncture points, you can send energy through the meridian system. There are also side channels that run between meridians, creating more connections.

EFT involves tapping on specific acupuncture points that are either at the beginning or end of various meridians, sending energy through an entire meridian from each point, and covering the whole system by tapping on a series of points. For it to work, you have to perform EFT while focusing on a specific issue you intend to clear. This focus sets up a disruption in the meridian system, which is then cleared by the tapping.

Gary Craig describes the basic principle behind his work in this way: "The cause of all emotional problems is a disruption in the body's energy system." It follows, then, that the primary function of EFT is to release the disruptions in the energy system by tapping on specific acupuncture points. And since disruptions in the meridian system are also associated with unconscious patterns in the mind that need to be addressed, in some cases, you also need to explore these patterns to achieve the desired results with EFT.

Sometimes we know we have unresolved emotions that need to be cleared to move forward in our lives. At other times, our next steps may be less obvious, but we know that we are not where we want to be. When this happens, ask yourself: Where in my life am I not experiencing joy, love, and freedom? Your answer will pinpoint what is preventing you from being your personal best. From there, you can begin to examine precisely what is in your way and release it with EFT and the other methods in this book.

We'll discuss holistic healing and its relationship to the techniques presented in this book after we present the basic EFT tapping sequences. In preparation, we want to give you an overview of what you will find in this book.

THE FOUR PARTS OF THIS BOOK

Before going any further, we want to provide an overview of what you will find in this book. It is divided into four parts that provide a structure for learning the techniques. This structure will help you to easily access any information you are looking for. You will also find many examples of processes that we have done with our clients and students, whose names have been changed to maintain their privacy.

Part 1: Getting Started

This part of the book provides some background on EFT and describes the techniques you will use most often with EFT — the tapping sequences.

No special knowledge is required to achieve success with these methods. Each EFT technique serves a specific purpose. We provide an overview of them here and explain each one in detail in the chapters that follow.

- **The Short Sequence:** This is the starting point for using EFT. The Short Sequence only takes about a minute and is effective most of the time. With each use, it clears one aspect of an emotion, so it is often repeated to entirely clear the emotion.

- **The Floor-to-Ceiling Eye Roll:** This short procedure helps when a blockage is almost gone. It will generally remove whatever is left, producing complete relief.

- **The Complete Sequence:** When you are not getting the desired results with the Short Sequence, you can switch to this longer tapping sequence. After using EFT over a period of years, Gary Craig says he hardly ever needs to use the Complete Sequence, because his success is so great with the Short Sequence. This has been our experience as well.

The Complete Sequence is like a sandwich with another technique, the Nine Gamut Process, wedged between two longer tapping sequences. While the Complete Sequence takes more time than the Short Sequence, it still only takes a few minutes and provides a wonderful tune-up. As with the Short Sequence, each time you use this sequence, it clears one aspect of an emotion, so it may need to be repeated.

Part 2: Exploring the Mysterious Depths of the Mind

Once you are familiar with the tapping sequences, you are ready to explore more ways to use them. This part of the book contains more possibilities than we can describe in a brief outline, exploring the nature of holistic healing and the soul. You will find more additions to EFT and going beyond, there are a number of effective methods that work well with EFT and/or as alternate approaches, when desired. They include ideas for both beginners and experienced EFT users.

If you are just getting started, we suggest learning the methods at your own pace, adding gradually to your healing toolbox. This part of the book includes the following:

- **Tips:** We start this part of the book with tips for optimizing your success with the EFT Sequences.

- **EFT Enhancements:** These are simple methods we have developed that enhance the positive results you get with

EFT. With these enhancements, you don't have to stop at feeling okay, you can go further and feel terrific.

- **The Use of Kinesiology with EFT:** It can increase your success rate by pinpointing what you have encountered. Kinesiology is a way to analyze different patterns that need to be cleared.

- **Psychological Reversal (PR) and Kinesiology:** If you are not receiving the desired results after using the Complete Sequence, you can determine the exact nature of a blockage where psychological reversal, an EFT term referring to sabotaging beliefs and judgments, is undermining your success. You will learn how to identify PR using kinesiology (muscle testing) and then to eliminate it with EFT.

- **A Holistic Approach to PR:** This approach can provide more awareness of the nature of any issue and also provides an alternate to using muscle testing, if desired. We include an overview of our holistic nature and a connection with the most powerful source of healing, the soul.

- **The SK Reframing and Anchoring Process:** This alternative to the tapping sequences accesses the power of the soul for healing. Like EFT, It is fast, easy, and effective.

- **Reaching Further into the Heart and Mind:** Here are more approaches that can enhance EFT and any healing approach, focusing on releasing limitations, enhancing your life force, and creating a joyful, loving existence.

Part 3: Special Challenges, Special Opportunities

This part of the book completes the EFT toolbox. Here we describe conditions that affect a small percentage of people and how to correct them. We again go beyond EFT with information that we have discovered in our own work. These special challenges include:

- **Neurological Disorganization (ND):** This condition is relatively rare, but good to know about, because it can thwart the success of EFT. We discuss this phenomenon and ways to correct it.

- **Energy Toxins:** Dr. Roger Callahan discovered that sometimes toxins in the environment, on the body or within the body can prevent a person from healing. This rarely occurs, but, as with Neurological Disorganization, it is helpful to know about it. We also describe how to use kinesiology to disclose the nature of energy toxins.

- **Compartmentalizing:** This kind of split-off thinking creates barriers to healing. When we divide certain areas of our lives, making examining them forbidden, then complete healing cannot occur.

- **The Seven Defense Patterns:** We all have weaknesses, and sometimes they can undermine the healing process. We describe seven specific defense patterns to be aware of to maximize our possibilities for healing ourselves and helping others.

Part 4: The EFT Experts

We already introduced the experts earlier in this chapter. In this part of the book, you have the opportunity of benefiting from their tips and ideas for a variety of EFT applications.

The Appendices –
Enriching the "Heart & Soul of EFT"

Included are three appendices that can be excellent resources.

- **Appendix A, Fostering Therapeutic Relationships,** provides some key concepts for helping others.

- **Appendix B, Glossary,** defines many energy psychology terms and concepts associated with this rapidly expanding field.

- **Appendix C, Resources,** offers you a list of holistic healing books and websites, including more resources from Holistic Communications, our publishing company.

MORE RESOURCES

In our descriptions of the techniques in this book, we have tried to be thorough and to provide as much information as we can put into words. Some people may understand the techniques better by seeing and hearing them in action, so we have also produced two DVDs/video tapes along with *Getting Thru to Your Emotions with EFT* that present the EFT techniques and more.

The DVDs/Video Tapes

Here we demonstrate each of the techniques, using real-life examples of EFT and GTT in action. These professionally produced works help to clarify the locations of tapping points, positions for muscle testing, and the nuts and bolts of each of the processes. We highly recommend them to anyone who is interested in mastering EFT and GTT.

Earlier Paperback Book

Our earlier book, *Getting Thru to Your Emotions with EFT,* includes the basic EFT information presented here along with other powerful Getting Thru Techniques that we have developed. *Getting Thru to Your Emotions with EFT* also details a variety of ways to apply EFT to common problems. Individual chapters address eliminating stress, overcoming insomnia, relieving pain, creating physical well-being, stopping smoking and other habits, reaching your ideal weight, increasing physical activity and performance, and achieving genuine freedom.

There is more information about the paperback book, DVDs, and audios in Appendix C, Resources, along with other resources. Also refer to the experts part of this book.

As you have gathered, you can find effective tools in this book for the full range of beginning to advanced users. If you are new to EFT, focus first on the basic techniques, rather than trying to digest everything at once. Once you have an overview, you can set a goal of learning and applying a new tool each week, or at whatever rate feels comfortable to you.

If you already know EFT, you can hone in on any section that draws you attention and add to your skills. Whatever your skill level, this volume provides a wealth of tips and strategies to help you succeed and expand your opportunities.

CHAPTER THREE

The EFT Tapping Sequences

*The important thing
is not to stop questioning.*

- ALBERT EINSTEIN

EFT is built on a foundation of two tapping sequences, the Short Sequence and the Complete Sequence, which provide relief with most troubling emotions. To benefit from the amazing power of EFT, you will want to have a good understanding of each of the steps in these easy-to-learn processes.

This chapter is an abbreviated version of the descriptions in *Getting Thru to Your Emotions with EFT*, which provides more thorough descriptions for beginners. In that book, we mentioned that we could recount hundreds of stories about dramatic changes our students and clients have experienced. By now, five years later, our students and clients have undoubtedly logged thousands of positive results. But to take one, here is a good illustration of the power of EFT.

EXAMPLE: HELPING HER FOR HER OWN GOOD!

Judy knew she needed to change her negative interactions with her sister Rose. Ostensibly, Judy thought the problem was about Rose's poor health and excess weight. In her concern, Judy offered "suggestions" about how Rose could eat better.

We all want to help the ones we love, sometimes even when they don't want it. Judy cared about her sister's health and the consequences of her poor eating habits, but there was more. Judy's real issue, the only one she could change, was her controlling attitude toward Rose.

Judy felt frustrated about Rose's eating habits. Phillip guided her through a round of EFT on that emotion, which then revealed a hidden fear: Judy was afraid that her sister's life would end prematurely due to her unhealthy ways. They then did some EFT using the following two affirmations (which are part of the process):

1. "Even though I don't want to give up influencing my sister, I love and accept myself and know I have many options available."

2. "I want to get over this fear that if I let go of my control of Rose, she'll get worse."

After a few rounds of tapping, a wave of sadness and tears came over Judy. She felt how deeply she loved her sister. Another round of EFT soulfully transformed her sadness into deep compassion for Rose. Judy realized, "It's her life, and I can't control it. I can just be there for her." Judy suddenly felt much closer to her sister.

Follow-Up

Two months after this session, Phillip spoke with Judy. She again expressed how helpful the session had been. She reported that her anxiety and anger toward her sister had vanished. Since Judy's session, Rose was hospitalized when she had trouble breathing. Fortunately, she came out of the hospital all right. Judy noted that she had no anxiety about this incident, which was far different than the way she used to react. She now related to her sister from a more neutral, unconditionally loving place.

GETTING STARTED

The basic EFT sequences involve repeating an affirmation and tapping on a series of key points on the meridian system. There are specific steps to follow and sequences for the tapping. To use EFT effectively, you will want to learn the steps and sequences, but it may help to know that EFT is forgiving; you do not have to do it perfectly for it to work. You will be asked to tap approximately seven times on each point, but you don't have to keep an exact count. Anywhere between five and ten is usually fine. People often get good results even when they are not tapping exactly on the right acupuncture points.

Pat Carrington, one of our EFT Experts, states "Gary Craig often reminds us that EFT is a very 'forgiving' technique, meaning that you don't have to be exact with it; you need not tap precisely on the spot you are supposed to or never miss a tapping spot, or say the exact words you have read in a manual. Most people make 'mistakes' while tapping, but this does not take away from the beneficial effect of EFT."

EFT includes a series of techniques that work like a team, and you may need to use more than one point to achieve results. You may also have to repeat the procedure to clear an emotional pattern completely. Using any technique or repetition of the process only takes a minute or two. With experience, you can often release even a complex emotional pattern in a relatively short time.

In this chapter, we explore:

- The Short EFT Sequence
- The Floor-to-Ceiling Eye Roll
- The Complete EFT Sequence

To attain the best results, you must keep your attention on what you are doing and on the blockage you intend to clear with the tapping. You need to have the disruption in place in the energy system when you do the tapping. This is done by focusing on the issue you intend to clear. For instance, if you want to clear a fear of public speaking, but think about relaxing on the beach in Hawaii while you are tapping, you will confirm that you had a good time in Hawaii. But, when you finish, you will still be afraid of speaking in public.

To help you maintain your focus throughout the procedure, you will be asked to repeat a "reminder phrase" at each tapping point. This phrase identifies the emotion you are clearing, and reminds the unconscious mind that you are working with a specific blockage.

THE SHORT SEQUENCE

We use the Short Sequence as the starting point for all of our EFT clearing processes. Once you identify the pattern you want to release, it takes less than a minute to complete the Short Sequence. There is a summary of the steps in this process in Figure 3.1 and the locations of the tapping points are shown in Figure 3.2.

Step 1: The Setup

To begin, it is important to understand that EFT works with specific emotions and the setup identifies an emotion to clear. Similarly, using EFT on physical symptoms is often more effective if you can identify the emotion(s) related to the condition. EFT Expert Betty Moore-Hafter describes it this way: "I find that the best results with physical issues are achieved when the underlying emotions are addressed. It's as if the body is holding the emotion in the affected area, which exacerbates the physical symptoms." You will learn how to access the underlying emotions in Chapter Six, where we describe the Holistic Process. In addition to providing deeper healing, this new understanding reveals a deeper meaning, which makes sense of what may otherwise seem like meaningless suffering. The experience can be transformational.

In the meantime, you can experiment with using EFT with the physical symptoms. This sometimes works, and it is worth a few minutes of tapping. If not, you will have an opportunity to take the healing to a deeper level with the Holistic Process or other techniques we cover later in this book.

Your Emotional Forest

You could compare your emotional world to a forest of trees. In this forest, each tree represents a specific emotional blockage in the meridian system. Most of us have a lot of them and find that it is very difficult to get anywhere in life without bumping into trees. Each tree also corresponds to an unresolved pattern in the unconscious mind so each one is connected with a specific emotional experience or piece of programming.

The goal of EFT is to move freely wherever you want to go. Eventually, you may want to clear the entire forest to create a more joy, love, and freedom. As Gary Craig says; "Every toppled tree represents another degree of emotional freedom."

Aspects

With any emotional pattern, there are one or more trees. Each tree is called an "aspect." In a case like fear from a dog biting you at the age of four, there may be only one aspect, and one

---

FIGURE 3.1
THE SHORT SEQUENCE

---

1. **THE SETUP:** Focus on bringing an emotion or issue into your awareness in the present moment. The key to the success of this process is to feel the emotion and set up the disruption in the meridian system.

2. **THE EVALUATION:** When you have brought the emotion up to its full intensity (or whatever intensity feels comfortable), measure how strong it feels between one and ten.

3. **THE AFFIRMATION:** While rubbing the "Sore Spot" (see the diagram in Figure 3.2 for the location) in a circular fashion, repeat the following affirmation three times: "Even though I have this _____, I deeply and completely accept myself."

    Note: If you cannot rub the "Sore Spot", you can tap continuously on the "Karate Chop Spot" instead, while repeating the affirmation.

4. **THE TAPPING SEQUENCE:** Using your index and middle fingers, tap with a medium pressure about seven times on each of acupuncture points in the order shown on the diagram while repeating the following reminder phrase once at each point: "This _____."

5. **THE RE-EVALUATION:** When you have completed the tapping sequence, take a moment to focus on the emotion or issue again and notice how it feels. Evaluate it again between one and ten to bring any difference in your experience into your awareness.

FIGURE 3.2
TAPPING POINTS FOR THE SHORT SEQUENCE

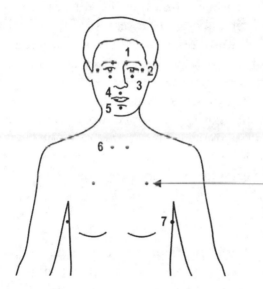

1. Eyebrow
2. Side of the Eye
3. Under the Eye
4. Under the Nose
5. Chin (just below the fold)
6. Collarbone

SORE SPOT

7. Under the Arm (tender
   area about 4" below
   the arm pit)

Note: You can tap on the points on either side. It doesn't matter which you use.

round of the process may completely clear the blockage. This is often true for phobic responses, which may be the result of a single highly traumatic experience. In other cases, there may be a whole grove of trees associated with a single emotion. For example, a child who was belittled by his father over a period of 10 years may have a dozen different aspects that are associated with the anger, fear, and resentment he felt and carried with him into adulthood. If each round of the process removes one aspect or one tree, you may think that he will need to do the procedure a dozen times to achieve results. Fortunately, this is not the case. Each time you do the process, you remove one tree, and the rest of the trees in the grove become shorter.

A dozen aspects is an extreme example, but after several rounds of EFT, the anger will generally be noticeably reduced as all of the trees become shorter, and the entire pattern may clear with as little as a few rounds. This is known as the "generalization effect," because the process starts to generalize through all aspects of a complex problem after a few rounds.

Multiple Emotions

From our experience, most patterns clear completely within about one to six rounds. An emotion may also change after doing one or two rounds. For example, a person may start with sadness, and after a round or two, experience anger. This means that anger is another aspect of the problem that was hidden under the sadness. With each round, you need to review the quality of the emotion and determine if it is actually the same one you felt before. And, as previously mentioned, you do not have to know where the emotion came from to use EFT effectively, but it is common for a greater awareness to come through while doing the procedure.

You may also start the process with more than one emotion related to a single problem. When this happens, decide which one is strongest and start there. If none is strongest, just start anywhere. Any related emotions will probably surface again later or may be cleared along with the strongest one.

One of the best things about using EFT is that it is gentle. If an emotion is painful, you do not have to bring it up to full intensity. It is necessary to focus on the issue to have the disruption in place in the energy system, but not to torment yourself. You may intentionally distance yourself from the emotion by imagining that there is a veil between you and the emotion, or by imagining that the emotion is a distance away from you. Loretta Sparks, one of our EFT Experts, also describes how she deals with painful emotions later in this book.

There may also be times when you are not able to bring an uncomfortable emotion to the surface. You may know that the emotion is a problem for you, but you are not feeling it right now. When this happens, focus on a time in the past when you felt the emotion. Focus on feeling the emotions you felt then. This will generally bring the discomfort to the surface so you can clear it with EFT.

The next step after bringing up the emotion is identifying it in simple terms you can use during the procedure. This is generally easy for emotions like anger and fear, but there may be times when you cannot identify an emotion. In this case, just call it whatever it feels like to you, like "this icky feeling," "this dumb emotion," or "this hollowness." The key is to know what you are identifying, so when you describe it you send a clear message to your mind about what you intend to clear.

Step 2: The Evaluation

Before you start tapping, you have to measure the intensity of the emotion between one and ten, where one is the lowest intensity imaginable and ten is the highest. The goal of the process is to bring the intensity down to zero, where there is no remaining trace of the feeling. As a note, you can measure the intensity of physical symptoms in a similar way.

The SUDs Level

This rating number is often called the SUDs level, a handy psychological term that stands for "subjective units of distress or disturbance." Identifying the SUDs level is a key part of the process, because it provides data you can use to evaluate your progress and ultimate success. If you are not sure where the intensity is between one and ten, just guess. If you cannot guess the intensity, or if you are dealing with something you cannot quantify, don't let that stop you. Just make note of how you feel, so you can compare it to how you feel after you finish the procedure. Your ability to identify the intensity will improve over time.

The Apex Problem

Why is identifying the SUDs level is so important? Dr. Callahan identified an interesting phenomenon connected with TFT, which we have also noticed with our clients. He calls it the "apex problem," referring to the fact that the brain is not working at its apex.

The apex problem is a form of denial that people who are new to these kinds of methods sometimes experience when doing subtle energy work. A challenge may be very intense when they begin, but, by the time the process is complete, they have forgotten how difficult it was earlier. They simply cannot believe the technique could produce such a profound transformation, so they go into a state of denial.

Quantifying the intensity of the emotion provides data for the rational mind to evaluate and brings more focus to the process. It removes much of the mystery, helps you to determine how to proceed, and measures the success of the process. Understanding this success then helps in the integration process. With awareness of the change that occurred, you also come to a deeper understanding of yourself.

Step 3: The Affirmation

This step addresses any unconscious blockages that may prevent you from achieving results with EFT. This phenomenon is known among users of EFT as Psychological Reversal (PR). We will explain PR in more detail in Chapter Five. For now, you just need to know how to eliminate it. You eliminate PR by repeating an affirmation that releases judgments and limiting beliefs. Craig estimates psychological reversal is only present about 40 percent of the time. But, using a generalized affirmation in the Short Sequence, PR is usually cleared. The affirmation is:

"Even though I have this _____,
I deeply and completely accept myself."

You fill in the blank with the specific emotion or problem you are aiming to clear. You would say something like: "Even though I have this anger, I deeply and completely accept myself," or "Even though I have this fear of public speaking, I deeply and completely accept myself," or "Even though I have this headache, I deeply and completely accept myself." This personalizes the affirmation to match the emotion or problem you have quantified.

Repeat this statement aloud three times aloud with conviction, while rubbing continuously on the Sore Spot shown in Figure 3.2. You can locate this spot by starting at the collarbone, then moving your fingers down past the first rib a few inches from the center of the chest. In keeping with its name, the spot usually feels tender to the touch.

If you have a medical reason for not rubbing on the Sore Spot, there is an alternative. You can tap continuously on the Karate Chop Spot shown in Figure 3.5 instead. This is the spot karate experts use to chop pieces of wood in half with their bare hands. It is located on the side of the hand below the little finger, right around the middle of the fleshy part of the hand.

The Karate Chop Spot is easier for many people to locate, but Craig has found rubbing the Sore Spot to be more effective, so we recommend using it whenever possible.

Repeating the affirmation statement with conviction is important, because you want to convince the unconscious mind to shift. If you are in a situation where you cannot say the affirmation aloud, you can say it quietly to yourself, maintaining the same conviction. If this does not work, you may have to wait until you are in a place where you can speak freely.

Step 4: The Tapping Sequence

You should start the tapping sequence immediately after completing the affirmation. The tapping is done by holding the index finger and middle finger of one hand together and tapping with the ends of these fingers on the points shown in Figure 3.2 in the order shown and described below.

As you tap on each point, you repeat a reminder phrase one time aloud. Repeating the reminder phrase helps you to stay focused on the issue you want to clear and sends a continuing message of your intent to your unconscious mind. The reminder phrase is "This _____," filling in the blank with the same name you used in the blank for the affirmation. If the affirmation was "Even though I have this grief, I deeply and completely accept myself," the reminder phrase is "this grief."

For the points that are on both sides of the body, you can tap on either side or both sides. You need to tap hard enough to send some energy through the meridians, but the tapping should not be painful.

The tapping points are acupuncture points, so they are generally tender to the touch. This sensitivity should help you to locate the points. We can also describe their locations a little more precisely, and recommend familiarizing yourself with the locations before you attempt to go through the sequence.

1. **Eyebrow:** This point is at the inside edge of the eye-

brow, above the inside corner of the eye. This is the Bladder 1 point in acupuncture.

2. **Side of the Eye:** This point is next to the outside of the eye, on the temple. This is the Gall Bladder 1 point in acupuncture.

3. **Under the Eye:** This point is just below the middle of the eye, near the edge of the bone. This is the Stomach 1 point in acupuncture.

4. **Under the Nose:** This point is in the indentation between the middle of the nose and the middle of the upper lip. This is the Governing Vessel 27 point in acupuncture.

5. **Chin:** This point is on the middle of the chin, just below the crease. This is the Conception Vessel 24 point in acupuncture.

6. **Collarbone:** This point is one of the trickier ones to locate. It is a tender area close to the end of the collar bone, next to the u-shaped indentation below the neck, just under the bone. This is the Kidney 27 point in acupuncture.

7. **Under the Arm:** This point is in the tender area on the side of the chest about four inches below the armpit, between ribs seven and eight, in line with the nipple. This is the Spleen 21 point in acupuncture.

Step 5: The Re-Evaluation

When you finish the tapping sequence, take a nice, deep breath and allow the energy to settle for a moment. You may also notice yourself automatically taking a deep breath during the procedure. This is a normal release, and it helps to allow yourself to breathe deeply.

Some people also feel physical sensations as the energy within and around them reconfigures itself. You may want to wait a moment before proceeding, if you are feeling the energy shift. This will help you to integrate the change.

Once you feel settled, you are ready to re-evaluate. Focus again on the emotion or issue, as you did at the beginning of the procedure. Measure the intensity between zero and ten, and compare it with the original intensity. In most cases, there is a significant difference. The emotion may be completely gone. If not, the important thing to notice is the difference. It often takes more than one round of the process to release an emotion completely. These are the possibilities to consider:

1. **Complete Relief:** The intensity is gone completely. In this case, focus on being in a situation you are likely to experience in the future that would previously have triggered the emotion or issue. Imagine yourself there to see if you get any emotional intensity. If you do, you can repeat the Short Sequence to clear the remaining intensity. If you cannot come up with any intensity, the pattern may be completely gone.

2. **Nearly Complete Relief:** The intensity of the emotion is down to two or less, so there is just a small residue left. In most cases, this residue will release with a short process called the Floor-to-Ceiling Eye Roll, which is described later in this chapter. Try this one next. If the emotion clears, you are done. If not, repeat the Short Sequence.

3. **Partial Relief:** The intensity of the emotion is lower than when you started, but it is still above a two in intensity. This means that there is another aspect of the emotion or issue to examine. The next step is to repeat the Short Sequence to clear the remaining emotion(s).

4. **Little or No Relief:** The emotional intensity has not

changed, or you have completed several rounds and the intensity has not changed much. When this happens, we recommend the Complete Sequence, which is described later in this chapter. We sometimes go directly to the "Magic Question" described in the next chapter or other methods described in this book. You will also find a few other tips in the next chapter that may be helpful.

When a pattern has cleared, you might want to take a moment to reflect on what has changed. People often experience a new sense of peace and calmness. When a blockage is removed, it allows you to be comfortable with yourself and to more fully experience the present moment. You may also have new understanding, including where the emotion or issue came from and the freedom you have achieved by releasing it.

There is no way of knowing whether an emotion will return or not. If it surfaces in the future, you can simply repeat the process. In any case, the clearing you have done has moved you closer to achieving emotional freedom.

Repeating the Short Sequence

If you have achieved partial relief after completing the Short Sequence, you are ready to repeat the process. When you evaluate the intensity of the emotion or issue again in Step 2, notice if it feels the same or if it has shifted to another emotion or issue. Physical symptoms may even move around in the body. This is positive. It means that they are releasing.

If what you are experiencing has changed, you can work on the new issue in the same way as the original one. Complex patterns with many aspects may have several different emotions connected with them. Moving from one to the next is an indication that you are making progress, even if the emotional intensity is the same.

One time, Jane did EFT with a woman who was afraid of driving on winding roads at night. Beverly started with a ten at the thought of the terror. After one round of the Short Sequence, Jane asked her if it had changed. Beverly said that it had not; she was still at a ten. When Jane asked her if the emotion had changed, however, Beverly said that she was now experiencing anxiety. Since the emotion had shifted, Jane knew that they were making progress and they did another round. At the end of the second round, the thought of driving on winding roads at night was neutral; the intensity had gone all the way down to zero. The whole process took less than ten minutes and provided Beverly with a welcome state of calm.

If you do not notice any difference in the quality of the emotion other than intensity, you can repeat the procedure with the same emotion. In this case, you need to distinguish it from the disruption you cleared in the first round by calling it something slightly different like "This remaining _____." If you said "This fear" the first time, call it "This remaining fear" the second time. When you repeat the affirmation, then you will say something like:

- "Even though I still have some of this _____, I deeply and completely accept myself."

    or

- "Even though I have this remaining _____, I deeply and completely accept myself."

    The reminder phrase will be:

- "This remaining _____."

Each time you repeat the process with the same emotion, you need to change the label slightly, with the understanding that each of the trees has a different label on it.

THE FLOOR–TO–CEILING EYE ROLL

This short process is very simple and only takes a few seconds to complete. Use it when you have reduced the intensity of an issue to two or less with the Short or Complete Sequence, but have not quite reached zero.

First you have to locate the "Gamut Spot" on your hand. You will find the location for this point, along with a description of the process, in Figure 3.3. It is located on the back of the hand just below the space between the little finger and the ring finger, near the knuckles. To do this procedure, tap continuously on this point while focusing on the emotion and completing a simple eye exercise.

You do the eye exercise while holding your head facing straight ahead. Begin with your eyes looking down as low as possible. If you are sitting in a chair, you should be looking straight down at the floor. Start tapping continuously on the Gamut Spot, hold your head still, remind yourself of the emotion, and gradually move your gaze upward over a period of about six seconds until you are looking as high up as you can. Keep tapping continuously on the Gamut Spot until you finish. If you are sitting in a chair, you should be looking at the ceiling when you are done, and your head should be in its original position.

This is the entire process and we have found it to be surprisingly effective. You may be tempted to settle with leaving a trace of imbalance, but we highly recommend clearing it once and for all with this simple technique.

When you are finished, take a nice deep breath. Then focus on the emotion again. In most cases, it will be gone. If not, you can repeat the Short or Complete Sequence to clear the rest of the emotion.

THE COMPLETE SEQUENCE

This sequence is used for stubborn emotions, when the Short Sequence is providing no results or minimal results. It is summarized in Figure 3.4. The process includes more points

FIGURE 3.3
THE FLOOR-TO-CEILING EYE ROLL

1. **THE EVALUATION:** Normally you will select this process after the Short Sequence or the Complete Sequence has brought the problem down to a one or two.

2. **THE TAPPING SEQUENCE:** Begin by holding your head facing straight ahead and tapping continuously on the Gamut Spot. Hold your head still. Now look down as far as you can toward the floor. While focusing on the problem and continuing to tap on the Gamut Point, gradually move your gaze upwards over a period of about six seconds until you are looking up as high as your eyes will go. While doing this, repeat once the reminder phrase you have chosen for the emotion: "This _____."

GAMUT SPOT (On the outside of the hand)

3. **THE RE-EVALUATION:** When you have completed the process, take a moment to focus on the emotion again and notice how it feels. Measure it again between one and ten. In most cases it will be gone. If not, you may want to continue with the Short Sequence or the Complete Sequence.

in the tapping sequence. The tapping is also done twice with another technique called the Nine-Gamut Process sandwiched in between.

Steps 1, 2 and 3: The Setup, Evaluation, and Affirmation

The Complete Sequence starts in the same way as the Short Sequence with the Setup, Evaluation, and Affirmation.

Step 4(A): The Long Tapping Sequence

Begin the tapping with the first seven points you covered in the Short Sequence, and continue with the following points on either of the hands. You will find the locations of these points in Figure 3.5.

8. **Outside of the Thumb:** This point is next to the fingernail.

9. **Side of the Index Finger:** This point is next to the fingernail on the side of the index finger facing the thumb.

10. **Side of the Middle Finger:** This point is next to the fingernail on the side of the middle finger facing the index finger.

11. **Side of the Little Finger:** This point is next to the fingernail on the side of the little finger facing the ring finger.

12. **The Karate Chop Spot:** This point is on the side of the hand below the little finger, in the middle of the fleshy part of the hand.

FIGURE 3.4
THE COMPLETE SEQUENCE

1, 2, and 3. THE SETUP, EVALUATION, AND AFFIRMATION: Refer to Figure 3.1, "The Short Sequence."

4. **THE TAPPING SEQUENCES:** The Complete Sequence, includes three parts.

   A. **THE LONG TAPPING SEQUENCE:** Tap as in the Short Sequence on each of the following points, in the order shown below, while repeating the reminder phrase:

   B. **THE NINE GAMUT PROCESS:** While tapping continuously on the Gamut Spot, go through the following eye movements while holding your head straight forward:

      1. Close your eyes.

      2. Open your eyes.

      3. Look down hard to the right.

      4. Look down hard to the left.

      5. Roll your eyes around once in a clockwise circle.

      6. Roll your eyes around one in a counterclockwise circle.

      7. Hum for about two seconds from any song, like "Happy birthday to you ..."

      8. Count aloud from one to five.

      9. Repeat the humming.

   C. **THE LONG TAPPING SEQUENCE:** Repeat the tapping sequence from Part A of the process.

5. **THE RE-EVALUATION:** Refer to Figure 3.1.

FIGURE 3.5
TAPPING POINTS FOR THE COMPLETE SEQUENCE

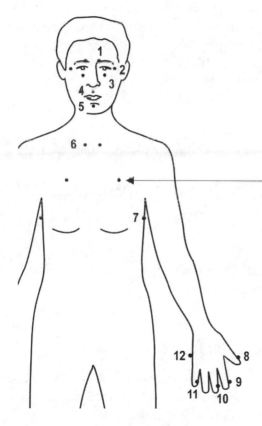

1. Eyebrow

2. Side of the Eye

3. Under the Eye

4. Under the Nose

5. Chin (just below the fold)

6. Collarbone

SORE SPOT

7. Under the Arm (tender area about 4" below the arm pit)

8. Outside of the Thumb

9. Side of the Index Finger

10. Side of the Middle Finger

11. Side of the Little Finger

12. Karate Chop Spot

Step 4(B): The Nine Gamut Process

When you complete the long tapping sequence, you do a series of exercises that stimulate and balance the different parts of the brain. The purpose of this process is to activate all of your resources. As with the Floor-to-Ceiling Eye Roll, start with your head facing straight forward, and hold it in the same position during the entire process. You also tap continuously on the Gamut Spot through the entire procedure. Once you start tapping, go through the following sequence of exercises:

1. Close your eyes.

2. Open your eyes.

3. Look down hard to the right.

4. Look down hard to the left.

5. Roll your eyes around in a complete clockwise circle.

6. Roll your eyes around in a complete counterclockwise circle.

7. Hum aloud for about two seconds from any song like "Happy birthday to you..."

8. Count aloud from one to five.

9. Repeat the humming for another two seconds.

According to Craig, you do not necessarily have to do the exercises in this order, but you do need to hum, count, and hum again in that order. You can mix up the rest, if you wish.

Step 4(C): The Long Tapping Sequence

Repeat the tapping sequence you went through in Step 4(A).

Step 5: The Re-Evaluation

Now you are at the end of the procedure. Take a nice deep breath like you did with the Short Sequence. Then focus again on the emotion and quantify the intensity between zero and ten. As with the Short Sequence, there are a few possibilities:

1. **Total Relief:** Focus on being in a situation you are likely to experience in the future that would normally trigger the pattern. Imagine yourself there to see if you get any emotional intensity. If you do, repeat the Short or Complete Sequence to clear the remaining emotions. If not, the pattern may be gone.

2. **Nearly Complete Relief:** The emotional intensity is down to two or less. Try the Floor-To Ceiling Eye Roll. If this clears the issue, you are done. If not, repeat the Complete Sequence.

3. **Partial Relief:** The emotional intensity is lower, but still above a two. The next step is to repeat the Complete Sequence to clear the remaining intensity.

4. **Little or No Relief:** The intensity of the emotion has not changed. Or you have gone through a few rounds, and it is not changing very much. When this happens, try the "Magic Question," which is described in the next chapter, kinesiology for addressing Psychological Reversal, which is described in Chapter Five, or the Holistic process described in Chapter Six.

You may be wondering if thinking about the emotion is a good indication of what your response will be the next time you encounter it in real life. In most cases, the answer is yes. Research with brain scans has shown that emotions consistently register themselves in the brain whether the situation is occurring externally or just being remembered. The unconscious mind does not know the difference between fantasy and reality. The exception would be if another aspect comes up when you get to the real life experience.

You can only know for sure by trying it out. Fortunately, if the real life situation brings up even a trace of the original intensity, you can use EFT again to clear whatever is left.

EXPERIMENTING WITH THE TAPPING SEQUENCES

With the sequences you have learned so far, you should be able to experience relief from a broad range of emotional challenges. Most people notice changes in their lives after addressing just one or two issues with EFT. If you practice on one new issue a day, you will be well on the way to making some dynamic changes in your life. Once you are familiar with the basic sequences, you will also be ready to supercharge your results with the enhancements provided in the next chapter.

CHAPTER FOUR

Supercharging Your Results

No dreamer is ever too small,
no dream is ever too big.

- UNKNOWN

As mentioned earlier, much has happened since we first wrote about EFT. We have used the techniques with thousands of people and we want to pass the benefits of our experience along to you. This chapter describes the following ways to optimize your effectiveness and the strength of your results:

- **10 Simple Tips:** These ideas can help you to get better results with EFT.

- **The Magic Question:** This is a simple question that can quickly provide clarity when the tapping sequences are not working.

- **The Healthy Expression of Emotions:** Understanding and encouraging the healthy expression of emotions is a key to the success of EFT.

- **EFT Positive Enhancements:** These ways to make EFT even more powerful and transformational are what we call the frosting on the cake.

- **Looking into the Future:** This is a wonderful way to strengthen the success of any clearing process by extending the positive results of the clearing out into the future.

- **Tapping Combined with Reframing:** This method uses EFT tapping to replace a negative image of oneself with a positive image.

The world of Holistic Healing is a creative work in progress. We and other users of modalities like EFT continue to explore the healing process and discover more ways to streamline our approaches. This again points to the fact that the tapping sequences are not cast in stone. In your explorations, you may discover some jewels of your own that will contribute to this evolving field.

10 SIMPLE TIPS

Sometimes, small changes in technique can produce big changes in results. These ideas may help you to broaden and streamline your approaches to the basic EFT Sequences.

1. **Be aware of the environment you are in when you use EFT.** Though it is not always possible to control your surroundings, be aware that EFT and any healing process will be most effective in a relaxing, toxin-free environment. Loud noises, toxic odors, and the presence of electromagnetic influences like TV's, computers, and fluorescent lights can affect your results. Also tight or unnatural clothing and perfumes can limit the effectiveness of these methods. We discuss this in detail in Chapter Nine, Exploring Energy Toxins, but we want to mention it here as a simple tip, be-

cause being more aware of your environment can make a big difference.

2. **Focus on the Short Sequence.** EFT users frequently ask us when we use the EFT Short Sequence and the Complete Sequence. We use the Short EFT Sequence almost all of the time, with wonderful results. To optimize these results with very intense emotions, when the SUDs level starts around nine or ten, we often do two rounds of tapping with the short sequence before stopping for the re-evaluation. This generally provides greater relief at a time when it is greatly needed, so the client is in a more relaxed state to proceed further, if required. Sometimes, if this is all that is required, bringing the SUDs all the way down to zero.

3. **Be as specific as possible when you identify the problem and when you select the affirmation phrase.** We discussed being specific when identifying the problem in the Setup part of the EFT Sequences, and want to reiterate this point. The specific emotion and the affirmation are the keys that open the door to healing and new possibilities. If the problem and the phrase are too general, they may not unlock the door. We have noticed with our EFT students and clients that the importance of being specific is often overlooked.

For instance, a problem with self-esteem generally has many, many aspects. Attempting to clear all of them with a generic phrase like "Even though I have this self-esteem problem, I deeply and completely accept myself" probably will not be very effective. Instead, focus on one aspect, like feeling uneasy around strangers or feeling incompetent learning to use a computer. Be as specific as possible, focusing on one aspect at a time.

4. **Add the "Thousand Meeting Places" point.** This is an additional point we use as part of the short sequence. It is located just behind the top of the head, so it is easy just to tap in the general area. In acupuncture, it is called "A Thousand Meeting Places" because many meridians converge here. This also makes it an effective tapping point that can easily be added to the short sequence.

5. **Use a series of different affirmations.** Another simple way to increase the effectiveness of the Short Sequence is to put all of your thoughts or have a client put all of his or her thoughts about an issue that you have chosen to address into a series of affirmations. As an example, a person who is feeling stressed at work might come up with the following series of affirmations:

    • Even though I feel pressured to work long hours, I deeply and completely accept myself.

    • Even though I am afraid that I will lose my job if I take time for myself, I deeply and completely accept myself.

    • Even though I fear that others will make fun of me if I take yoga classes, I deeply and completely accept myself.

    There may be even more than three affirmations that apply. It is fine to say as many as one wants. This is a simple way to address different aspects of an issue together while bringing up unconscious thoughts and feelings that may facilitate the healing. We find it particularly helpful with complex issues and freeing for the person who has an opportunity to express all of his or her feelings.

6. **If the Short EFT Sequence is not working, consider adding the Nine-Gamut Process.** The Nine-Gamut balances the brain and may temporarily correct Neurological Disorganization, a condition we discuss later in Chapter Eight. Rather than adding all of the extra tapping points in the Complete Sequence, we sometimes just add the Nine-Gamut Process to the short sequence and finish off by tapping on the Under-the-Nose, Collarbone, and Under-the Arm points, something that Roger Callahan does.

7. **Allow a little time and a few clarifying breaths before doing the re-evaluation.** People are generally impressed with EFT's speed and effectiveness. At the same time, remember that powerful changes are occurring and allow room for the transformation to occur.

   We sometimes refer to this as being spacious, giving the recipient a few minutes to settle down energetically after completing the tapping. Interestingly, many people notice the SUDs going down for a period of time, so taking a few deep breaths and just hanging out for a minute or two can be beneficial, particularly with a deep clearing. It also allows time for the recipient's conscious mind to adjust to the possibility that the problem is really gone.

   One of our students recently mentioned telling another student who was working with her in a practice session that her SUDs was at three after completing a round of EFT when she actually could not find any traces of the emotion she had been clearing. She said that she did this partly because she couldn't believe it was actually gone and also that her mind was making some allowance in case it came back.

   With practice, you can recognize this kind of distortion. If you ask the recipient to take a few nice deep breaths, as you breathe along and feel yourself being centered, enjoying the peaceful space, your effectiveness will improve.

8. **Use the Short EFT Sequence as a simple tune-up.** Doing one or two rounds of tapping can be refreshing when you feel like you could use a little extra energy. Since the tapping sends energy through the whole meridian system, we find that we generally feel better after tapping, even when we are just tapping along with our clients, which we usually do. We also do a round or two when we want to boost our energy levels.

9. **Be willing to change the Affirmation.** Remember, EFT is flexible; missing a point in the sequence or tapping in the wrong place does not generally seem to diminish the effectiveness of the process. Likewise, the affirmation is not cast in stone. In fact, sometimes a variation on the basic "Even though I have this _____, I deeply and completely accept myself" may be more effective. For some people, saying "I deeply and completely accept myself" is difficult. In such cases, the normal affirmation might actually aggravate the problem and interfere with the healing process.
   Here are some alternative affirmations:

   - "Even though I have this _____, I love and accept myself enough."

   - "Even though I have this _____, I know I'm okay."

   - "Even though I have this _____, I choose to move on with my life."

   - "Even though I have this _____, I know I have many options, resources, and possibilities available to me."

- "Even though I have this _____, I'm willing to see things differently."

- "Even though I have this _____, I'm ready to let go."

- "Even though I have this _____, I really want to get over it."

- "Even though I have this _____, I'm safe and secure."

- "Even though I have this _____, I am open to the possibility that I can deeply and completely accept myself."

- "Even though I have this _____, I want to completely and deeply accept myself."

- "I release _____, and choose peace (or love, freedom, etc.)"

As you start to use alternative phrases, others may come to mind. When helping others, you can empower them by inviting them to participate in the wording. You may also be able to intuit a statement for yourself or another person that is uncanny in its precision. Just confirm that the person you are helping feels comfortable with the phrase before starting the process.

One time Phillip was helping a client named Susan with the affirmation. Susan was dealing with her husband's promiscuity. Based on her comments, Phillip suggested the EFT affirmation could be "Even though I feel devalued and dishonored, I can still deeply love and accept myself." Then Phillip asked Susan to complete the sentence, "and I choose to..."

Susan's immediate response was "I choose to be

completely attractive to my husband." Recognizing that Susan's wounded ego had gained the upper hand and knowing that she needed to address her own feelings rather than her husband's response to her, Phillip helped Susan to center herself (refer to the Centering Process in Chapter Six). Together, they then changed the affirmation to "Even though I felt devalued and dishonored, I'm getting over this, letting go of my anger, and feeling more at peace."

After a round of tapping, Susan realized more deeply that she could protect and value herself. This change showed that the EFT was working and she was coming to a deeper understanding of the problem. Susan then added the affirmation, "Even though I feel devalued and dishonored by my husband, I can still value who I am and respect myself." She rapidly transformed her feelings and released the negativity.

This example illustrates how resistance to healing can be subtle. It can lie under the surface of the initial responses the person gives. If EFT is not working, you might want to check the affirmation to confirm that the wording feels right for the issue at hand. Underlying aspects might be ready to spring forth if you take an open, exploratory approach. Then healing can progress more easily.

10. **Support those you are assisting by tapping along with them.** When we work with clients in person or by phone, we tap along as they are doing EFT. This adds energy to their healing and gives us an energetic boost at the same time.

These ten tips should help you to hone your approach to EFT. You can also find great advice from the EFT experts who have contributed to this book in Chapter Twelve. For starters, here are a few of their insights:

- David Lake states, "I have found from much experience that the more actual tapping done in the presence of the problem, the more likely a 'deeper' and better result. Thus I am content to do a lot of tapping — without stopping. I call this *continual tapping*."

- Patricia Carrington suggests, "Experiment to find ways to make EFT more suitable for your own personality and needs. No two people approach EFT in exactly the same way. Some prefer to repeat their Reminder Phrase twice at each acupoint instead of the 'recommended' once; others like to say their complete set-up phrase rather than just the Reminder Phrase at each acupoint; some benefit most from EFT by doing exactly the steps they learned without deviating at all from the protocol."

- Steve Wells, who specializes in achieving peak performance, recommends identifying "how you would like to see yourself — the ultimate, successful you — and conduct some tapping on 'being' that person now."

- Marilyn Gordon suggests, "Tap with your fingers or with your mind, as both are effective."

- Phillip Friedman states, "When a person gets stuck, I use any of the following approaches: 1.) access an earlier or deeper upset/affect; 2.) tap the nine-gamut; 3.) Tap the karate-chop point ..."

- Sandra Radomski, who specializes in allergies, recommends treating for "whatever is causing my symptoms."

- For those who help others, Betty Moore-Hafter makes this important point: "I take lots of notes when a client is describing a problem and then use the client's own words to create set-up phrases for EFT. Clients are the experts on themselves and using their own words is the best way to 'tune in' to the ways their minds are working."

With experience, you will find that simple changes in technique can produce dramatic changes in your results with EFT. In addition to the tips already mentioned, we have found the magic question to be particularly insightful.

WHEN EFT IS NOT WORKING, ASK THE MAGIC QUESTION

The upcoming chapters offer detailed explanations of what may be happening psychologically and energetically when EFT is not working, along with providing a variety of ways to address the imbalances. As an overview of what is happening when EFT is not helping to release stuck emotions, we have found that most often there is something the client needs to understand. So this is where we look next. The series of affirmations mentioned earlier may bring up the needed awareness. We also have discovered a simple question that frequently does the trick.

In EFT terms, this kind of unconscious blockage is a symptom of Psychological Reversal which we describe in the next chapter, along with how to use kinesiology (muscle testing) to detect the exact nature of the problem. Before doing that, however, here is the Magic Question that may provide the answer:

"Can you think of anything that could be stopping you from releasing this _____?"

The responses are often surprising and enlightening. The answer may be just below the surface and one simple question will evoke the awareness that is needed for EFT to be successful. For what you are addressing, you may need a variation on the question, like:

- Can you think of any reason you can't overcome this disease?

- Do you really want to be free of this fear?

- Is there any reason you couldn't succeed at fulfilling your dream?

- Could anything you can think of be preventing you from earning the income you desire?

- If you could be completely free of this difficulty, would that present any problems?

Here is an example. Phillip was helping a woman named Martha with her relationship to her grandchildren. She felt hurt because they forgot to call her on Grandmother's Day.

To help with these feelings, Phillip showed Martha how to do EFT. She started with an intensity of eight out of ten for being hurt. After several rounds of EFT the intensity had only dropped slightly, to six. EFT is usually much more effective, so Phillip knew something else was holding Martha back. He asked Martha, "Do you want to get rid of this hurt feeling?" Without thinking, she responded, "Why no! Then my grandchildren would never notice me!"

As Martha heard the words that were coming out of her mouth, an "ah-ha" realization occurred. Although she didn't know the term "psychological reversal," she immediately realized how she was sabotaging herself and reinforcing her pain. Martha intuitively understood that she had been using her self-victimization as a magnet to attract her grandchildren's attention. With this new realization, Martha did another round of EFT, this time saying, "Even though I don't want this hurt to disappear, I can still deeply and completely accept myself." With this one round, the hurt disappeared.

THE HEALTHY EXPRESSION OF EMOTIONS

A huge key to success with these and other healing methods is being comfortable with emotional expression. People often feel embarrassed when they are affected by intense emotions. This is not surprising, since American culture is generally uncomfortable with emotions. It is important as an EFT user, and particularly as a person helping others with these methods, to eliminate any related nervousness or fear.

As mentioned earlier, our focus in using these methods is on normal people with normal problems. If you help such people with these methods, you are like an anchor of strength that they can depend on to help them through the kinds of stormy emotions people normally have. You need to feel comfortable with emotional expression. Uncomfortable clients need to know that they are in a safe place where they will be accepted and supported.

The healthy expression of emotions is not something to be avoided. In fact, it is generally the repression of such feelings that we are addressing with EFT, so having them surface is an integral and necessary part of the healing process. We encourage clients to express their feelings to the degree that they feel comfortable doing so, without ever pushing them to go into areas where they are not comfortable. Fortunately, with these powerful clearing techniques, the discomfort generally fades in minutes, often forever. A little momentary discomfort is a small price to pay for the lifelong emotional freedom it ultimately provides.

One time a man who had purchased our earlier EFT Book and videos phoned us. He was concerned because his daughter started to cry when he used EFT with her. In fact, he was so concerned about seeing his daughter cry that he decided not to use the techniques again, in spite of our insights about emotions. Unfortunately, he was teaching his daughter to repress her emotions; this will most likely lead to bigger problems for her later in life.

For normal people with normal problems, bringing up stuck emotions in the process of releasing the painful feelings is a necessary step that we encourage, as long as the recipient is willing. When it is done in a supportive environment, accompanied by a quick and powerful clearing tool like EFT, the process can be transformational, releasing tremendous amounts of tension and bringing a wonderful sense of peace and harmony. Discouraging this expression buries the emotions deeper, which is unhealthy, adding more stress. Over time, emotional repression can also lead to physical problems.

ENHANCING YOUR RESULTS

As we experimented with EFT and SK, we realized that even more is possible. The healing model in our culture focuses on getting rid of discomfort, but releasing old limitations generally brings new understanding of ourselves and new possibilities. Focusing on positive, uplifting emotions like love, joy, gratitude, and peace that emerge in the healing process is a key to creating a healthy, fulfilling life. When we started using EFT, we were quite happy with the way problems quickly disappeared. At the same time, we began to sense that our clients were being left in a vacuum, because the process ended when the negative state was gone, without focusing on a positive outcome and the wonders that lie ahead in the future. What replaces the unwanted habit or feeling? The soul seeks balance and wholeness; as old negative energy is released, it fills the space with positive, soulful qualities. If we fail to recognize this additional step by focusing on these wonderful qualities, we and/or those we help are missing the best part of the process. It is like leaving the frosting off the cake.

Without paying attention to the positive, the void leaves an opportunity for the wounded ego to interfere. This is often what is happening when positive results obtained with EFT quickly disappear. Why not fill this space with uplifting qualities? When we started to explore the positive states and new understanding that naturally emerge as limitations are released, our results, which were good before, became even better and more transformational. They were supercharged.

Installing the Positive

We use two different processes to enhance the emergence of positive qualities:

1. The EFT Enhancement Sequence, which we use to tap in positive affirmations, colors, sounds, and feelings

2. Looking into the future with Future-Pacing

These methods are to be used when the SUDs level has been reduced to zero or very close to zero. They are not intended to replace the clearing, as the blockages have to be released for the positive qualities to emerge. Just as you could not redecorate a house that is still filled with old, worn-out furniture, you cannot beautify a mind that is cluttered with old, negative thoughts.

TAPPING IN POSITIVE EMOTIONS

EFT works as well at raising the intensity of the positive emotions that emerge from the clearing process as it does at reducing the intensity of old, stuck emotions. Jane once helped a woman we will call Judy, who was reluctant to move in a new direction in her life, starting a holistic healing practice. When asked to describe her feelings, Judy said that she was afraid of the criticism that comes from doing something unconventional. Such feelings are common, since society typically ridicules that which it does not understand.

With EFT, Judy's fear went quickly from an eight to a zero. When the fear was gone, Jane asked her to close her eyes and reflect on what she was experiencing now that the fear was gone. With a smile on her face, Judy described feeling light and joyful, sensing the presence of a new ease in her ability to share information about holistic healing. Together, they came up with the affirmation "I am light and joyful; I can share my understanding with ease," drawing on the words that had just come into Judy's mind.

When asked how strong the positive state was now, with one being mild and ten being strong, Judy said five. Then they did another round of EFT, replacing the usual affirmation with the phrase "I am light and joyful; I can share my understanding with ease" and using "light and joyful" as the reminder phrase. After one more round of EFT, Judy's smile was even bigger. The positive state was now close to ten in intensity. Feeling elated, she said she felt confident and ready to move ahead with her new direction.

From this example, you can see that Judy was doing okay after they finished clearing her fear with EFT, but she was superb after the Enhancement Sequence, feeling fully prepared to move forward. The positive affirmation was the frosting on the cake. It was also an affirmation that Judy could repeat to herself in the future, as she reached for her goal.

The EFT Enhancement Sequence

Here are the steps in the process, mirroring the steps in the Short Sequence:

1. **The Setup:** Focus on bringing the positive feelings that are emerging from a clearing process into your awareness. As with the normal setup, the key is to feel the emotions, so you may want to close your eyes, take a nice deep breath, and focus on what you are experiencing. If any uncomfortable feelings emerge, this just means that the clearing wasn't complete. Once you release the old, stuck emotions, a clear, positive state will emerge. When it does, pay close attention to the exact words that come up into your awareness and use them in the affirmation, because these are the words that have the deepest meaning to the mind. If the words are not coming, you can refer to Figure 4.1, Positive Soul Qualities, to access a menu of positive qualities.

2. **The Evaluation:** Now measure how strong this positive state feels between one and ten. This time one is the low measure, meaning that the positive state is mild, and ten is the high measure, meaning that the positive state is strong.

3. **The Affirmation:** Now you replace the standard EFT affirmation with your new positive affirmation. From the example above, the phrase would be "I'm light and joyful; I can share my understanding with ease." While rubbing on the "Sore Spot," repeat the affirmation aloud three times, with conviction.

4. **The Tapping Sequence:** Tap on each of the points, as you would in the Short Sequence, while repeating a reminder phrase. In Judy's example, the phrase was "light and joyful."

5. **The Re-Evaluation:** When you have completed the tapping, take a moment to focus on the positive state again and notice how it feels. Evaluate it again between one and ten to bring any change in your experience into your awareness.

As with any of the EFT sequences, you can do several rounds of this Enhancement Sequence to bring the positive state up to around ten in intensity. Enjoy the results.

Variations

Rather than focusing on a statement, you may relate more to involving other senses with the use of imagery or a sound.

- **A Color or Symbol:** Even if you have trouble visualizing, it is easy to access a color, or a symbol. When you have completed an EFT clearing, just think of the first color or symbol that comes to mind as you focus on how you are feeling now. You can also add a shape to the color. For instance a blue sphere or yellow triangle.

- **A Sound**: Maybe the sound of a chorus, a soft breeze, or a particular song comes to mind. You can use this, too.

- **A Feeling/Sensation**: As mentioned in the example above, you may notice a particular feeling in your body, like a lightness, airiness, or openness.

- **A Combination**: Combining two or more senses can deepen your awareness. You could have an affirmation, a color, and a feeling, or any other combination of sensory experience, including scent and taste. Interestingly, if you focus on the taste in your mouth before and after clearing with EFT, you may notice that a difficult state is generally accompanied by a bad taste, while a positive state is generally accompanied by a pleasant taste.

Whatever combination of senses you choose, the key is simply to focus on them as you rub on the sore spot and tap on the points. Here is an overview of how the enhancement might occur. If you are eliminating fear of criticism and the fear is reduced to zero after a few rounds of EFT, then you would close your eyes, take a couple of nice deep breaths, and ask yourself what now replaces the fear. If you feel that you now have more acceptance of criticism or calmness when criticized, then ask yourself what the color and shape of the calmness is. Let's say it is gentle azure blue waves washing over you. You may also notice that your body feels light and gently relaxed.

Next, ask how much acceptance you now have, from one to ten (ten being the strongest). You should already have some of the positive after using EFT. As an example, say it is three out of ten. Now focus on the gentle blue waves and the light feelings in your body as you rub the sore spot and tap on the points. The goal is not necessarily to reach a ten, but to boost it to what you might consider an optimal level (maybe seven to nine will feel fine).

Some other points to consider:

• Use intuition (in other words, your "sense" of what is needed) to determine what is a good level to currently achieve. Bear in mind, that further enhancement work and repetition of these strategies can bolster the results.

• If the positive quality has a low number, even after doing several rounds, more clearing may be needed. Just ask yourself what is in your way, focus on your emotions again, and notice what comes up.

• After clearing with EFT, the positive quality may already be a nine or ten and more tapping is not necessary. In this case, just take another deep breath and allow yourself to be fully aware of the wonderful shift you have experienced.

Integration of the energetic changes will continue over time, and the number may rise further. Try to remember to return your focus to the clearing in the coming hours and days, and notice what is different. As a follow up, consider:

• using positive enhancements as part of a regular healing regimen.

• incorporating the color/symbol/affirmation/sound into a meditation practice.

• visually displaying an affirmation in a prominent place, like on the refrigerator, in the office, or in your car.

• doing rounds of tapping during the day with the positive enhancement(s).

You can also combine several of these suggestions. You will find that these positive states blossom with nurturing.

Using this Process with General Affirmations

We sometimes use this Enhancement Sequence with general affirmations, like "I feel vibrantly healthy and alive." It is fine to use it with any affirmation, though it will not be effective if you do not truly believe the affirmation or if the affirmation has brought up painful feelings that you have not cleared. The clearing always comes first. With this in mind, the Enhancement Sequence works wonderfully well for enhancing positive states that lie "in waiting" in your consciousness, ready to be brought more strongly into your awareness.

LOOKING INTO THE FUTURE

Future pacing is a concept drawn from NLP that we used in the Reframing Process in *Getting Thru to Your Emotions with EFT*. It is a wonderful way to integrate the success of any clearing process, focusing on the positive state that has emerged with the clearing and extending it out into the future. It demonstrates the concept that when we change, our reality changes to accommodate the shift that has occurred.

Here is an example from a session Jane had with a man who was nervous about an upcoming surgery. When they initially discussed the procedure, George rated the intensity of his nervousness at five. In this case, Jane used the SK Reframing and Anchoring Process (R&A) described in Chapter Six to clear the nervousness. As mentioned, this process and EFT are interchangeable, so the results are similar.

After one round of R&A, George's nervousness was down to one. Jane had him take a couple of deep breaths, since it can take a bit of time for the clearing to complete itself. Then he said the nervousness was gone completely. At that point, Jane asked him to close his eyes and describe what he was feeling. He described feeling light and free, like he was floating. Jane asked him to continue to focus on those feelings and imagine a color that would represent them. He said a beautiful, light teal.

In this case, Jane didn't ask George to measure the strength of the feelings, but she could have. Instead, with his eyes still closed, she asked him to imagine his future lying out before him and to send the beautiful teal color and feelings out into the future, to the time when he would be having the surgery and recovering. Then she asked him to imagine stepping into that future with those feelings. With the upcoming surgery, she walked him through each step of the process, from the night before, through the drive to the hospital, checking in, preparing, going into the surgical room, going to sleep, coming out of the surgery, and recovering. She had him describe what it was like in each place, surrounded by the beautiful teal color, feeling light and free.

At the end of the process, each stage of the experience was wonderful in George's mind. Though she did not ask him how strong the state was between one and ten when they were done, she knew that he was at a ten.

This example relates to an event in the immediate future. Often, issues apply to a longer timeframe, in which case you could imagine sending the color out as far as you can imagine into the future, and going out a week, then a month, then six months, or even longer, noticing what the future is like. As with the positive affirmation, if difficult emotions come up in the process, it simply means that there is more to clear. Once the clearing is complete, the future will look bright.

The Future-Pacing Process

Here are the steps in the process:

1.   **The Setup:** As with the EFT Enhancement Sequence, you focus on bringing the positive feelings that are emerging from a clearing process into your awareness. The key is to feel the emotions, so you might want to close your eyes, take a nice deep breath and focus on

what you are experiencing. If any uncomfortable feelings emerge, this just means that the clearing wasn't complete. Once you complete the clearing, a positive state will emerge. When it does, pay close attention to the exact words that come up and make note of them. Then notice how your body feels. Ask yourself what color or colors would represent these positive feelings and imagine completely surrounding yourself with the color(s). Again, if any uncomfortable feelings emerge at any time in the process, clear them before continuing.

2. **The Evaluation:** Now measure how strong this positive state feels between one and ten. This time one is the low measure, meaning that the positive state is mild, and ten is the high measure, meaning that the positive state is strong.

3. **Look/Sense into the Future:** With your eyes closed again, imagine that your future is laid out before you, and send the color and feelings out into the future. If a long-term focus applies, you can imagine sending them out as far as you can possibly imagine, filling your entire future with the color and the feelings. Note that a color is like a hologram that energetically represents the positive state that you have created. Sending it out into the future gives a strong message to your mind about your intent for this future.

4. **Move into the Future:** Now, surrounded by the wonderful color and feelings, imagine moving into the future, maybe a week ahead, then a month ahead, then six months ahead, going at whatever intervals feel appropriate for the subject. At each stage, focus again on being there with the color and the feelings, and notice what the future is like. Notice how it is different from the way it was before you did the clearing.

5. **The Re-Evaluation:** When you have completed the future-pacing, take a moment to focus on the positive state again and notice how it feels. Evaluate it again between one and ten to bring any change in your experience into your awareness.

As with the affirmations, the color and feelings are something you can use as a reminder in your daily life. Any time you want to strengthen the positive state, just imagine being surrounded with the color and feelings.

INTEGRATING A MORE SOULFUL PERSPECTIVE ON LIFE

You can also look at the use of EFT and positive affirmations from a higher, more soulful perspective. As we release old stuck emotions with EFT, new opportunities open. We are different people than we were before, and more connected with the soul's essential nature.

With this in mind, you may be able to install more than one positive affirmation, since these soulful qualities interrelate. For instance, a person who "taps" into more of a sense of deserving may also feel more joy and confidence. Just as when eliminating one blockage can reduce or eliminate others, so too can building one positive quality activate others. On the other hand, if you boost one positive quality, say deserving, while another quality like trust remains low, it suggests another area to explore for healing and growth.

Soulful Balanced States

In Leslie Temple-Thurston's insightful book *The Marriage of Spirit*, she describes what she calls "ascended balanced states." These soulful states, such as honoring, peacefulness, or playfulness, are cleared emotional states, which are loving and heart-centered. They promote balance and maturity, reflecting the soul's presence and guidance.

Temple-Thurston points out that we are composed of polarities, or opposites. Interestingly, the opposite of a negative quality may not necessarily be any higher in relation to consciousness. Often, the soul's presence is reflected in a third, ascended state that represents balance between the two. For instance, being polite to others rather than being mean is not the ultimate solution, as there are times when being kind may not be appropriate, such as when a person is taking advantage of you. What might the ascended state be in this case? It could be a neutral state of genuineness that can help you stand up for yourself in an appropriate way, when necessary.

One time, Phillip did EFT on himself for the feeling of restlessness. After quelling the restlessness, he figured that he had reached his destination, the opposite of restlessness, which was stillness. Yet he sensed that this quality was not truly the goal. By centering himself and reflecting on being still, he realized the true "ascended state" was clarity. He then installed clarity into himself through a round of tapping.

The Marriage of Spirit provides a handy reference list of soul qualities, which you can use for your positive enhancement installations. We have adapted Temple-Thurston's list here in Figure 4.1. You can also add to this list. To determine the appropriate ascended state you can:

- use your intuition

- muscle test

- meditate

- journal

- allow the quality to emerge from the depths of your awareness

- write out opposites and what the ascended quality might be (Temple-Thurston calls this process "Triangles")

FIGURE 4.1
POSITIVE SOUL QUALITIES

Acceptance	Honoring
Balance	Humility
Bliss	Joy
Centeredness	Kindness
Clarity	Knowing
Compassion	Light-Heartedness
Confidence	Neutrality
Deserving	Nurture
Detachment	Patience
Equality	Playfulness
Flow	Peace
Forgiveness	Purity
Generosity	Tolerance
Grace	Trust
Gratitude	Truth
Groundedness	Unconditional Love
Harmlessness	Unity
Harmony	Wholeness
Healing	Wisdom
Health	

You can also focus on the list and notice if any of the qualities stand out. Note what you experience as you focus on one of them. If it brings up any negativity, you can clear it with EFT and proceed with the enhancement. If you feel fine, but feel drawn to having more of it, you can do so now.

On a larger scale, these are the qualities that will help our society to transcend the complex problems we face. Activating more soulful awareness with these methods is a valuable contribution to humanity's future.

An Example of a Positive Installation

One of our clients was angry about waiting for her husband to support her emotionally. After releasing her anger with EFT, she was ready to install the positive. Here were the positive installations Phillip helped Lana find:

- For the quality of joy, she saw a green starburst. The accompanying sound was a firecracker (for celebrating).

- For the quality of optimism, she saw a blue square. The accompanying sound was a hum. Together, the image and sound made her feel grounded and solid in her positive installations.

- The affirmation she came up with was "I'm optimistic about what's going to happen in my life, and I deeply and completely accept myself."

When Lana tapped on the points, she would alternate using the different senses: visualizing the images, hearing the sounds, and saying the affirmation using the key word "optimistic." As a follow up, she tapped while saying this positive affirmation daily as part of her meditation and daily routines. Her dedication paid off; many positive, synchronous events magically started to occur in her life.

Lana's story is typical of results we have witnessed when

people take the extra step of enhancing the results they receive with the clearing and reflect regularly on the positive, soulful qualities that emerge organically from the process. As Mahatma Gandhi once said, "In the attitude of silence, the soul finds the path in a clearer light, and what is elusive and deceptive resolves itself into crystal clearness."

Holistically, the ultimate goal in any healing process is to reach a higher, balanced state, which can rise above the opposing poles without tilting to one side or the other. You can do this with the enhancements provided in this chapter. We also discuss working with polarities and higher emotional states in detail in our *Getting Thru to Your Soul* book.

When People are at a Loss

As healing progresses, higher emotional states often emerge spontaneously, and we generally focus on helping our clients to bring these states out without adding any suggestions. A person's own words and realizations have the strongest meaning for them. There are, nonetheless, times when clients are at a loss as for what would fill the void. They are probably still integrating the shifts they experienced. They are also often so glad to be rid of the negative state that the idea of replacing it with a positive one is hard to consider.

When we ask such people about their positive resources after clearing an issue, they often are uncertain. Not surprisingly, they appreciate suggestions, which we provide by offering a menu of several possibilities.

One of Phillip's clients cleared her fear about money being destructive. To help her choose a positive quality, he suggested she could replace the fear with qualities of deserving, confidence, and joy. She decided to focus on deserving. Then she was able to successfully do an enhancement to elevate the positive results of her clearing up to a high level.

TAPPING COMBINED WITH REFRAMING

Reframing is an important concept in healing. It is an NLP term that refers to replacing an undesirable state with one that is desirable. The SK Reframing and Anchoring Process that we have included in Chapter Six is a powerful technique that we use regularly. Roger Callahan also combined a reframing visualization with tapping. Here is how you can use these two powerful healing modalities together. As a note, if you have difficulty visualizing, just "sense" the scene. The key is having a strong awareness of it.

- Start with an image or behavior that you would like to change. If the goal is to eat healthier foods, you could start by remembering a time you made an unhealthy food choice.

- When you picture the image of unhealthy eating, make a note of how *clear* the image or sense of the scene is. One is very dim; ten is total clarity. Generally, the number is high, indicating the high intensity of the problem.

- Then mentally erase this negative image/behavior and replace it with a desired one. For instance, see/sense yourself eating a healthy meal.

- Now you are ready for the tapping. As you tap on each point, using the complete sequence with the eye movements, keep visualizing the desired outcome.

- After a round of tapping measure the clarity of the desired scene. Compare it to the clarity of the undesired scene. The desired scene should be considerably clearer, while the undesired one should have become dimmer and fainter.

- If desired, repeat the process.

CONCLUSION

The methods described in this chapter have provided a variety of ways to improve your effectiveness with EFT. With the 10 tips, healthy expression of emotions, the Magic Question, EFT positive enhancements, and other alternative approaches, you can rise to amazing heights. You have also learned how to deepen any EFT healing process and connect with a more soulful perspective. The enhancements actually do more than just enhance. They can help you to expand, access deeper levels of your awareness, and realize your full potential.

Continuing on, there is still much more to explore and we remind you to do so at a pace that feels comfortable to you.

Part 2

EXPLORING THE
MYSTERIOUS DEPTHS OF
THE MIND

CHAPTER FIVE

Psychological Reversal and Kinesiology

*Whether you think you can
or think you can't – you are right.*

- HENRY FORD

If the EFT Tapping Sequences are providing little or no relief, the next recommended step is adding kinesiology (muscle testing) to shed some new light on the subject by testing for a condition known in EFT terms as Psychological Reversal (PR). We sometimes use this approach, though we may also use the Magic Question mentioned in the last chapter or the Holistic Process, which is described later. The Magic Question is fast and easy, so it is generally worth the time. Then the choice between testing for PR and using the Holistic Process is generally one of personal preference, or, when assisting others, selecting the method that seems most appropriate for them.

Kinesiology is a powerful tool for accessing information from the body's innate wisdom and the unconscious mind. It works by testing how the strength of a muscle is affected by focusing on an external stimulus or part of the body. With kinesiology, you can test how an individual is affected by the introduction of specific foods, vitamins, scents, music, environmental factors, and verbal statements. You can also test the strength of different systems in the body and its surrounding energetic structure.

Kinesiology has many applications and we cannot cover them all here. This chapter focuses on using it with EFT. For more about kinesiology, refer to Appendix C, Resources.

USING KINESIOLOGY WITH EFT

We used kinesiology before we learned EFT and we have used it even more in recent years with both EFT and Spiritual Kinesiology. It is a great way to uncover more unconscious information about any condition that is not responding positively to EFT. This unconscious information is generally known as Psychological Reversal, and commonly called PR.

As mentioned earlier, when tapping alone is not working, there is generally something unconscious that the user needs to understand. Pinpointing the exact nature of the reversal is sometimes required to overcome it, so the kinesiology can effectively increase your success rate with EFT, along with providing some fascinating food for thought. Muscle testing will quickly tell you if psychological reversal is blocking your success and provide valuable information about what is happening in the unconscious mind.

THE NATURE OF PSYCHOLOGICAL REVERSAL

What causes PR? According to Gary Craig, "the principle cause is negative thinking. Even the most positive thinkers among us carry around subconscious negative, self-defeating thoughts. PR is the usual result. As a general rule, the more pervasive this type of thinking, the more prone we are to becoming psychologically reversed."

The way we understand it, PR is related to having a limited perspective about ourselves and our possibilities, creating self-sabotage. Holistically, it relates to the mental and spiritual levels, which are more subtle than the physical and emotional levels, so these limitations may not be as obvious to us as a pain in the neck or feelings of insecurity, though both have mental and spiritual aspects. If, at a deep level of the unconscious, we believe that life is difficult, that we will never succeed, or that we do not deserve the best, these beliefs become self-fulfilling prophecies. The "Levels of PR," as they are known in EFT terms, make uncovering these limitations easy.

As mentioned before, Gary Craig found that PR is present less than 40 percent of the time. The affirmation in the EFT tapping sequences addresses PR in a general way that works most of the time. Sometimes just saying the affirmation with the Short Sequence or the Complete Sequence will bring up more understanding of what is in the way. When this happens, you can tailor your affirmation to the exact nature of the limitation you have encountered. When the affirmation does not work, the Levels of PR are more specific.

Kinesiology can uncover self-defeating patterns that may be blocking your success with EFT. It also demonstrates how unconscious patterns influence the ability to recover. And, in the spirit of EFT, testing for PR is relatively easy to do. It only takes a few minutes and it can greatly enhance your success with EFT.

It is worth noting that some conditions are frequently linked with PR. Gary Craig has noticed that people who are prone to addictions, depression, or chronic diseases are almost always psychologically reversed in relation to these problems. PR is also linked with procrastination, pervasive negative thinking, learning difficulties, and problems with athletic performance. This seems logical, because all of these conditions are forms of self-sabotage. To the degree that you have such problems, you probably also have a corresponding inability to make positive changes in your life.

OVERCOMING PSYCHOLOGICAL REVERSAL

In its use with EFT, the goal of muscle testing is to fine-tune the affirmation and release the PR with the Short or Complete Sequence. We described all of this in detail in *Getting Thru to Your Emotions with EFT*, and we start with more or less the same description here. We have also added more tips for successful use of muscle testing and information about the significance of inconsistent results.

The PR Test Statements

The test statements used to determine the nature of PR related to overcoming obstacles are shown in Figure 5.1. Testing these statements with kinesiology demonstrates how the unconscious mind develops ineffective strategies to cope with challenges. The test muscle will remain strong when given a statement that agrees with your unconscious programming or a statement that is true to you. Testing each of the statements on this list will show you if there are any limiting beliefs or judgments that need to be cleared before a pattern can be released. Remember muscle testing tests your unconscious/body responses.

You may be surprised by the results you get with kinesiology. These results may explain why you may be working diligently to overcome an obstacle and getting nowhere. Unconsciously, you may not actually want to get over it or believe that you deserve to get over it. These sabotaging strategies may include an inability or unwillingness to overcome physical and/or emotional symptoms. The mind may see the symptoms as a way to get attention, avoid unpleasant situations, or protect you from danger.

Let us explain these examples. We all need to be nurtured

and loved, so we seek ways for this to occur. Some people are unable to reach out to others and create mutually loving relationships, or find themselves alone. In such cases, they may unconsciously manifest painful physical or psychological symptoms as a way to get others to care for them. A doctor or nurse's care, then, is better than no care at all.

Illness is also a way to avoid stressful situations, such as going to work or to school. And conditions like carrying extra weight may provide protection for a person who feels unsafe around other people, particularly the opposite sex. When this is the case, the individual may work diligently to lose weight with little or no success. These are just a few examples. The possible interpretations of the unconscious mind are endless.

It follows that when the symptoms are providing a hidden benefit, it is unlikely that EFT or any other clearing technique will be successful. Using kinesiology to muscle test the statement "I want to get over this _____" will often expose this form of psychological reversal. If the muscle tests weak, it means you do not want to get over it on an unconscious level. The statements "I want to completely get over this _____" and "I will get over this _____" are also helpful when a person is receiving partial success, but doesn't seem to be able to release a blockage completely.

Since a strong response means that a statement is true to your unconscious mind, a weak response means that the statement is false, indicating the presence of PR. If the muscle tests weak for any of these statements, your unconscious mind does not want to overcome the problem. You need to eliminate the PR to make progress with EFT.

PERSONALIZING THE TEST STATEMENTS

Whatever you are dealing with, you need to tailor the statements to the condition. Here is an example of what the test statements would be for the fear of flying:

FIGURE 5.1
THE LEVELS OF PR FOR OVERCOMING OBSTACLES

When PR is present, one or more of the statements will probably produce a weak response with muscle testing:

- I want to get over this _____.
- I want to <u>completely</u> get over this _____.
- I <u>will</u> get over this _____.
- I believe that I can get over this _____.
- I deserve to get over this _____.

Here are a few more variations you can try:

- I will do everything necessary to get over this _____.
- I will allow myself to get over this _____.
- It is possible for me to get over this _____.
- Getting over this _____ will be good for me.
- Getting over this _____ will be good for others.
- It will be safe for me to get over this _____.

Also, if none of the statements listed above identify the problem, you or the person you are helping may be able to provide a more precise statement than those listed above, as a person's own words have the most power in his or her mind.

FIGURE 5.1
CONTINUED

When there is no PR, you will receive a strong response for all of the above statements. To confirm your results, you can test the opposite statements. With no PR, they should all produce a weak response. With PR, the response should be strong for the following statements:

- I don't want to get over this _____.
- I don't want to completely get over this _____.
- I won't get over this _____.
- I don't believe I can get over this _____.
- I don't deserve to get over this _____.
- I won't do everything needed to get over this _____.
- I won't allow myself to get over this _____.
- It is not possible for me to get over this _____.
- Getting over this _____ won't be good for me.
- Getting over this _____ won't be good for others.
- It won't be safe for me to get over this _____.

- I want to get over this fear of flying.
- I want to completely get over this fear of flying.
- I will get over this fear of flying.
- I believe that I can get over this fear of flying.
- I deserve to get over this fear of flying.
- And so on...

Testing statements related to realizing goals is similar. Statements used to determine the nature of PR related to achieving goals are shown in Figure 5.2. In this regard, it may help to start with the premise that we are where we are in the different areas in life because of the beliefs we have about ourselves, which are generally unconscious. If you are finding it challenging to find success, to lose weight, or to realize any of your dreams, this checklist can help you to identify what is happening in your unconscious mind. A prime example is wanting to lose weight. Most people who are not able to reduce excess weight are dealing with PR. In this case, the test questions could be:

- I want to weigh 135 pounds (or your goal weight).
- I am totally committed to weighing 135 pounds.
- I will weigh 135 pounds.
- I believe that I can weigh 135 pounds.
- I deserve to weigh 135 pounds.
- And so on...

You can use these questions with different weights to find out what your unconscious mind wants to weigh and why.

Here is another example:

- I want to be a successful lawyer.
- I am totally committed to becoming a successful lawyer.
- I will be a successful lawyer.
- I believe that I can be a successful lawyer.

- I deserve to be a successful lawyer.
- And so on...

We have seen numerous examples of people who are trying to become successful in areas that are not of interest to them on a deeper level. A woman may be trying to become a lawyer because it is her father's dream, rather than her own. Such realizations can be transformational, ultimately leading to more joy, freedom, and success in areas that are in alignment with one's true purpose.

It is worth noting that you can also just ask the PR questions directly without muscle testing, as suggested with the "magic question" discussed earlier. This approach will not go as deep into the unconscious mind as kinesiology, but sometimes the answer is just below the surface and easy to access. We generally prefer muscle testing, because it is faster than discussing each question and generally more effective.

Tricia's PR Story

Tricia found it disturbing that her boyfriend was not "environmentally sensitive." To narrow down the problem, she focused on one incident when he didn't recycle. The memory made her feel annoyed, at about a level six intensity.

After two rounds of EFT the annoyance was at a two, but Phillip sensed something was holding her back from releasing the feeling completely. He went through the Levels of PR with her, and Tricia said that she didn't feel that she could completely release the annoyance. Her reason for holding on to it was that she didn't believe the problem could go away so quickly. It had taken less than 10 minutes to do the EFT process at that point, and she had built up this annoyance for years.

The solution was to change the EFT Affirmation to, "Even though I don't believe I can let go of this annoyance so quickly, I still deeply and completely accept myself." After just one

---

FIGURE 5.2
THE LEVELS OF PR FOR REACHING GOALS

When PR is present, one or more of the statements will probably produce a weak response with muscle testing:

- I want to _____.
- I am totally committed to _____.
- I <u>will</u> _____.
- I believe that I can _____.
- I deserve to _____.

Here are a few more variations you can try:

- I will do everything necessary to _____.
- I will allow myself to _____.
- It is possible for me to _____.
- _____ will be good for me.
- _____ will be good for others.
- It will be safe for me to _____.

Also, if none of the statements listed above identify the problem, you or the person you are helping may be able to provide a more precise statement than those listed above, as a person's own words have the most power in his or her mind.

FIGURE 5.2
CONTINUED

When there is no PR, you will receive a strong response for all of the above statements. To confirm your results, you can test the opposite statements. With no PR, they should all produce a weak response. With PR, the response should be strong for the following statements:

- I don't want to _____.
- I am not totally committed to _____.
- I won't _____.
- I don't believe I can _____.
- I don't deserve to _____.
- I won't do everything necessary to _____.
- I won't allow myself to _____.
- It is not possible for me to _____.
- _____ won't be good for me.
- _____ won't be good for others.
- It won't be safe for me to _____.

round of tapping, the remainder of the annoyance disappeared and Tricia had a smile on her face.

GETTING STARTED WITH KINESIOLOGY

You can use kinesiology alone or with another person. We will describe ways to do both. Receiving accurate results requires focused awareness, some practice, and an ability to be neutral about the results. Both the provider and receiver need to be open to the information that is coming up from the unconscious without drawing any premature conclusions about the results. If you think you already know the outcome, your bias may influence the results.

For those who are inexperienced with kinesiology, we recommend doing EFT to clear any doubts you may have about your ability to use muscle testing successfully. Many people become psychologically reversed when trying something new. EFT can help to overcome any fear or anxiety you may have related to kinesiology.

Preparation

Before testing with kinesiology we suggest the following:

1. Be sure the environment is neutral with no distracting music, scents, and so on.

2. If possible, have the person receiving the kinesiology drink some water. This optimizes brain functioning. Also deep, diaphragmatic breathing can help oxygenate the system.

3. Be in a neutral emotional state and centered. If you are working on another person, be sure that he or she is also in a centered state. You may know ways to center. If not, we describe the process we use in Chapter Six.

4. If you are testing another person, only do so with his or her permission and understanding of the importance of being neutral.

ARM TESTING WITH TWO PEOPLE

When you are centered, you are ready to start muscle testing. One of the easiest ways to use kinesiology is with a partner. We suggest the following arm testing method:

1. **Position the Receiver:** Have the receiver of the testing stand erect, holding one arm out straight to the side. The elbow and hand should be extended, so they form a straight line that is parallel with the floor, with the palm of the hand facing down. Either arm may be used for the testing, as long as it is in healthy condition. You should not perform this type of muscle testing on an area of the body that's sore or hurt.

2. **Position the Provider:** The person who is to perform the testing then stands either in front of or behind the receiver, facing the extended arm. The provider places one hand on the receiver's shoulder for stability and the other hand on top of the extended arm, at the wrist, so the provider's hand is touching the wrist lightly, but not exerting any pressure. Placing the hand on the wrist before starting the testing allows the receiver to become accustomed to the touch.

3. **Review the Testing Procedure:** To test, the provider provides a phrase for the receiver to repeat aloud, starting with "My name is _____." When the receiver has completed the statement, the provider pushes straight down on the extended arm, at the wrist. Here are a few tips:

   • Allow the receiver to complete the statement and push on the arm itself, not on the hand. If you push on the hand, you are testing the wrist, which is generally not strong enough for this type of test.

- To be sure the receiver is paying attention, the provider should say "resist" or "hold" just before exerting pressure on the arm.

- Hold the hand that will be pushing flat, and push straight down with the palm, gradually increasing the pressure to test the resistance.

- Avoid any jerky or chopping movements or gripping the receiver's arm.

4. **Test for accuracy:** The first few tests should be designed to determine the strength of the receiver's arm and the accuracy of the results. Start with the receiver's name, then test for another name and a few other easy questions, like the date, the location you are in, and so on. A true statement should generate a strong response and a false statement should generate a weak response. In addition to testing the accuracy of the results, the first few questions provide base data on the difference between a positive and negative response.

If the receiver does not provide accurate results to the first few tests, do not proceed further until you have corrected the problem. There are a couple of easily correctable things that may be happening:

- The receiver may be dehydrated. Have him or her drink at least a full glass of water and try a few deep breaths. Retest and proceed if the results are accurate.

- The receiver may not be centered and grounded. Repeat the Centering Process to bring him or her into the present moment. Retest and proceed if the results are accurate.

- You can ask something similar to the magic question described earlier to find out if there is any reason why the receiver would not test accurately. Here you are looking for the presence of anxiety, fear of appearing weak, fear of the response, or fear of addressing a traumatic issue. The question might be something like "Do you notice any feelings that might interfere with this process?" If so, you can do EFT on the feelings and return to the muscle testing.

- With a holistic approach, everything is viewed as connected. If fear, anxiety and/or other feelings are affecting your ability to effectively address the issue at hand, clearing them is a positive and necessary step in the healing process.

If none of these options help, consider the Holistic Process, which is described in the next chapter. This will access any limiting beliefs or judgments that could be interfering with the muscle testing and with the effectiveness of EFT. If you want to explore the inaccuracies further, you can find more information on possible reasons for inaccurate testing later in this chapter.

5. **Test for PR:** With accurate results, you are ready to test anything you wish. For use with EFT, test "The Levels of Psychological Reversal" in Figure 5.1 or 5.2.

If you are new to muscle testing, we recommend starting with a partner and practicing arm testing until you feel competent. This is one of the easiest forms of muscle testing. Then you can move on to self-testing.

SELF TESTING

If no one else is around, you can test yourself. We offer two methods here.

The One-Hand Method

There are several ways to perform self-testing. We prefer the One-Hand Method, because it leaves the other hand free if you want to test a substance. We will discuss this more later when we explore energy toxins. Here is our technique:

1. Hold one hand with the middle finger extended straight out from the hand. We generally recommend using your non-dominant hand, because this leaves your dominant hand free to hold a substance you want to test, if desired.

2. With this method, the middle finger serves the same purpose as the extended arm in arm testing, and the index finger corresponds to the hand of the provider who is exerting pressure on the arm. Hold the index finger over the middle finger, touching lightly.

3. Proceed with statements just as you would with arm testing, resisting with the middle finger and exerting pressure with the end of the index finger. This may take a bit of practice, but you can confirm the reliability of your results by testing a series of questions to which you know the answers and testing the responses you receive.

As a note: some people prefer to use the index finger as the "extended arm" and the middle finger to exert pressure. You can experiment with both and decide if either one feels comfortable to you. If not, you may prefer using two hands.

The Two-Hand Method

This is one of a number of ways to muscle test with two hands.

1. Hold the first hand out and form a loop with your thumb and index finger. This hand will be the equivalent to the extended arm. You can use either hand, but may prefer your non-dominant hand. With this method, you will test your ability to hold the thumb and finger of the first hand together.

2. Hold the thumb and index finger of your second hand together inside of the loop you have formed with the thumb and finger of the first hand. You have created two interlocking rings with the thumb and index finger of each hand.

3. Proceed with statements just as you would with arm testing, resisting with the thumb and finger loop while you try to pull the loop apart with the thumb and finger of your second hand.

INTERPRETING YOUR RESULTS

Once you have completed the testing, you need to interpret the results. You are drawing information from the unconscious mind and the body's innate intelligence, so the results may not match the receiver's conscious intent, thoughts, or desires. A strong response to a question indicates that the statement is true to the receiver or that the condition described is understood as beneficial in the mind of the receiver. A weak response indicates that the statement is untrue to the receiver or that the condition described is not understood as beneficial to the receiver.

As mentioned, responses to statements like "I want to be successful in life," "I want to get over this fear," or "I want to be my ideal weight" are easy to understand. A strong response means this statement is true, and a weak response means this statement is false. Responses to other statements may be less obvious. The key is to remember that you are testing the response to whatever you are instructing the person to focus on.

Once you've encountered a blockage using kinesiology, you need to decide what to do next. In some cases, the response to the muscle test may trigger new understanding in the receiver that will provide a direction for EFT. In other cases, the recipient may not have any conscious understanding of the response. This is fine, too. All you need to know is the nature of the PR. With the basic levels of PR, you can usually overcome the blockage by changing the standard affirmation to address the specific nature of the reversal and continuing with EFT in the usual way. Figure 5.3 gives examples of affirmations to use with each of the levels of psychological reversal.

TIPS FOR SUCCESS AND ACCURACY

Small changes in technique can create big changes in your results. As mentioned earlier, successful use of kinesiology takes practice. The following suggestions, which have been gathered from a variety of people who use muscle testing on a regular basis, may also help you to increase your effectiveness.

1. **Avoid testing on an area that is sore or injured.**

2. **Be aware of differences in response.** Some people test more clearly than others. Their arms may drop dramatically; whereas, for others, the arm might just go slightly weak. Some results may also be subtle. If a person tests slightly weak, the influence may just be having a mild affect, while a very weak response may indicate a stronger effect.

3. **Use a neutral tone of voice.** If you use a questioning, doubting voice, the person is more apt to go weak as a

FIGURE 5.3
AFFIRMATIONS FOR OVERCOMING PR

LEVEL OF PR	AFFIRMATION TO USE IN THE EFT SEQUENCE
"I want to get over this _____."	"Even though I don't want to get over this _____, I deeply and completely accept myself."
"I want to completely get over this _____."	"Even though I don't want to completely get over this _____, I deeply and completely accept myself."
"I will get over this _____."	"Even though I don't think that I will ever get over this _____, I deeply and completely accept myself."
"I believe that I can get over this _____."	"Even though I don't believe I can get over this _____, I deeply and completely accept myself."
"I deserve to get over this _____."	"Even though I don't believe that I deserve to get over this _____, I deeply and completely accept myself."
"I will do everything necessary to get over this _____."	"Even though I am unwilling do everything necessary to get over this _____, I deeply and completely accept myself."
"I will allow myself to get over this _____.	"Even though I won't allow myself to get over this _____, I deeply and completely accept myself."

response to your tone of voice, not necessarily responding to the subject you are asking about.

4. **Keep the ego out of the way.** Muscle testing is not a
   contest. Any kind of competitive battle, where the provider and/or the receiver are trying to prove something,
   will interfere with the results. Being neutral about the
   results is the key to successful muscle testing for both
   the provider and the receiver.

   It sometimes is tricky to not let your biases or intui-
   tions show. Have empathy without being overly sympa-
   thetic or trying to please the other person. Be as detached as possible from the outcome, while still being
   supportive. The challenge of being detached about
   oneself is also the reason it can be harder to self-test.
   Practicing muscle testing will increase your confidence
   and accuracy.

5. **Be sure the receiver is ready.** Always finish the statement you are testing before applying pressure and be
   sure the receiver is resisting. Say the statement, like
   "My name is _____," and have the receiver repeat it
   aloud, or at least make sure the receiver has heard the
   statement. Then say "hold" just before pushing to be
   sure the receiver is resisting. Calibrate to the individual receiver's reaction time. Note how long it takes for
   a person to hear the question and take it in before you
   exert pressure on the arm.

6. **Use statements rather than questions.** Questions can
   produce confusion. Instead of asking "Is your mind
   strong?" for example, say "Focus on your mind."

7. **Use a light steady pressure above the wrist.** A sugges-
   tion would be to use two fingers, while holding the receiver's shoulder with the other hand. Avoid jerking or
   bouncing when you push on the arm.

8. **If in doubt, repeat the test.** Be sure that both you and the receiver are focusing on the test statement. If there is any doubt about whether the receiver was distracted or whether the result was strong or weak, repeat the test. You can also use the opposite statement, such as "I deserve…" and "I don't deserve…" to confirm the result. Just remember to trust that muscle testing works. At the same time, realize that just as in any test, inaccurate results can be due to lack of experience and not being aware of the importance of subtleties like the ones on this list.

9. **Be sure the receiver is not pushing upward.** The receiver should be resisting the downward pressure, not pushing upward. Pushing upward involves other muscles, and it will interfere with the accuracy of the test. Pushing up indicates the conscious mind is responding to the test, which can interfere with the results.

10. **Communicate with the receiver.** Encourage the receiver to have an open, exploratory attitude. Issues like deserving to improve or having the ability to improve in an area of a person's life are subtle, but the receiver may know where the problem lies or experience a sudden recognition about the source of the problem. When you get significant test results, ask if the receiver understands what they mean.

11. **Relax and take your time.** Test responses are sometimes confusing, so it is important not to rush. You may have to stop and think for a moment to be sure that you understand what the result of a test means.

12. **Give yourself positive suggestions.** Just before performing a test on yourself, tell yourself something like "I'm an easy read," "Muscle testing is easy for me," or "I am open and neutral." Let the experience be natural

and just let things unfold. You can also do a round of EFT, using an affirmation like "Even though I have doubts about muscle testing, I can deeply and completely accept myself."

13. **Have the receiver look down at the ground.** NLP research has shown that looking down grounds a person in the body, which is balancing. On the other hand, looking elsewhere may be distracting. Some people also find it helpful to concentrate by closing their eyes.

14. **Recognize when you or the receiver is losing focus or tiring.** Muscle testing is an intentional, focused act. Be sure to pause between questions, so there is no overlap. If you rush or get tired, your results will suffer.

UNDERSTANDING INCONSISTENT RESULTS WITH MUSCLE TESTING

You may wonder what is happening if you are having difficulty muscle testing yourself or with another person who is not testing accurately even with the tips. Judith Swack, originator of the Healing from the Body Level Up system, has muscle tested thousands of clients and reports the following considerations when a person can't be muscle tested accurately:

- **The muscle tests strong for both "yes" and "no."** Swack reports that this is the most common problem. If "yes" and "no" are equally strong, or if the "no" reaction is not well defined, Swack equates this with the presence of a phobic anxiety. If the "no" response is actually stronger than the "yes" response, like a reflex jerk, this indicates that the recipient is overcompensating for a fear of saying "no" or a fear of showing weakness. In any of these cases, you could discuss these possibilities with the recipient and do EFT on the fear or anxiety.

In his book *The Energy Psychology Desktop Companion*, David Gruder also equates the strong "yes" and "no" with Neurological Disorganization which is discussed in Chapter Eight. This would be the next thing to explore if you are not receiving results exploring fear and anxiety.

- **The muscle tests weak for "yes" and strong for "no."** Swack reports that this indicates the presence of a limiting belief or beliefs. These can be accessed without the further use of muscle testing by doing the Holistic Process, so this is where we would go next.

- **The muscle tests weak for both "yes" and "no."** This could indicate a number of different things, including anxiety, as described for the strong "yes" and "no." It may also suggest that the recipient needs food, has low blood sugar, or is being affected by energy toxins, which we describe later, or the receiver might be affected by a trauma. David Gruder also mentions that a weak "yes" and "no" may indicate apprehension about addressing the problem at hand. Larry Nims also notes that such responses can indicate that the receiver is confused.

    To find out what is happening with the weak "yes" and "no," you could simply ask if the receiver feels hungry or confused, if he or she has been traumatized, if he or she has some apprehension about addressing the problem. With being traumatized and with apprehension, you can start by doing EFT on the apprehension or whatever the client identifies related to feelings about addressing the problem at hand. If none of these seem to apply, your next option is to explore energy toxins, which are discussed in Chapter Nine.

Once the origin of the inaccurate testing is resolved, the recipient should muscle test accurately. And the fact that the recipient has cleared the blockage and muscle tests properly evidences great progress.

Lilly's Story: Correcting Muscle Testing

In a session with Phillip, Lilly tested strong for both yes and no. She sensed that she felt unable to say no or show weakness, because of her family's strong, domineering religious background. Upon questioning, she revealed that, as a child, she continually received the message from authority figures not to complain, so she repressed her feelings and pain. She remembered standing on her feet for long hours in church at age eight. If she fidgeted, her grandmother would tap her on the head and embarrass her. Lilly also recalled being chastised as a child for not practicing her scriptures properly. If she drank milk during certain holy days, she was harshly reprimanded. When focusing on her fear of expressing her pain and desires, she reported a SUDs of ten.

Phillip and Lilly started with the affirmation, "Even though I wasn't able to express my pain and my desires, I still can accept myself enough and have many options available," and completed the short sequence with the reminder phrase "this pain and desire." Afterward, Lilly recalled a friend of hers who had recently disapproved of her taking an alternative healing class. The next affirmation then was, "Even though I couldn't get credibility with my friend, I still can deeply accept myself and move on with my life." This round of EFT took her SUDs from ten to two.

To increase her awareness, Phillip then guided Lilly through the Centering Process. As she relaxed and connected with her soul's guidance, Lilly received a message to stand on her own two feet, and come from love and conviction in her heart. To enhance this new understanding, they did an EFT Enhancement, tapping while saying "I'm gaining more love and conviction." After tapping, Lilly's positive numbers on love and conviction rose from a four to an eight.

Lilly then recalled the original incidents: having to stand in the church and being chastised for erring with her scriptural practice and for drinking milk during the holy period. The SUDs was now at a two. Phillip asked her if she could completely remove these fears in just one minute, would it create any problems for her? She replied that she would be rejected. Lilly then did a round with the affirmation, "If I express my desires, I will be rejected, but I can still deeply and completely accept myself enough and really want to get over this."

With another round of EFT, Lilly's fears of rejection and expressing herself were gone. Phillip again muscle tested her for yes and no, and she muscle tested fine, with a clear yes and no. Lilly felt great about being able to muscle test, which she had really wanted to do.

MASSIVE PSYCHOLOGICAL REVERSAL

Our discussion of PR would not be complete without examining a condition known as Massive Psychological Reversal. It may sound a bit ominous, and in some ways it is, because it is the result of having PR in a lot of areas. Fortunately, this pattern can be addressed.

The key here involves examining how we respond to the events in our lives. As mentioned earlier, most of us have PR in one or a small number of areas in our lives, so we can succeed easily in some areas and encounter difficulty in other areas. A small percentage of people have very little PR and are able to overcome seemingly insurmountable obstacles with ease. On the other end of the scale are those for whom any small obstacle seems insurmountable or for whom almost everything seems to go wrong. These generalized reversals are symptoms of Massive PR.

Let's look closer. As Roger Callahan pointed out, Massive PR is evident in individuals who test weak when saying "I want to be happy" and test strong when saying "I want to be miserable." In these people, the energy flow through the body is disturbed in a way that makes both physical and emotional healing difficult. They test weak for achieving positive results in most aspects of life. Not surprisingly, as mentioned earlier, they have difficulty improving their health and realizing their goals they tend to procrastinate and are prone to self-destructive thinking.

These tendencies create an understandably negative attitude, so Massive PR is also linked to depression, chronic pain and fatigue, and addictions. This pessimistic perspective may even create a reluctance to try to change or seek help, because everything seems futile. Homeless people and criminals provide extreme examples of pervasive reversals.

As with many things, there are degrees of imbalance. Minor stress, like a cold or small shock, may cause a temporary energy reversal that soon corrects itself. If not automatically corrected, the minor reversal can be balanced in a relatively stable person with some simple energy tapping, massage, deep breathing, exercise, hydration, rest, or meditation. For a person with Massive PR, recovery from even the most minor disruptions may seem to be difficult or impossible.

Identifying Massive PR

You can pinpoint the presence of Massive PR with either of the following muscle tests.

- **The Hand-Over-the-Head Method:** Have the recipient place the palm side of either hand just above the top of the head and muscle testing the other arm. It should test strong. Then have the recipient turn the hand above the head over so the back of the hand is just above the top of the head, with the palm pointing up. Now the muscle should test weak. If the muscle tests weak when the palm is down and strong when the palm is up, the person has Massive PR.

Another possible result of this test is that both hand positions test strong, In this case, Neurological Disorganization is the likely culprit. We describe this condition and how to address it in Chapter Eight.

- **The Happy Test:** Test the recipient for the statements "I want to be happy" and for "I want to be miserable." The first statement should test strong and the second statement should test weak. If the subject tests weak for wanting to be happy and strong for wanting to be miserable, Massive PR is the likely cause.

Temporary Correction of Massive PR

To correct this condition temporarily and continue with EFT, we suggest using either of the following approaches:

1. Tap the karate chop point while saying "Even though I don't want to be happy, I deeply and completely accept myself." Then retest the Hand-Over-the-Head Method. If you now receive a normal response, you can continue with EFT. This method comes from James Durlacher, author of the book *Freedom From Fear Forever*.

2. Do the Short or Complete EFT Sequence using the affirmation "Even though I am miserable, I deeply and completely accept myself." and the reminder phrase "this misery."

Correcting Massive PR Permanently

Recognizing that Massive PR tends to be the result of pervasive negative thinking, permanent correction generally requires a change in thinking. With a holistic model, which we will discuss more in the next chapter, this means transforming limiting beliefs and judgments into positive beliefs and love. This book provides a variety of ways of doing this, including the following:

- Repeat the second procedure described above every waking hour for a week, then retest the Massive PR on a regular basis and focus on positive thinking.

- Use the Diamond Approach described in Chapter Seven to create a "high thymus outlook."

- Practice the Soul Centering Process described in Chapter Six regularly, focusing on your value and self-worth. The Soul honors the wonderful uniqueness of each individual, particularly oneself; it provides positive input that you can reinforce whenever you think of it.

- Use the Holistic Process described in the next chapter regularly to access limiting beliefs and judgments and clear them with EFT.

- Observe when you procrastinate. Even if you test normal for Massive PR, most of us procrastinate at times. And wherever we procrastinate, we are withholding energy that could be used beneficially. Observing what is happening when you procrastinate is a way to uncover emotional blockages, limiting beliefs, and judgments that need to be addressed. You can do this by focusing on a time when you tend to put things off and using the Holistic Process. You may be surprised at your unconscious reasons for procrastinating.

- Refer to the Forgiveness Section in Chapter Seven.

- Refer to the section Appreciating Yourself and Your Possibilities in Chapter Seven.

- Use Affirmations: Since Massive PR is related to negative thinking, you may want to interject positive thoughts as frequently as possible. Gary Craig calls the thoughts that constantly run through our heads "the writing on our walls." If you are writing a lot of negative stuff, this is what you will most likely have in your life. If you write more positive things, your life will change for the better.

It can help to write down positive thoughts and place them in prominent locations in your home, like on the refrigerator door and the bathroom mirror. This will remind you of your goals. Also remember that you can strengthen positive affirmations, as described earlier.

All of these methods require consistent focus over time to change the "writing on the walls" and correct Massive PR permanently. For all of us, this also shows how important the quality of our thoughts is to our well-being and our ability to create the life of our dreams. We can all benefit from the practices described above.

CONCLUSION

As you have seen, exploring Psychological Reversal and its negative impact can be quite illuminating. Eliminating it is freeing, opening a new world of possibilities. Correcting PR along with the holistic healing tools you will find in the next chapter will exponentially increase your ability to create more emotional freedom and transform your life.

CHAPTER SIX

A Holistic Approach to PR

Each soul is potentially divine.
The goal is to manifest this divine within.

- VIVEKANANDA

If you are not drawn to using kinesiology to deal with Psychological Reversal, you have other options. As mentioned, PR is related to having a limiting perspective on one's possibilities and oneself. We can understand these limitations better from a holistic perspective. The methods presented in this chapter are not part of Gary Craig's toolbox. They are tools we use regularly to deepen awareness of what is happening in the body, mind and spirit; increase the effectiveness of the EFT Tapping Sequences; and provide alternatives to the tapping itself, when needed. These tools include the following:

- The Holistic Process

- Centering and Grounding

- The Reframing and Anchoring Process (R&A)

The word holistic means "relating to or concerned with integrated wholes or complete systems rather than with analyzing or treatment of separate parts." When we approach healing holistically, we connect the part to the whole; in fact, the part contains the whole. Analyzing and fragmenting only work when they are integrated into the seamless whole. From this perspective, any kind of dysfunction is regarded as fragmentation from the whole and healing is viewed as a return to wholeness.

This approach, then, acknowledges that everything is connected. When we address problems at any level, physically, emotionally, mentally, or spiritually, we understand that they are also connected to each of the other levels. Those who have experience with the human energy field understand that the physical, emotional, mental, and spiritual levels are distinct parts of the self with distinct perspectives that are also connected with each other and with the wholeness of the entire energy system.

THE NATURE OF HOLISTIC HEALING

With a holistic approach to healing, then, the part is seen in reference to the whole. Each issue is understood in relation to the entire person, including the body, emotions, mind, and spirit. And the whole person is seen in relation to the world in which he or she lives. Any dysfunction related to a physical ailment, emotion, belief, attitude, or judgment is brought back into harmony with the whole.

This approach can provide the basis for viewing health and healing in a new way based on learning about oneself and making positive, lasting changes. Examining the physical, emotional, mental, and spiritual aspects is enlightening and opens to powerful healing. Figure 6.1 shows where the journey to wholeness takes us on each of the four levels.

As you can see, the entire system is considered, rather than

FIGURE 6.1
THE FOUR LEVELS OF HEALING

THE HEALING JOURNEY TAKES US	FROM	UNCONSCIOUS EXPRESSION OF THE EGO
	TO	CONSCIOUS EXPRESSION OF THE SOUL
Physically	From	Pain, discomfort and illness, where physical vitality is suppressed
	To	A sense of physical well-being, comfort, and vitality
Emotionally	From	Painful unresolved emotions and a lack of joy
	To	Emotional understanding and a joyful experience of life
Mentally	From	Limiting beliefs and attitudes, which create limited possibilities in the world
	To	Unlimited thinking and possibilities in the world; genuine freedom
Spiritually	From	Judgment of self and others, feelings of shame and separation
	To	A loving existence with feelings of being a part of a unified whole

limiting the focus to addressing symptoms at just one level while ignoring dysfunction on the other levels. Doctors, often only address problems on the physical level, leaving any related emotional pain, limiting thoughts, and judgments toward ourselves and others in place.

This form of healing is incomplete. Fortunately, it is becoming widely recognized that physical problems are often related to emotions that have not been acknowledged. If we can acknowledge these emotions and clear them with EFT, we have improved our potential for healing. And, even better, if we can address emotions before they affect the physical body, we can avoid potential illness and enjoy life more.

From the physical level, each level also provides a deeper level of healing. The emotional level is deeper than the physical level and the mental level deeper than the emotional level, with the spiritual level providing the deepest and most complete healing. This demonstrates why EFT may not work when addressing a problem at the physical or emotional level: there may be something at the mental and spiritual levels that still needs to be addressed to complete the healing. Once this occurs with the Holistic Process, EFT generally works on troubling emotions, and this may also be reflected on the physical level as well.

THE HOLISTIC MAP

The Holistic Process we described in *Getting Thru to Your Emotions with EFT* provides an easy–to–use map of the physical, emotional, mental, and spiritual levels of the energy system. Though we do not want to repeat the entire process here, we want to offer a simple way to access these four levels and to address PR without using kinesiology.

This method is similar to the Magic Question, with the addition of more awareness. You are essentially asking four questions, with some variations, to access the four levels. You start with the physical level, because it is the most concrete. From there, each level becomes more subtle. Recognition of what is occurring at each level also becomes progressively more subtle, though the answers are generally there when we open to them.

This brings us to an important point: the Holistic Process requires honest self-examination. Though we may be hoping that EFT will act like a magic pill that will instantaneously eliminate all of our problems, this is not always the case. Realizing that we have to learn some things about ourselves can sometimes be difficult, because many of us are concerned about what we might discover. We do not want to dig down into the unconscious programming mentioned earlier and find out what is really happening, for fear of discovering something bad about ourselves.

These kinds of fears are unfounded, because the limited parts of ourselves that we are afraid of confronting are not really us. They are the fragmented parts that need to be brought back to wholeness so we can recognize that we are wonderfully unique, deserving of love, and in possession of infinite possibilities. Discovering the deeper truth about ourselves and realizing our full potential is the purpose of the Holistic Process.

THE FOUR KEY QUESTIONS

To reach an open, balanced starting place, you can do a brief Centering Process, or just close your eyes and take a few nice deep breaths to relax your mind and body. You need to start with a specific issue, as you would with EFT. Generally, the issue is either physical or emotional, though it can be at any level. As with EFT, be as specific as possible when you define the issue and if you have more than one issue, address them one at a time.

With one issue in mind, just relax and open yourself to whatever comes into your awareness when you ask the questions listed in Figure 6.2. As you proceed, you are going from the most easily accessible level, the physical level, to the emotional level, mental level, and the deepest level, the spiritual level. The levels of PR focus on the mental and spiritual levels, and these are generally the places where you will discover what you need to understand to complete the process with EFT.

Awareness of what is happening on each level is more subtle as you go, so just take your time with each question and, to maintain your focus, you may want to close your eyes for a moment again to connect with the deeper levels of your mind. Then write whatever comes to mind down, so you can review it when you are done. Notice if you feel an urge to avoid any of the questions. If so, take another deep breath and open to loving self-examination. Since all the levels are energetically interconnected, there are generally corresponding blockages on all levels. Remember, whatever comes up reveals the limitation that is blocking the truth, which is always freeing.

Once you have gone through the four questions, you can use EFT for clearing the emotions. Then, go back through each of the levels and ask the questions again, noticing the changes in your awareness at each level. They are generally dramatic and transformational.

Also notice that you may find variations on these questions that work better for you. For identifying the emotions behind physical symptoms, EFT Expert Betty Moore-Hafter says:

> A favorite question is, "If there were any emotion in that part of the body (or in that pain, stiffness, etc.), what would it be?" The body is also highly metaphorical, as our language indicates. A person with neck pain can be asked, "is there anything or anyone who is a pain in the neck for you?" Amazingly, a core issue is often then revealed and tapping on that core issue may resolve most of the discomfort.

FIGURE 6.2
THE FOUR LEVELS OF HEALING

LEVEL	QUESTION
Physical	Focusing on the issue, where do you feel it physically and how does it feel in your body? Notice any and all sensations related to the issue at hand.
Emotional	Focusing on the feelings in your body, what do you feel emotionally? On this level, there may be more than one emotion, so you need to ask if there is more until it feels like you have uncovered all of the emotions.
Mental	Focusing on the emotions, how does this issue relate to your possibilities in the world? This question may seem a bit obscure to some people, so you may have to rephrase it. Here you are aiming to access beliefs and attitudes that are related to the emotions. Another way of saying it might be "How does this emotion relate to your sense of power in the world?" or "How does this emotion relate to achieving what you want?"
Spiritual	Focusing on the emotions and beliefs, how do you feel about yourself? From this perspective, how do you evaluate yourself?

Understanding Limiting Beliefs

Most people can understand the physical and emotional levels pretty easily. The mental and spiritual levels can be a bit trickier, so we want to provide some examples to assist you.

The mental level, which relates to our power in the world, could be seen as the externalization of a problem, how it plays out in one's life. It expresses itself in beliefs and attitudes, through which we create our reality. If, in the deepest recesses of your mind, you think that life is a bowl of cherries, this expansive belief is what you get. On the other hand, if you think that life is the pits, this limiting belief is creating your reality.

Understanding the beliefs that are creating our reality is critically important if we want to be free to live joyful, fulfilling lives. EFT Expert Carol Tuttle discusses limiting beliefs related to money this way:

> If you're not making as much money as you'd like, then you're holding onto some negative beliefs about yourself and how much money you're capable of flowing. Money is a resource with a neutral energy that we project our beliefs onto. Money takes on that energy and that is the experience we get with it. When you change your beliefs about money, money changes for you. When you choose wealth, and start to believe that wealth is spiritual and abundant, wealth finds you.

We would add, if you have more money, you have more resources available to make a positive contribution to the world.

Of course, most of us have limiting beliefs in many areas. With the levels of PR, statements like "I don't want to release this _____" or "I cannot release this _____" expose beliefs about why one's possibilities are limited. The following are some other examples of limiting beliefs. If any of them sound true to you, fill in the blanks and you may learn something new about yourself. They may also help you to recognize other limiting beliefs or attitudes that are preventing your from realizing the life of your dreams.

- I cannot be powerful, because...
- My possibilities are limited, because...
- I cannot achieve my goals, because...
- Life is difficult, because...
- I cannot assert myself, because...
- People take unfair advantage of me, because...

These statements may also trigger awareness of other limitations to examine. When we are in touch with our wholeness and value ourselves. these limitations fall away, along with the excuses that support them. Once we recognize them, EFT can work wonders.

Judgments

On the deepest level, we have judgments about ourselves that prevent us from experiencing wholeness. Here are some examples. Again, if any of them sound true to you, fill in the blanks, and you may learn something new.

- I don't deserve the good things in life, because...
- I am flawed, because...
- I am inadequate, because...
- I cannot open my heart, because...
- I don't deserve love, because...
- I shouldn't exist, because

Also, note that we tend to judge others when we don't feel good about ourselves. Some people cannot admit that they feel insecure, but it is obvious in their judgments of others. When we love ourselves, we feel whole and complete. In a very simple sense, we are okay and everything else is okay. We can accept others as they are, even when we do not agree with them. Spiritually, we are connected with the soul and all is well.

The deepest and most complete healing occurs at the spiritual level. In our work, we always strive to achieve this level of healing, because it eliminates the likelihood that there are deeper levels of dysfunction that could cause the symptoms to recur. You could say that dysfunction begins when we lose our sense of wholeness or okayness and a part of us is fragmented from the unity of the soul. This fragmentation cascades down from the spiritual level to the mental level, the emotional level, and finally, to the physical level. The Holistic Process turns this pattern around by bringing healing to all levels and returning us to wholeness. It works on just about any emotional, mental, and spiritual issue, and may also work wonders on physical conditions as well, though, as mentioned earlier, this is not as reliable. At any rate, with physical conditions, there is always something to learn, and the Holistic Process combined with EFT can be a big help in dealing with physical problems.

Example of the Holistic Process with Chocolate Cravings

Once Phillip was showing a class how to overcome chocolate cravings with EFT. It generally works like a charm for such carvings, as shown on *Getting Thru to Your Emotions with EFT DVD/Video 1*. The demonstration starts out with the volunteer smelling a piece of chocolate, then after doing EFT, rating how much craving is left. In the hundreds of cases we have done, the craving usually starts somewhere between six and ten and it almost always goes down close to zero after one to three rounds of EFT. In this demonstration, however, Ginger's SUDs level was hardly dropping after several rounds of EFT.

Phillip knew he needed to go deeper to address the problem, even though he had a limited amount of time for the presentation. Going into the Holistic Process, Phillip started to ask the four key questions. On the physical level, Ginger noticed that she felt pain in her heart. Emotionally, she experienced sadness and loneliness. Mentally, she believed it was a lonely world. Spiritually, she judged herself as being inadequate. She was reminded that her mother fed her chocolate as a young child. Back then it was a treat and having it now reconnected her with those treasured times with her mother.

Nowadays Ginger felt that her life was lacking love and comfort. She wasn't lacking in chocolate, though, as she consumed frequently. Based on the Holistic Process, Phillip suggested that she change the affirmation from "Even though I have this chocolate craving,..." to "Even though I'm sad and lonely and want comfort and love, ..." After one round of EFT, she showed a great relief. She looked much lighter and no longer wanted the chocolate that was in her hand. Holistically, all of the energetic levels had shifted. Now, Ginger's heart felt soothed. Emotionally, she was peaceful. Mentally, she saw the world as friendly, and spiritually, she felt good about herself. The whole process took about ten minutes.

An added note about the Holistic Process: people really like it. They are amazed at what has been hidden away in the unconscious mind and grateful for the new awareness this process so easily brings. As the layers are uncovered and healed, it is like finding hidden treasure. EFT alone often works wonders, but when deeper unconscious blockages are present, the Holistic Process can deepen the healing and increase awareness.

SOUL CENTERING AND GROUNDING

The Holistic Process shows that healing at the spiritual level provides the most complete healing and creates possibilities for bringing more joy, love and freedom into our lives. From this perspective, disconnection from the truth and wisdom of the soul is where dysfunctional patterns begin. The feelings of shame and separation promote limited thinking, painful emotions, and even physical symptoms.

The Soul Centering Process reverses this process of creating limitation and pain. It is transformational, connecting us both with our higher awareness and our bodies. The ascended state Soul Centering produces facilitates healing with EFT or any method. It aligns us with our higher wisdom, an intelligence that is far vaster than our normal awareness. At the same time, it grounds us, aligning the body and the earth. Together, these alignments create a profound state of well-being and balance.

Here are four ways to center:

1. **Use the Soul Centering Process,** which follows.

2. **Imagine yourself as a tree**, with deep roots and branches extending to the sky, with the sun acting like your higher self, sending energy down through your body.

3. **Remember a time where you felt whole and complete,** like a time when you were in nature, were surrounded by beauty, or felt much love.

4. **Visualize going to a sacred place** to meet with your higher self.

The Soul Centering Process

The following process is from our *Soul News* Email Newsletter. You can find it, along with more related information on our website at www.gettingthru.org/sn0599.htm.

For those who are not familiar with guided visualization processes, the key is to relax, disconnect from the active, rational mind, and connect with the receptive side of your nature. The easiest way to do this is to shift your focus away from the thoughts that normally occupy your attention and focus on the sensations you feel in your body and the emotions you are experiencing. As you do this, allow the experience to unfold without expectation and involve all of your inner senses to deepen the experience.

This centering process is designed to be easy enough for anyone to do and short enough that you can do it every day to strengthen your connection with your soul. It will not work, though, if you are in a hurry, because, as we mentioned before, you connect with your soul through the receptive side of your nature. Be sure to allow ample time when you begin to use it; as you become familiar with the process, you will find that the connection will come quickly and easily.

This process is designed for you to read each word slowly and close your eyes at intervals to focus on the experience. Before you start, you may want to focus for a moment on an issue that you would like to address as you connect with the energy of your soul and your higher self. Now we can begin.

As you start to read this process and prepare to relax, take a few deep breaths and feel the tension beginning to melt from your body. Fill your lungs completely with pure, clear air with each inhale and allow the tension to continue to release with each exhale, so that with each breath, you feel more and more relaxed and balanced, and your body becomes lighter, allowing the tension to drift down through your arms, legs and feet and into the earth. Now, imagine that there is a cord extending from the base of your spine deep into the earth that provides firm grounding and stability. As you continue to focus on your breathing, feel yourself becoming balanced within your body and more stable with every breath.

Now bring clear energy into your mind with each inhale, so all of the cells of your brain can relax and your mind becomes more and more clear with each breath. Allow any thoughts you do not need right now to drift away so your mind can become completely clear and relaxed. And allow the clear energy to move down so that your entire head is relaxed, traveling down your neck and shoulders now, and allowing all of the organs in your body to relax. Now allow a wave of clear energy and relaxation to move gently down your arms, all the way down to the tips of your fingers. And feel another wave of relaxation moving down your spine to your legs and feet, traveling all the way to the tips of your toes, so your entire body is relaxed and filled with clear, pure energy. You may want to stop reading for a moment and focus on relaxing your entire body, from the top of your head to the tips of your toes.

You can use the simple steps above for a quick centering or continue on to connect with the soul, which provides even more stability and a higher level of awareness.

As you continue, begin to focus your breath on the area around your heart, where your soul connects with your body. Imagine that you are sending pure energy into this area, so that with each breath, there is more and more energy there and, as you continue breathing, you can feel the energy intensifying so it may seem like there is a ball of light around your heart. Allow this ball of light to become brighter and brighter, radiating its energy out in all directions, so that you feel yourself completely surrounded by the energy and you can feel this energy permeate every cell of your body with its beautiful light. As you do this, if any pain comes up in your heart, simply allow the pain to come out into your awareness and ask the breath to release it. You can also clear it with EFT before going further. Letting go of this pain will help you to completely embrace the love you hold in your heart. You may want to stop reading again for a moment and focus on experiencing the energy of your soul in your heart and radiating out around you.

Now you can shift your focus to the area just above your head and imagine that there is another light there. As you imagine it there, allow this light to begin to pour down through the top of your head and fill your entire body, so that you can see and feel yourself filled with this light all the way down to the tips of your fingers and the tips of your toes. As it becomes brighter and brighter, it overflows so that you are completely surrounded with

this light and you can feel yourself in perfect harmony and bal-
ance with everything that is around you. You can also feel the
energy of all of the others who are building this connection and
allow it to help you to strengthen the experience for you. Take a
moment now to feel this harmony and how you are connected
with all that is.

From this place of peace, you can ask for guidance about any
problem you may be experiencing. This is especially useful if you
focused on a problem before starting the process and can recall
how it felt to you then. You should find that your perspective is
different than it was before. From this place of clarity, you can
bring in new levels of awareness to help you in any aspect of your
life. If you are focusing on a problem, you may want to stop read-
ing for a moment and view it from this higher perspective.

If you were not able to fully experience the energy of your
soul, just continue to practice this process and focus on releasing
any painful emotions that come up. You will notice a shift as you
release the emotions and open to the loving energy of your soul.

Now it is time to come back to the present time and feel your-
self where you are, sitting or lying down, making note of your
body's position. And, as you breathe, allow your breath to bring
you back to your normal waking state, feeling alert and alive. As
you prepare to go off to other activities, make sure that you are
grounded with the cord that extends from the base of your spine
to the center of the earth.

Along with creating a wonderfully relaxed and balanced
state, being centered is a key to helping others; it provides a
firm foundation for healing. It also generally produces grounding, but grounding is important enough to merit focusing on it
specifically.

Grounding

When we are ungrounded, we feel spacey and disconnected.
With grounding, we feel stable and more able to cope with the

twists and turns of daily life. You can ground yourself using any of the following techniques:

- Sense your feet attached to the floor, or like magnets grounded to the earth.

- Do some deep breathing and feel yourself being connected with your body.

- Imagine a grounding cord from your tail bone to the center of the earth.

- Take a walk. Strolling through grass with bare feet is particularly grounding.

- Drink water.

- Name the objects in the room.

- Bend over with your knees slightly bent, feet firmly planted on the floor, while breathing slowly. Then gradually rise to a standing position.

- Eat some food (yet avoid unhealthy foods and overeating, which are ungrounding).

- Hold a stone like hematite, jasper, onyx, or petrified wood.

Grounding connects us with the body and creates stability. As you saw, the Soul Centering Process also includes grounding. In a sense, one could say that it brings us into a perfect sense of alignment between heaven and earth.

Our studies of the healing power of the soul have led us to another holistic method that draws directly on the soul's energy for healing. The Spiritual Kinesiology Reframing and Anchoring Process, or R&A for short, is another easy, fast, and effective method that can replace the tapping sequences, if desired. Since it also works so well, we will provide a brief description of it here.

THE SK REFRAMING AND ANCHORING (R&A) PROCESS

This is a wonderful method that we use interchangeably with the EFT Tapping Sequences. When PR is present, R&A may work better than tapping, because it heals at the spiritual level, which, as mentioned earlier, is the deepest and most complete level of healing. We describe R&A in detail in our *Getting Thru to Your Soul* book, along with the other SK Techniques. The description provided here is drawn from that material.

Anchoring

R&A includes the use of two powerful techniques: anchoring and reframing. Anchoring is a term derived from Neurolinguistic Programming (NLP) that refers to how a memory in one of the senses stimulates a response in one or more of the other senses. Hearing an old song brings back wonderful memories. Or maybe it's the smell of a particular perfume or the color of a special dress that recreates that special feeling. These are examples of naturally occurring anchors.

We have many anchors that help us to get along in our environments. Red and green traffic lights stimulate drivers to stop and start at the right times. The sound of the school bell reminds students that it is time to go to class. Anchors provide a way for the unconscious mindto sort and retrieve information. Unfortunately, if we are not aware of them, they may be using us more than we are using them. With awareness, however, we can replace unproductive anchors with positive resource anchors. This can help us to function better, enjoy life more, and achieve our goals.

To use the soul's healing power, we can anchor in the soul's wisdom and bring ourselves more into alignment with our true purpose. This is what we do with R&A, with remarkable results. We first need to understand how anchors are created:

- **The recipient's internal state is the key.** In everyday life, we have no control of the anchors we unconsciously install in ourselves. This, of course, is the problem. Fortunately, with R&A, we can consciously anchor a positive soul-aligned state.

- **Timing is critical.** Anchors occur naturally during a heightened experience. This tells us that when setting anchors, we want to install them at the height of an experience.

- **Repetition strengthens an anchor.** If you repeat the experience you desire, you can strengthen the anchor.

Reframing

Reframing is another powerful NLP technique that clears blockages by replacing an unbalanced pattern with a balanced one. *Getting Thru to Your Emotions with EFT* includes a reframing process that replaces a painful image with a positive one. We will go a step further here by reframing with the soul's energy and wisdom. With this technique, you can anchor your soul's wisdom into all aspects of your life and realize your dreams. The R&A Process quickly changes a painful, unbalanced pattern in the unconscious mindand energy system to a balanced one.

The R&A Technique

The general process for R&A is similar to the EFT Tapping Sequences in that you determine a specific issue to clear, measure the SUDs level, and perform rounds of the healing process. Each round of R&A takes about as much time as a round of EFT tapping, so it is equally quick and easy. The healing process is slightly different and may even seem to be too simple to work, but based on our experience with thousands of individuals and on extensive feedback from others who use it, we have found it to be just as effective as EFT.

Before starting this process, it is necessary to establish that the receiver is able to make a connection with the soul. We generally ask our clients if they have a way that they connect with their spiritual selves. If they do, we have them describe how they do it. If not, we guide them with one of the methods mentioned in the Centering and Grounding section.

Step 1: Setup

This step corresponds to the EFT Setup, where you decide on a specific issue to clear. As with EFT, you want to be as specific as possible.

Step 2: Evaluation

The purpose of this step, which directly corresponds to the Evaluation in EFT, is to measure between one and ten the intensity of the issue you want to address.

One of the benefits of using R&A is that it is not necessary to know the source of a problem to clear it. If there is no emotional intensity or physical sensation to measure, you can skip this step. On the other hand, if you can quantify it, you will have a way to evaluate your progress when you finish.

Step 3: Balancing

The Reframing and Anchoring Technique (R&A) shifts an unbalanced energy pattern, which is anchored physically on the shoulder, to a balanced one, which is anchored physically on the arm. This process may look so simple that you may think it could not possibly work. We had these thoughts ourselves, until we tried it and saw the results. In the eight years that we have been using it, we have found it to be as simple and effective as EFT.

Figure 6.3 illustrates hand positions for using this process with another person. Here is the process:

- The provider can stand or sit next to the receiver. For the purpose of this example, imagine that the provider is sitting to the right of the receiver. As the receiver focuses on the unbalanced pattern, the provider lightly places his or her left hand on the right shoulder of the receiver to anchor the pattern. After silently counting to 10, the provider releases the hand. If you are doing this process alone, place your left hand on your left knee or another place on your body.

- Now it is time to reframe. You have two choices:

  1. **Anchor the Soul's Energy:** The provider says something like: "Focus on connecting with that soulful part of yourself. Imagine the light of your higher self above your head and allow the perfect energy to come down from this light to balance _____ [describe the pattern you are working on]. Feel the energy coming down, surrounding you with its healing light. When you feel yourself completely surrounded by this balanced energy, say okay."

  2. **Recall a Soulful Experience:** This is similar to the approach Carl Carpenter uses with Hypno-Kinesiology, the precursor of Spiritual Kinesiology. The provider instructs the receiver by saying something like: "Think of time in your life when you felt whole, complete, and confident."

- While the receiver continues to focus on the balanced pattern, the provider places his or her right hand on the receiver's right arm above the elbow to anchor it and says

FIGURE 6.3
HAND POSITIONS FOR R&A

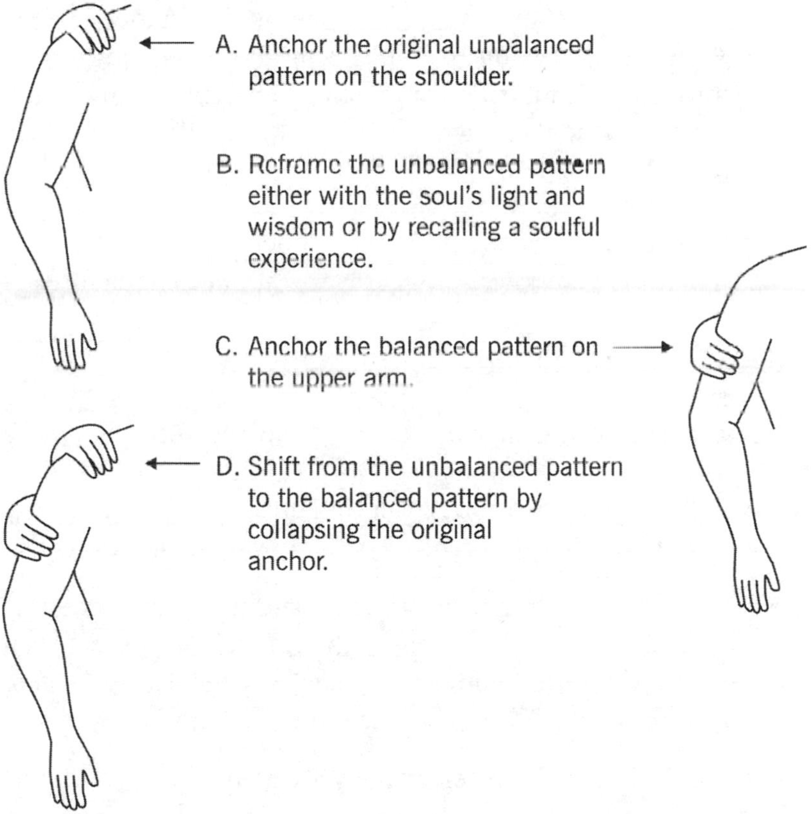

A. Anchor the original unbalanced pattern on the shoulder.

B. Reframe the unbalanced pattern either with the soul's light and wisdom or by recalling a soulful experience.

C. Anchor the balanced pattern on the upper arm.

D. Shift from the unbalanced pattern to the balanced pattern by collapsing the original anchor.

something like: "Continue to focus on this energy and feel it becoming even stronger." After silently counting to ten, the provider releases the hand. If you are doing this process alone, place your right hand on your right knee or another place on your body.

- The provider asks the receiver to think about nothing and again places his or her hands on both anchors. In our example, the left hand goes on the right shoulder and the right hand goes on the right arm above the elbow. The provider counts silently to ten, then removes the hand from the shoulder. This releases the negative anchor. He or she then counts to five while leaving the right hand on the arm to reinforce the positive anchor, then releases this hand. If you are doing this process alone, place your hands on your knees or wherever you put them before.

Step 4: Re-Evaluation

When you have finished balancing, have the receiver take a deep breath to allow the energy to reconfigure. The receiver may feel the energy shift over a period of a seconds or minutes. Then there are a few different ways to re-evaluate the changes.

- Have the receiver focus on the issue in the same way he or she did initially. Measure the intensity again between one and ten, and notice any changes. In most cases, there is a substantial change or the issue is completely gone.

- Discuss how the receiver feels about the issue now. The balancing process often brings unconscious information into the individual's awareness. Discussing it can lead to profound recognition of the change that occurred. While it is not necessary for the receiver to share this experience, this can help to integrate the changes. We generally offer the possibility of sharing.

If you determine that you are finished using SK, simply wipe off the anchor points with a few gentle sweeps of your hand, like you are removing dust, to complete the process. If you determine that more work needs to be done, you can do another round of balancing, just as you would with EFT.

Although one round of R&A sometimes releases the blockage, several rounds are often required to bring the intensity of the issue all the way down to zero. As with EFT, this simply means that there are different aspects of the imbalance to release. With each round, ask the receiver if the emotion has changed, such as from fear to anger, and continue with whatever emotion has surfaced.

With a little practice, R&A is easy to do and amazingly effective. As one client commented, "It is deceptively simple, but profoundly effective in obtaining real shifts with lasting results." Of course, there may be times when you do not receive the desired results. If, after several rounds of the process you do not seem to be making progress, there is probably something the receiver needs to understand consciously for the pattern to clear. When this happens, you can use the Holistic Process to find out what is occurring.

Lisa's R&A Story

After being her mother's caretaker for many months, Lisa's mother died. Since she had been training in our Holistic Healing Class how to do EFT and Spiritual Kinesiology, she had done relatively well going through the grieving process. Nonetheless, a month after her mother's passing, some distressing issues rose up from her unconscious.

Although she had spent many hours with her mom, Lisa was at work the day she passed away. Lisa now remembered her thoughts while driving to work on what turned out to be her mother's final day. She recalled focusing on hurtful things her mother had said to her during her life. She now felt a strong guilt about focusing on the negative during last day her mother was alive, instead of all the wonderful things that they had shared.

Her guilt was at a nine intensity. Using R&A, Phillip helped her to reframe the experience with her soul's awareness. She connected with light and her spiritual source. After one round, Phillip asked her if there was a message and Lisa reported understanding that there was a lot of love between them and her guilt had gone down to a three.

As the energy reconfigured, Lisa immediately felt sadness, which she tearfully rated at ten. She was sad that she couldn't be with her mother during her last day. Another round of R&A brought her the message, "your mother is in good hands." Her mother had been embraced by the higher realms. Lisa could feel the soulful connection very strongly now.

Lisa's guilt and sadness were completely gone after two rounds. A smile burst through her drying tears. Phillip asked her to think of a positive anchor and Lisa envisioned a quilt that she and her mother had sat on. The quilt was made by her grandmother from dresses the children had worn. Lisa planned to put this treasured heirloom in an appropriate place in her house.

When people do get messages from their souls or higher guides, we have found that it dramatically accelerates healing and integration. Using Reframing and Anchoring can be applied to any issue, like EFT, and it works particularly well on resolving grief.

EYE MOVEMENTS

Another way of recognizing how everything is connected is through the exploration of eye movements. As discussed earlier with the Nine-Gamut Process, eye movements access different parts of the body-mind. They also can balance different parts of the brain, helping to restore balance in the entire energy field. NLP (Neurolinguistic Programming), EMDR (Eye Movement Desensitization and Reprocessing), and Rapid Eye Technology use eye movements to help find imbalances and correct them. Note: if a person has a physical visual impairment, this might hamper the use of these techniques.

Eye movements may also help access unconscious patterns that are preventing healing. Here then are two related techniques that can come in handy:

1. This approach is a different use of the Floor-to-Ceiling Eye Roll. Its purpose is to access unconscious blockages. Have the person you are helping roll his or her eyes slowly upward from the floor to the ceiling, and notice if there is a jump in the eye movement somewhere along the way. If so, have the recipient go back and refocus on the area where there was a jump. Ask what he experiences when his or her eyes focus there. Find out if this movement brings up any emotions or images. If some "charge" is detected, it can be a doorway to a revealing process.

2. Here is another variation on using eye movements, drawn from a video by Steve Reed, psychotherapist and creator of the Remap Process. While addressing an issue, have the recipient follow the following movement. Hold your finger or a pen up and have his/her eyes follow your movements as you slowly circle the air. As the receiver follows your circular movement, have her tell you when she experiences an emotional charge or discomfort, or if she sees an image. Repeat, moving your finger or pen along the sensitive area. Use the recipient's reaction as a starting point for accessing an issue.

    You can identify where the client is looking with the time on the clock. For instance, the discomfort might be at the 4:00 position, the area where the eye focuses on the practitioner's circular movement.

For a more extensive examination of eye movements and working with meridians, Steve Reed has an energy technique called the Remap Process. Clients do various eye movements as they hold a series of acupressure points. With the possibility of using any of the 361 acupuncture points and all the meridians, Reed helps them find the exact locations to release emotional pain. Once the client connects with the point, Reed has him or her do eye movement patterns to access emotionally charged material, process blocked memories, integrate positive insights, and balance the brain hemispheres. For more on Steve Reed's videos, visit www.psychotherapy-center.com.

"A Natural Balance"

Here is an example of using eye movements for healing. Sally was having trouble relating to her ex-husband, whom she still saw regularly because of their children. Though Bob told her that he "missed the beauty that she brought him," Sally said she was angry and envious of his new girlfriend. He was taking the new girlfriend to exotic vacations, just as he once took Sally. Ironically, Sally didn't used to enjoy being with him on these lavish vacations, despite the beautiful surroundings.

While having Sally focus on this issue, Phillip motioned a pen in a circular pattern. As Sally's eyes followed the movement, she felt feelings of sadness at 2:00 and 11:00 positions, and experienced feeling free at the 10:00 position. The sadness was accompanied by a sense of being in a closed-in space.

Using sadness as a doorway to healing, Sally formulated the affirmation, "Even though I'm disappearing from my previous life and that distresses me, I deeply love and accept myself and am ready to fully experience my new life." After two rounds, the sadness went from six to zero. Then they focused on the freedom, which was originally a five and now had risen to an eight. They enhanced the process by identifying the freedom as an emerald crystal, that was tintinabulating, sounding like tingling glass. After tapping in that freedom energetic — the image and sound — Sally felt more uplifted. Grinning, she said she now had a "joyful exuberance" about relating to her husband. She now experienced "a natural balance" by being apart from her former mate.

The process showed Sally two things: that she could release the envy and sadness and that she could acknowledge the immeasurable gains she had made by separating from her husband. Her new freedom image (the emerald, tingling crystal) had overlapped the old negative, jealous image.

IMPLEMENTING THE HOLISTIC MODEL

Sally's process is a beautiful example of the ease with which you can merge EFT with other powerful modalities. With the levels of the Holistic Process, you have a precise tool for monitoring what is happening at the physical, emotional, mental, and spiritual levels. It creates a map for healing that you can use with any issue. This map can help you to understand more about what is happening within you or those you are helping with EFT. Recognizing each level as a person describes and addresses an issue can help you to be more targeted in your exploration of the nature of a problem and in your approach to correcting it.

CHAPTER SEVEN

Reaching Further into the Heart and Mind

*Your vision will become clear only
when you look into your heart.
Who looks outside, dreams.
Who looks inside, awakens.*

– *CARL JUNG*

You can learn a lot about the workings of the mind with the Levels of PR and the Holistic Process. Both increase the effectiveness of EFT. Once you have mastered the tapping sequences, you may want to learn both of these methods, along with the SK Reframing and Anchoring Process. As you have seen, they are all fascinating and illuminating, accessing the mysterious depths of the mind. And remember, if you are not drawn to the use of muscle testing or find yourself having difficulties with it, the Holistic Process and R&A are both effective for addressing PR.

You may still want to learn more, to open to your full potential. With this in mind, we are ready to delve further into the workings of the heart and the mind, to explore creating a totally fulfilling and joyful life. As with the last chapter, the information you will find here is related to EFT, but not part of Gary Craig's methods. We will examine:

- Adding the Diamond Approach
- Connecting with your heartfelt joy and excitement
- Addressing two common fears
- Forgiving yourself and others
- Appreciating yourself and your possibilities

THE DIAMOND APPROACH

In his book *Life Energy*, Dr. John Diamond describes an effective meridian-based healing method using muscle testing. Diamond reached a disappointing time in his career in psychiatric and preventive medicine when he recognized that the methods he and his colleagues were using were not as effective as he would like them to be. From this place of disillusionment, he discovered a simple way to determine which emotions are holding a person back and how to quickly correct the imbalances. When he started using this approach, his clients began to make dramatic shifts, even in cases he had been treating for years. His book describes some of the wonderful results, along with how to do the process.

One of the delightful aspects of Dr. Diamond's approach is the way he describes life energy and its connection to well-being and life purpose. He discusses how he recognized that connecting oneself with a genuine, positive sense of purpose produces more life energy, along with promoting health and well-being; conversely, losing this sense of purpose drains life energy, along with reducing health and well-being. Diamond's success with this approach clearly illustrates the fundamental importance of having a sense of purpose, which we, of course, relate to the soul. Being connected with the soul's excitement and joy adds energy and vitality; being disconnected depresses energy and vitality.

Diamond's main focus is simple: show clients through muscle testing how their health and well-being relates to having a healthy thymus gland and help them to anchor positive imagery and a positive outlook. Diamond considers the thymus gland, which is located in the middle of the chest, above the heart, to be the master gland of the body, controlling its life energy or life force. This "master switch" also serves as the key link between the body and mind. He discovered that when people are affected negatively by any influence, their thymus glands invariably test weak and that this in turn has a negative impact on their health and happiness.

The following list pinpoints some important differences between the perspectives on life of individuals with healthy thymuses, who have what Diamond calls a "high thymus outlook," and those with unhealthy thymuses, who have a "low thymus outlook."

HIGH THYMUS OUTLOOK	LOW THYMUS OUTLOOK
Positive outlook on life (belief systems)	Pervasive negative thinking and beliefs
Following heart's (soul's) desire	Ignoring heart's desire
Enhanced life force, excitement	Depleted life force, depression
High will to be well	Low will to be well
Sense of well-being	Sense of being stressed
Faith and trust in divine order	Fear of death and suffering
Gratitude	Mourning fate
Joyful and loving	Fatalistic, settling for unhappiness

Though Dr. Diamond does not use the term Psychological Reversal, one could draw a comparison between a low thymus outlook and the negative affects of PR on the energy system. This perspective may be limited to a single issue or a small number of issues; it could also be pervasive, as is the case with Massive PR. It follows that achieving a high thymus outlook would eliminate PR, and we have confirmed this in our work.

To create greater health, well-being, and healing potential on all levels, then, the goal is to shift to a high thymus outlook and focus on maintaining this perspective as often as possible throughout the day. A positive, high thymus outlook is a key ingredient in activating the energy system's ability to heal and balance itself. We need to take responsibility in this area and anchor a positive outlook in our daily lives. John Diamond's approach makes this easy.

Examining a Low Thymus Outlook with EFT

To create a high thymus outlook, you can use EFT to clear limitations associated with a low thymus. Just go down the list above and measure your SUD's level for each of the low thymus traits. For any items with a high SUDs reading, ask yourself why the reading is high to get more understanding of what is occurring. You can also use the Holistic Process to increase your awareness in an area where you have a high reading.

Realize that any blockage you release with EFT will boost your life energy. As EFT Expert Carol Tuttle states,

> By using EFT to clear these energy blocks [referring to limiting beliefs, fear, doubt, anger, and a myriad of other thoughts and emotions], you are freeing your life force energy to have more radiance and a clearer vibration, so you are free to attract into your life more of what you desire. When your life force energy is flowing vibrantly, you are a powerful creator to manifest more of your dreams and life purpose.

Once you transcend the limitations associated with a low thymus outlook, you can supercharge your results and enhance the high thymus traits with EFT, as described in Chapter Four, and create a tremendously high thymus outlook. Transforming such limitations into strengths is a gift you can give to yourself that will pay off every day. You will also feel terrific. EFT provides amazing tools for creating a positive, joyful, loving, fulfilling life. All you have to do is use them.

Diamond's Thymus Test

John Diamond provides an interesting method for activating a high thymus outlook that you may wish to explore. This approach can also help you to connect more with your life purpose and create positive goals. Diamond muscle tests the thymus gland, which is located in the center of the chest, roughly right between the EFT sore spots. You can easily recognize the spot, because it is sensitive to the touch. The thymus is the regulator of the body's immune function and a good indicator of your general well-being. To test the thymus:

- For a general test, place your middle and index fingers on the thymus and muscle test.

- For a specific issue, focus on the issue, place your middle and index fingers on the thymus gland and muscle test.

As a note, tapping on the thymus activates it, just as tapping on the EFT points activates them. This can be done every day to increase vitality and well-being.

Diamond found that the thymus usually tests weak initially with a general test. In these cases, he talks with his clients about what is occurring in their lives and retests as they focus on statements related to different aspects of their lives. Some examples might be:

- I want to stay at my current job.

- I want to become a professional chef.
- I want to live with my brother here in Seattle.
- I want to live in New York City.
- I am satisfied with my relationships.
- My marriage is fulfilling.
- I want to have children.
- I want to work just four days a week (rather than the six days I work now).

The point in asking these kinds of questions is to determine what brings the heartfelt joy, excitement, and fulfillment that are associated with being connected with one's purpose and, on the other hand, to determine what is blocking this connection. When we settle for a life that lacks fulfillment, our life energy is drained and we are bound to have problems. Ultimately, we want to be fulfilled in all areas of life. Through these thymus tests, Dr. Diamond helps clients to develop what he calls a "homing thought," which you could also call a purposeful or soulful thought. This thought provides the keys to envisioning a vibrant future. Remarkably, Diamond documents helping patients eliminate even critical conditions by continuing to focus on their homing thought.

For a woman in the hospital, this purposeful thought may be a simple statement about becoming well, like "I see my condition improving so well that I can leave the hospital next Thursday," accompanied by frequently visualizing herself as vibrantly healthy. For a person who is dissatisfied with his life, this thought may be more connected with what he really wants to do and where he wants to be, like "I am developing a career as a professional writer working in Philadelphia." With each client, the focus and statement are both unique, with deep personal meaning.

Even if your thymus tests strong initially, it can be worthwhile to retest as you focus on different aspects of your life, like where you live, your profession, your relationships, and so on. This will help you to identify areas where you are less connected with your purpose. By testing different possibilities, you can discover new ways to perceive your possibilities.

For maintenance, Diamond recommends retesting regularly, since our perspectives and heartfelt desires change over time. A thought that is purposeful today will not necessarily be purposeful next year or possibly even next month.

CONNECTING WITH YOUR HEARTFELT JOY AND EXCITEMENT

Let's return for a moment to the questions in Chapter Two: "Why am I here?" and "What do I want to do with my life?" As you use EFT and make positive changes, how can you tell for sure that you are heading in the right direction? In addition to the methods related to the thymus, we use a simple approach: connecting with your heartfelt joy and excitement.

In the last chapter, the Centering Process demonstrated the connection between the heart and the soul. To produce a soulful thought and soulful goals, simply connect with the joy and excitement in your heart. This is a variation on Diamond's approach, since the thymus gland is also connected with the heart. Along with honest self-examination, your heartfelt joy and excitement leads you toward your soul's true purpose.

The heart, then, is like a barometer that can tell you whether you are heading in the right direction. We describe this in relation to setting goals in our *Awaken to your True Purpose* Manual:

> Goal setting is just a matter of pursuing your heartfelt joy. Joyfully following your purpose adds life energy and excitement, while stifling your purpose drains life energy and creates depression. If we could all be joyful, we would have little need for guidelines or a program to help us. Your heartfelt joy tells you what to aim for.

By centering yourself, connecting with your heartfelt joy, and reflecting on an issue or on different aspects of your life, you can find out what enhances your life energy and what drains this vital force. With this approach, you can come up with a soulful homing thought to focus on throughout the day. The benefits of the homing thought include:

- Handling life's many stresses better, including common environmental factors that you face regularly

- Being more centered

- Experiencing considerably more life energy

- Gaining clarity about personal goals and having a new confidence

- Enjoying life

We have experimented with how our clients and students respond to stressful situations while focusing on a soulful homing thought and consistently found that their thymus tested strong. *Getting Thru to Your Soul DVD/Video 1* shows a compelling example of this approach. In the video, Juanita tests weak when muscle tested while the audience thinks negative thoughts about her. Then she focuses on a soulful homing thought that connects her with her higher purpose. Now she tests strong while the audience again projects negative thoughts toward her.

In his book *Life Energy*, Dr. Diamond also describes a system for balancing the meridian system in relation to specific issues. This system includes muscle testing trigger points for each of the acupuncture meridians. We use a variation of this technique with Spiritual Kinesiology and have found it to be well worth exploring.

TWO COMMON FEARS

To create a truly vibrant and joyful life, there are two common areas of PR that are worth examining: the fear of getting well and fear of success. Here are overviews:

1. **Fear of getting well:** Illness may provide hidden pay offs that prevent us from becoming well or from functioning optimally. Blockages that can interfere with embracing vibrant health can include feeling it's not possible to recover, fearing loss of attention, and believing it is somehow unsafe, to name a few. It is surprisingly common for people who are in need of love to become ill in a misguided unconscious desire to have their families pay attention to them or even to receive the support of the doctors and nurses in a hospital.

2. **Fear of success:** Some of the reasons people unconsciously sabotage their potential to succeed include perfectionism, not wanting to surpass the accomplishments of their parents, meeting their parents' low expectations, changing/losing relationships, fear of boredom and loneliness, addiction to the past, feeling punished by God, or blaming God. The seven chief defenses, which we describe later in this book, fuel all of these fears.

On the path to wholeness, we all have to take an honest look at ways we may be sabotaging ourselves. Here are two ways to overcome these fears.

1. Test the Levels of PR Statements for these fears

2. Build on the positive

In the EFT Experts part of this book, Carol Look also discusses how she uses EFT to neutralize blockages to success and abundance. She states, "When you have comfort zones – ceilings to what you believe you can achieve – you will always stay within them. After using EFT for my own comfort zones, I increased my income by over 20% the first year."

Testing the PR Statements

By testing the PR statements in Figure 7.1 for either of these fears, you can gather information on sabotaging beliefs and judgments. Alternatively, just ask yourself the PR statements and notice if you detect any sabotaging beliefs or judgments in either or both of these areas. If you feel particularly stuck or uncover a number of blockages in either of these areas, you may want to return to them over time. This could transform your life.

Building on the positive

To fully overcome these common fears, it is important to develop a positive attitude, as discussed earlier with the "high thymus outlook." Failing to remember or acknowledge our successes is often a reason we fall short of succeeding with our goals. This fire is fueled by the tendency of our culture to criticize and analyze shortcomings more than compliment and celebrate achievements.

We suffered from this form of blindness ourselves when we started our holistic healing practices and classes. We read numerous books describing wonderful healings and transformational experiences people had using different methods, but it took some time to recognize that such changes were not reserved for others. The same kinds of transformations were occurring all around us in our students, clients, and ourselves. As we developed and refined our methods, we gradually recognized the power of the techniques we were using, and learned to acknowledge our successes.

From a soulful perspective, each of us came into this life

with unique gifts to share and a joyful purpose to realize. As you take an honest look at yourself, be sure to acknowledge your strengths and successes, even if they seem small. By examining how they were created, you can learn to draw more and more on your talents, strengths, and knowledge. Also remember to connect with your heartfelt joy and excitement. Focus on where your heart is leading you, giving more time and energy to the activities that bring joy. This is an important part of living a soulful life and realizing your purpose.

With the puritan work ethic, some may think that this is self-centered. From another perspective, by empowering yourself and creating an exciting and joyful life, you are contributing to the creation of a more positive world. As EFT Expert Dr. Alex Lees mentions, "Empowered people contribute positively to the workings of the world, making it a much more pleasant journey for all."

The next step is to focus on integrating your successes and joy into your daily life. This might include tapping in positive statements as described earlier, meditating on previous accomplishments, going out for a special occasion to commemorate an achievement, and finding other ways to celebrate successes. The idea is to plant seeds for more success, to promote a positive attitude, and create an exciting, joyful existence.

FORGIVENESS

Learning to forgive is another important element on the journey to wholeness and particularly in addressing Massive PR. Focusing on appreciating yourself may bring up some judgmental feelings that need to be addressed. Forgiveness is a key.

There are times in all of our lives when we are wronged by others or are in the wrong ourselves – and these transgressions sometimes stay with us, along with resentment and hatred. From Dr. Diamond's perspective, such feelings produce a low thymus outlook and drain our life energy. On the other hand,

---

FIGURE 7.1
THE LEVELS OF PR FOR PERMISSION
TO HEAL OR SUCCEED

When PR is present, one or more of the statements will probably produce a weak response with muscle testing:

1. I want to heal/succeed _____.

2. I want to <u>completely</u> heal/succeed _____.

3. I <u>will</u> heal/succeed _____.

4. I believe that I can heal/succeed _____.

5. I deserve to heal/succeed _____ _.

6. I will do everything necessary to heal/succeed _____.

7. I will allow myself to heal/succeed _____.

8. It is possible for me to heal/succeed _____.

9. Healing/succeeding _____ will be good for me.

10. Healing/succeeding _____ will be good for others.

11. It will be safe for me to heal/succeed _____.

FIGURE 7.1
CONTINUED

Affirmations to overcome the levels of PR:

1. Even though I don't want to heal/succeed _____, I completely accept myself.

2. Even though I don't want to completely heal/succeed _____, I deeply and completely accept myself.

3. Even though I don't believe that I will ever heal/succeed _____, I deeply and completely accept myself.

4. Even though I don't believe that I can heal/succeed _____, I completely accept myself.

5. Even though I don't believe that I deserve to heal/succeed _____, I deeply and completely accept myself

6. Even though I am unwilling to do everything necessary to heal/succeed _____, I deeply and completely accept myself.

7. Even though I I will not allow myself to heal/succeed _____, I completely accept myself.

8. Even though I don't believe that it is possible for me to heal /succeed _____, I deeply and completely accept myself.

9. Even though I don't believe that healing/succeeding _____ will be good for me, I deeply and completely accept myself.

10. Even though I don't believe that healing/succeeding _____ will be good for others, I deeply and completely accept myself.

11. Even though I don't believe that it is safe for me to heal/succeed _____, I deeply and completely accept myself.

forgiveness frees us to create a high thymus outlook, strengthen our life energy, and move forward with vibrance and love. Forgiveness is actually a gift we give ourselves as much as or more than those who have wronged us. And, whether we have been the victims or perpetrators, forgiving and loving ourselves is an essential element of the journey to wholeness. Once we realize the importance of forgiveness, we can heed Samuel Johnson's advice: "A wise person will make haste to forgive, because he knows the true value of time, and will not suffer it to pass away in unnecessary pain."

Gaining this wisdom requires maturity and understanding. The path to creating a loving and joyful life is strewn with personal betrayals, transgressions, and violations. We all need to learn how to deal with them effectively and release any related negativity. Stuck emotions occupy space in our consciousness and make us prisoners of the past. They take us away from our true selves and our ability to live in the present moment, along with the higher, positive emotional states we want to cultivate. In addition to being happier, people who are more forgiving report fewer health problems. Forgiveness reduces stress, blood pressure, muscle tension, and depression. Forgiveness is sometimes the missing ingredient in a complete healing.

Many people find it hard to forgive because they equate forgiveness with condoning other's damaging behavior. This is not the case. We forgive for ourselves, to transcend judgment, increase our life energy, and experience love and joy. As EFT Expert Phillip Friedman simply states: "Forgiveness (of oneself and others) is a key to happiness." We may also fail to recognize that we have all been on both the giving and receiving end of such behavior. When wrestling with forgiveness, it is easy to overlook one's own transgressions. Perhaps we might not have harmed others as much as we have been hurt ourselves. Awareness of being a transgressor as well as a victim can help us to be more forgiving and compassionate.

Myths about Forgiveness

Forgiveness is often misunderstood. In their helpful little book *How to Forgive When You Don't Know How*, Jacqui Bishop and Mary Grunte identify some common misconceptions about forgiveness:

- Forgiving means forgetting.
- Some people don't deserve to be forgiven.
- Forgiving means you have to trust the other person.
- Forgiving condones the person's actions and makes the person unaccountable.
- Forgiving is a sign of weakness.
- The other person has to apologize before you can forgive him or her.

None of these limiting beliefs get to the heart of the problem: holding grudges, judging others, and experiencing negativity. We need to forgive others for our own benefit, to release the stuck emotions and move on to more positive pursuits. Forgiveness allows us to find peace and create an environment where love can flourish. It requires us to take responsibility for our feelings and to clear related blockages. Then we can live in the present and not be controlled by past memories.

When seeking forgiveness, you can use the above list of misconceptions to muscle test or identify areas that stand in the way. From a holistic perspective, these misconceptions are limiting beliefs and judgments on the mental and spiritual levels, and they are often unconscious. In EFT terms, they are forms of PR that commonly interfere with EFT clearing.

Beliefs that Make It Hard to Forgive

Fred Luskin, author of *Forgive for Good*, describes how forgiveness helps a person to take things less personally, which also indicates one is taking a more soulful perspective. In addition to the myths listed above, what else stops people from attaining the freedom that forgiveness provides?

Luskin found some of the main roadblocks to forgiveness are the unenforceable rules that people create. These rules, which are all limiting beliefs about the way life should be, come in absolute terms and tend to cause reactionary behavior when others break them. The rule makers may also obsess on correcting those who violate their rules.

Beliefs that make it hard to forgive include:

- My partner has to be faithful.
- People must not lie to me.
- Life should be fair.
- My life has to be easy.
- My past should have been different.
- My parents should have treated me better.
- People must be kind to me or care for me the way I want.

When under the sway of such dogmatic and often unconscious thoughts, we try to force reality to fit into these parameters. We will never be able to control others and such rules just end up creating a lot of stress and suffering when they are violated. On the path to wholeness, forgiveness becomes a great healer and balancer. It is one of the best correctives for an overly rigid approach to life. Through forgiveness, we can find the deeper meaning in experiences that created restrictive beliefs. Forgiveness also becomes a powerful reality check. It helps us to create realistic dreams and goals that we can achieve regardless of what others do.

It is also important to recognize that forgiveness can be a large goal. Most people are in the process of recovering from some harmful act or acts. It can take some time and healing before a person is ready to forgive him- or herself or another.

Even with EFT, a period of healing may be needed to fully deal with complex emotional pain, while also allowing for the possibility of a ten minute wonder. However long it takes, the results are worth the effort. Forgiveness may be a final and necessary component of complete healing that cannot be forced or rushed. It may come in stages and pieces before full forgiveness occurs. Sometimes a person may be able to forgive another in increments, until full forgiveness occurs.

"If I Forgive, Then..."

Another barrier to forgiving is the fear that something bad would happen. A woman may be afraid that her family would not pay any attention to her if she didn't complain that they were inconsiderate. Another person may believe that people will take advantage of him if he forgives his past grievances. Such fears are often unconscious. Once they are identified, EFT or the Forgiveness Process described later in this chapter can help remove them

To understand what might be holding a person back, Bishop and Grunte recommend completing the following statements by writing or saying them:

- "If I forgive, then... *I'll have to...*"

- "If I forgive, then... *I won't be able to...*"

- "If I forgive, then... *life will never ...*"

- "If I forgive, then... *no one will ever ...*"

- "If I forgive, then... *people will...*"

- "If I forgive, then... *my parents will/won't...*"

- "If I forgive, then... *God will/won't...*"

When using this list, just say the first thing that comes to mind. Avoid analysis or "thinking" about it. By going through the "If I forgive, then..." statements, you can easily uncover beliefs that restricting you. Once you identify a blockage, you can use EFT or one of the other tools in this book for clearing.

Interestingly, people sometimes include God as part of the problem, believing that God is blaming or punishing them. By doing a forgiveness process, this kind of fear can also be understood and cleared.

Self Forgiveness

As mentioned, in addition to forgiving what someone did to us, we also need to be able to forgive ourselves. Luskin found four categories of self-forgiveness:

1. Those upset with themselves for failing at something they considered important, such as graduating from college, getting married, or having children.

2. Those who failed to act at certain times, to help themselves or others.

3. Those upset about hurting someone else, like cheating on their spouses, behaving poorly as parents, or managing a business poorly.

4. Those ashamed of self-destructive behavior like alcoholism or laziness.

The process may also need to include forgiving oneself or others for the consequences of the grievance. If a man abused his sister as a child, he may need to forgive himself both for the offense and all the unpleasant results. As an EFT set-up phrase, you could say, "I forgive myself for _____, and all the suffering and negative consequences it caused, and I deeply and completely accept myself."

The Stages of Forgiveness

In the Lazaris audio *The Incredible Force of Forgiveness* (www.lazaris.com), he examines the process of forgiveness in stages, similar to those involved with grieving and illness. When forgiveness is difficult, examining each of these stages can be beneficial:

1. denial
2. self-blame
3. self-pity
4. indignation
5. then becoming more conscious in order to do a forgiveness process for integration

You can ask yourself how each one applies and use EFT to release any associated emotional charges as part of this process. With the speed and ease of EFT, completing all five stages need not take a long time, perhaps only an hour or a day. Even if it takes longer, the relief it brings is well worth the effort.

Be Set Free Fast (BSFF) Forgiveness Process

In addition to using EFT, we want to share another forgiveness process we use in combination with EFT. It comes from psychologist Larry Nims, author of *Be Set Free Fast*, another meridian-based healing modality.

1. Ask if you are ready to forgive. If not, process more or wait until another time.

2. If ready, tap on the point next to the nail of the little finger, which is on the heart meridian, on the ring finger side, while affirming "I now release my anger toward [name of offender] for [the particular action]."

3. Tap on the point next to the nail of the index finger, which is on the large intestine meridian, on the thumb side, while affirming "I now forgive [name of offending person] for [particular action]."

4. Repeat the anger release taps in Step 2, this time releasing anger toward yourself.

5. Repeat the forgiveness tapping in Step 3, this time forgiving yourself.

Larry Nims views clearing anger as an integral part of the forgiveness process. He also finds, as we do, that forgiving someone else includes forgiving yourself. You can also add affirmations that address related issues, such as how the forgiveness will affect your life and the consequences it has for others.

Bob's Story: Forgiving His Father

Phillip once helped a client named Bob, who was in the process of forgiving his father for being controlling and abusive. They first did EFT to clear Bob's anger toward his father. Once that was done, Phillip instructed Bob to tap on his little finger and say aloud, "I release the anger I have toward my father for his interference and excessive forcefulness." With Phillip's prompting, Bob then tapped on his index finger and said, "I forgive my father. I understand where he was coming from. I can accept his actions and their consequences, learn from them, and move on with my life."

With Phillip's guidance, Bob moved back to tapping his little finger and said, "I let go of any remaining anger I have toward myself on this issue." And moving again to his index finger, he said, "I forgive myself and accept and love my father for the many good things he gave me, like laughter and independence. No one is perfect. Dad, I want you to find peace in yourself, so we can all be peaceful. In any event, I am at peace.

I'm free to move on and live my life."

When the process was complete, Bob let out a big sigh, feeling relaxed and tranquil toward his father and himself. In just twenty minutes, Bob completely released extreme emotional pain that had plagued him for over forty years.

Additional Notes

A few things to keep in mind when expressing forgiveness:

- When helping another, you can provide possible words to say for releasing anger and forgiveness. These suggestions can facilitate the process, just be sure the person you are helping feels the words are right. Also invite the other person to come up with his or her own wording.

- When determining the words to use for forgiveness, let your soul be your guide. Connect with the feelings in your heart, as described in the Soul Centering Process in Chapter Six. Once you are familiar with the process, you can just breathe pure energy and light into your heart, open to the love there, and let the words flow. If you are coming from a centered place, the words will feel right, devoid of judgment and intellectualizing. Heart-centered words promote forgiveness.

- Be wary of saying "I forgive him for he did the best he could." To take Bob's example above, abusing a child is clearly not the "best" his father could do. So it's good to accept and, if possible, understand why the father was abusive, but not to endorse the abusive acts. Bob did a nice job of balancing the abuse with thinking of positive things that his father gave him, such as fostering a sense of humor. If the person you are helping cannot think of any "gifts" from the transgressor, then just reflect on what was learned from the situation and how the experiences can be used for personal growth, turning manure into compost.

It helps to include what the person learned from the experience, regardless of how terrible it may have been. By pointing out the positive, such as the personal growth resulting from the experience, the person can more easily integrate the experience and forgive.

- Philip Friedman discusses some additional ways to use forgiveness in the EFT Expert section in this book.

Forgiveness may be best viewed as a journey that evolves over time. Making steps toward forgiveness, even if not complete, is valuable. It is far healthier than repressing emotions and holding grudges.

APPRECIATING YOURSELF AND YOUR POSSIBILITIES

A theme that has woven through this chapter is learning to love ourselves and uncover our unique possibilities. As Ralph Waldo Emerson observed, "To be yourself in a world that is constantly trying to make you something else is the greatest accomplishment."

If you suffer from Massive PR or just want to increase your focus on creating the life of your dreams, Figure 7.2 provides some statements about how you view yourself that you can muscle test. This list is a variation on one developed by Larry P. Nims, a psychologist who also uses meridian-based techniques. You will want to test positive for all of these things to move forward into a life filled with joy, love, and freedom. Any areas where you test weak are worth deeper exploration. Since they are keys to your internal world, you may want to use the Holistic Process to learn more about precisely what is happening on the physical, emotional, mental, and spiritual levels, and clear away the garbage once and for all.

Learning to fully appreciate ourselves is an essential part of our personal and spiritual development. We all have the precise qualities we need to realize our dreams, but most of us have not fully recognized the beauty of our uniqueness. Exploring the tools in this chapter can help you to appreciate yourself and explore exciting new possibilities for your direction in life.

FIGURE 7.2
TEST STATEMENTS FOR MASSIVE PR

- I am a good person.

- I want to be happy.

- I want to be successful.

- I deserve to be loved.

- I deserve good things in life.

- I have many talents and skills.

- I have a resourceful mind.

- I am a capable person.

- I have a good body.

- I want to be healthy.

Part 3

SPECIAL CHALLENGES, SPECIAL OPPORTUNITIES

CHAPTER EIGHT

Correcting Neurological Disorganization

All life is an experiment,
the more experiments you make the better.

EMERSON

If you have used some of the methods presented thus far, you have probably had some wonderful successes. These experiences are the most common by far. Nonetheless, there may still be times when you or those you seek to help do not respond well or at all to EFT, even after addressing PR and exploring some of the other methods described so far. This part of the book focuses on these special challenges and the opportunities they provide.

This part of the book focuses on four common impediments you may encounter. We explore these conditions in the rare instances when we are not having success with our usual methods. They are also good to know about for general reference, because overcoming these limitations can enhance your well-being even where EFT is already providing positive results.

Chapters Eight to Ten examine these four impediments:

1. Neurological Disorganization (ND)
2. Energy Toxins
3. Compartmentalizing
4. Strong Defense Patterns

Neurological Disorganization, which is the subject of this chapter, and Energy Toxins, in the next chapter, are the final elements of the EFT toolbox that Gary Craig recommends addressing if you are not receiving the desired results with the tapping sequences or with the Levels of PR. We discussed them briefly in *Getting Thru to Your Emotions with EFT*. Since then, we have gained more experience, which we share here.

Compartmentalizing and strong defense patterns are not part of EFT. We are adding them in Chapter Ten, because we find them to be pivotal factors that can influence the success of EFT or any healing process.

WHAT IS NEUROLOGICAL DISORGANIZATION?

In a very small percentage of cases, which Gary Craig estimates at less than 5 percent, an energy imbalance known as Neurological Disorganization, Switched Circuit, or Switching thwarts the effectiveness of EFT. Just as a car can become misaligned and malfunction as the result of wear and tear, so too can the energy system become misaligned and malfunction as the result of a variety of factors including trauma and/or prolonged stress. When this condition is present, muscle testing and healing are both impaired.

This chapter shows you how to muscle test for the presence of Neurological Disorganization (ND), along with ways to address it. Physically, ND is a condition that involves misinterpretation of nerve impulses within the central nervous system. It is also related to a polarity imbalance in the functioning of the right and left hemispheres of the brain. Affected individuals may have difficulty accessing emotions due to right brain dysfunction; they may also have difficulty with logical thinking and problem solving, due to left brain dysfunction.

This may seem a bit obscure, and, fortunately, you do not need to understand the exact nature of ND to use EFT successfully. Also, there are some simple ways to recognize Neurological Disorganization. Indicators may include some or all of the following:

- awkward gait
- clumsiness
- reversing letters
- confusing left and right
- saying the opposite of what one means

People who seem spacey and ungrounded, or beside themselves and unable to cope probably have ND. After being around such people for awhile, you may feel a bit disoriented yourself. In a sense, ND is contagious. Though this is generally temporary, it again reinforces the importance of being centered and grounded, particularly if you are helping others.

Unfortunately, for those for whom ND is the norm, healing and achieving goals can be difficult. We need to look at such conditions without judgment, and remember that ND is a polarity problem, not a character defect. As noted with the Holistic Process, imbalances generally include judging ourselves. Healing ultimately must include love and with this in mind, we approach these tendencies from a loving perspective.

CORRECTING NEUROLOGICAL DISORGANIZATION

Fortunately, Neurological Disorganization is at least manageable if not correctable, though this generally takes some time and consistency. In *Getting Through to Your Emotions with EFT*, we described a process Gary Craig included in his EFT toolbox called Collarbone Breathing to address this condition. We are not including that process here, because, over the years, we have found that we do not use it. As far as we know, Gary Craig does not use it either. Instead, we will examine a variety of ways to detect and correct it.

Kinesiology Tests for ND

You have already encountered ND in the Kinesiology accuracy tests mentioned earlier in this book. You may also have encountered a situation where nothing you have learned so far seems to work. The next thing to do is test for ND. The following ways of performing this test have been recommended by experts in the field.

1. **True-False Method:** James Durlacher, author of Freedom From Fear Forever, suggests testing a series of obvious true-false questions. Muscle test the statement "I was born in (place of birth)." Then test the statement "I was born (somewhere else)." Or muscle test "2 plus 2 equals 4," then "2 plus 2 equals 7." If the testing is off, ND may be present.

2. **Index Finger Method:** With this method from Fred Gallo, another renowned expert in the field, have the recipient place the palm side of either index finger at the bridge of the nose, and test. The muscle should test strong. Place the nail side of index finger on the bridge of the nose. Now the muscle should then test weak. If the test produces different results, ND may be present.

3. **Hand-Over-the-Head Method:** Have the recipient place the palm side of either hand just above the top of the head and muscle test the other arm. It should test strong. Then have the recipient turn the hand above the head over so the back of the hand is just above the

top of the head, with the palm pointing up. Now the muscle should test weak. If the tests show both conditions strong, Neurological Disorganization is probably present. As mentioned earlier, if the muscle tests weak when the palm is down and strong when the palm is up, this indicates Massive PR. This method also comes from James Durlacher.

Corrections for ND

As with testing for ND, innovative experts in the field have discovered a variety of ways to correct it. These methods generally provide a temporary correction, which will allow you to continue with EFT on a specific issue. Achieving permanent results and a consistent grounded state is another matter. The correction methods are not time consuming, but achieving permanent results generally requires practice throughout the day over a period of time. In some cases, a neurologically disorganized person may also need to start with general balancing for a period of time before he or she can successfully address any specific issues.

Here are the methods for correcting ND. Many of them are described in David Gruder's book *The Energy Psychology Desktop Companion*, which catalogs information from a number of experts in the field.

1. **Thymus Thump** (from John Diamond)

   - Smile

   - Think of someone you love and

   - Thump on the thymus (sternum), humming or saying "ha, ha, ha, ha..."

2. **Belly Button Correction** (from David Gruder's book)
   Press firmly on the belly button and simultaneously:

- Rub under the nose with your free hand, then switch hands and repeat.

- Rub under the lower lip with your free hand, then switch hands and repeat.

- Rub both collarbone points with your free hand, then switch hands and repeat.

- (Optional Step) Massage the tailbone with your free hand, then switch hands and repeat.

3. **Cross Crawl**

- Touch the right hand to the left knee, then the left hand to the right knee. If possible, exaggerate the leg lifts and arm swings. Even more effective is tapping the opposite knee with your hand or elbow as you lift your leg. The most important motion, though, is to cross the midline of the body.

- You can add to the above exercise: counting, then humming, then circling eyes in each direction, similar to the nine-gamut process.

- Continue this exaggerated "march" at a slow pace for at least a minute, deeply inhaling through your nose and exhaling through your mouth. You can also intuit or muscle test the amount of time needed to complete the exercise.

4. **Over-Energy Correction:**

- Cross the left ankle over the right one (can be done standing or sitting).

- Outstretch your hands in front of you, back to back, thumbs pointing downward.

- Place the right hand over the left hand and interlock your fingers.

- Fold your arms inward, resting interlocked fingers on the chest.

- Note: For some people, the opposite ankle and hand are used. Use muscle testing or intuition to determine the positions.

- Put the tip of the tongue on the roof of the mouth during the inhale.

- Rest the tongue on the floor of the mouth during the exhale.

- Do this for approximately one to two minutes.

5. **Figure Eights:** Draw them in the air with a finger, tracking the movement with your eyes; or walk in a figure-eight pattern.

6. **Diamond Approach:** The techniques described in Chapter Seven for creating a high thymus outlook are also effective with ND. Those who do not feel drawn to physical exercises like cross crawls or figure eights regularly may find this approach more enticing. It also adds more awareness of the need to create balance.

7. **Reduce Stress:** Since Neurological Disorganization is linked to stress, finding ways to feel relaxed and buoyant throughout the day is essential. The Soul Centering Process, EFT, and the Holistic Process all can help in developing a Stress Reduction Program. There is also an entire chapter on stress management in our book *Getting Thru to Your Emotions with EFT*.

As mentioned earlier, unlike many of the other blockages to success with EFT, permanent correction of ND generally takes time. Pick methods that seem easiest and most enjoyable or use different ones on different days for variety. And focus on stress reduction along with all of the other methods.

We recommend performing a corrective process several times a day, particularly during and after stressful periods, then retesting for ND. If you are helping another person, you need to emphasize the importance of correcting this condition, because the affected person may find staying focused on a goal challenging. Remember that it only takes about a minute to complete this procedure. And if you miss it once or twice and feel defeated, just do EFT on the feelings of being defeated, then proceed with the goal.

CHAPTER NINE

Exploring Energy Toxins

Dreams are renewable.
No matter what our age or condition,
there are still untapped possibilities within us
and new beauty waiting to be born.

– *DR. DALE TURNER*

We all know that we live in a toxic environment. For those who do not respond well to EFT, even after addressing PR and Neurological Disorganization, energy toxins may be the problem. These cases include:

- people who do not respond at all
- those who respond slowly
- those whose problems return quickly

Dr. Callahan found that the reason some of his treatments didn't hold was energy toxins. Sensitivities to certain substances one consumes or comes in contact with can disrupt the energy system. Though Gary Craig has found energy toxins to be the culprits in only a very small percentage of cases, they deserve examination. In addition to increasing your effectiveness with EFT, eliminating energy toxins can help to maximize your well-being on all levels: physically, emotionally, mentally, and spiritually.

Unfortunately, our culture does not does not teach us to be sensitive to the effects of substances and environmental influences on our bodies, so we may overlook obvious hazards. The human body also has a way of adjusting, so we may not even have noticeable symptoms related to toxins that are interfering with our health and well-being. Energy toxins include toxic substances and negative energies that irritate the energy system. The culprits we are discussing here are toxins in:

- foods we eat
- substances we put on our bodies
- the environment around us

Common energy toxins include a variety of foods, cigarette smoke, mold, cleaning products, vaccines, stuffy rooms, and more. Depending on the individual, virtually any substance can be an energy toxin and if one is weakening the energy system, EFT may be ineffective.

Fortunately, EFT and other energy treatments may also eliminate negative reactions to the disturbing substances and there are other strategies that can be used, which are described in this chapter. Naturopathic doctor Sandra Radomski, who specializes in treating allergies, also describes her approach in the EFT Expert part of this book.

OUR INCREASINGLY TOXIC WORLD

Most people are not aware of the toxic dangers that lurk almost everywhere in the environment. Colleen Huber who is trained in naturopathy has written:

> The EPA (Environmental Protection Agency) estimates that there has been no "clean air" in the United States

for more than 25 years. Even relatively pristine areas are not immune because global air currents carry pesticides... Indoor air pollution is even worse. The formaldehyde and other solvents leaking out of our walls, furniture and especially carpets keep many, perhaps most of us, in a limbo between good health and vague malaise.

Since 1945, over a 100,000 new chemicals have been introduced into our lives. This is approximately three new chemicals a day, which are increasingly present in our food, substances we use on our bodies, and our environment. Our diets have also changed dramatically during the last century, shifting from whole natural foods that were largely free of toxic substances to prepared foods that are often filled with chemicals and additives. Over 3,000 chemicals are added to our food supply and more than 10,000 chemical solvents, emulsifiers, and preservatives are used in food processing. Is it reasonable to assume that our bodies are capable of dealing with this ongoing onslaught of foreign substances?

Human fat tissue sampled in the United States has shown 700 chemical contaminants that have not been chemically identified. Chemicals that are foreign to the body tend to accumulate over time. The liver is designed to filter out these harmful substances, but with an ever increasing workload, it can be overwhelmed. This overload shows up in allergies and sensitivities, and has been linked to many forms of disease.

A 2004 study in a British medical journal estimated that perhaps 75 percent of most cancers are caused by environmental and lifestyle factors, including exposures to chemicals. The Columbia University School of Public Health estimated that 95 percent of cancer is caused by diet and environmental toxicity. In addition to cancer, toxins have been linked to neurological disorders like Parkinson's disease, Alzheimer's, and attention deficit disorder, hormonal imbalances, muscle and vision problems, fatigue, headaches, obesity, and more.

Those of us with strong constitutions and healthy bodies

may think that this does not apply to us, not recognizing that the body is under stress. The body can adjust to the presence of toxins, so one can be unaware that there is a problem. This is the case with cigarette smoking. Most of us have tried it and recall the initial reactions: coughing, choking, and dizziness. Regardless, through continued exposure, most, if not all, of these symptoms disappear. The same thing happens with irritating perfumes, foods, and other toxic substances.

We have had some startling examples in our own lives. One of the most memorable involved a cologne Jane used for over thirty years. She first received it as a gift as a teenager and began to use it regularly. During that time, she was aware that she was sensitive to fragrances and could not find any others that did not cause an allergic reaction. It baffled her that this single cologne seemed to be fine, and she kept using it, even though she knew it contained synthetic ingredients.

More recently, when she was facing some health challenges, Jane decided to stop using the fragrance to reduce any potential stress on her body. She eliminated it for at several months. Then, one evening when we were going out to dinner, she put some on just as we were going out the door. As we drove to the restaurant, she had such a tremendous reaction to this cologne that she had to wash it immediately when we arrived. Have you ever wondered how a person could reek of perfume and seemingly not notice it? The fact is, the individual's system has probably "adjusted" to it, blocking it out of his or her awareness. This does not mean it is not having a negative affect.

A similar thing happened when Jane stopped eating potatoes, along with a number of other foods. During the time that she was on this limited diet, she experienced consistent improvements in her health and well-being. She also noticed that she felt lighter and more joyful. Such changes can be subtle, so it can be easy to overlook them or fail to make a connection. Then we were traveling several months later and since restaurant breakfasts often come with potatoes, Jane thought she would have some just once, not thinking that a potato could do much harm. She enjoyed them, but about fifteen minutes later, she suddenly became extremely angry and distraught, which is unusual for her. For us, this was a clear demonstration of how the foods we eat affect us on all levels.

With exposure to chemicals like perfumes and exhaust, symptoms of energy toxins may appear immediately upon exposure, so they are easy to identify. With foods and some other substances, symptoms may appear between fifteen minutes and, with delayed reactions, a day or more after exposure, so identifying the culprit can be tricky. We also have to remember that there may not be any noticeable symptoms at all with regular exposure, or there may be symptoms that we are not associating with the offending substance.

LEARNING FROM OUR BODIES

Body awareness is severely lacking in our society. We spend much more time analyzing the ideas that run through our heads than we do sensing the messages that are coming to us through our bodies. With practice, this can change and we can learn a lot from our bodies. Doris Rapp, an environmental medical practitioner who specializes in helping children and adults with energy toxins, recommends identifying these threats to your well-being by increasing your awareness of what you eat, touch, and smell. Rapp, a leader in her field, is the author of *The Impossible Child* and has an enlightening website at www.drrapp.com.

Almost any symptom can be related to energy toxins, including brain fog, fatigue, digestive or respiratory problems, menstrual difficulties, anxiety, depression, learning disabilities, hyperactivity, and pain. Also look for redness on the face or ears and bags under the eyes. Weight gain, puffiness, and bloating may also be related to energy toxins. If the body considers a food to be poisonous, it may retain water and accumulate fat in an attempt to neutralize the energy toxin.

Doris Rapp identifies five areas that can reveal the effects of inhaling or ingesting an energy toxin. Watch for changes in:

1. **Behavior.** Bouts of anger, depression, and more may be linked to energy toxins.

2. **Appearance.** Red earlobes, dark eye circles, nose rubbing, throat congestion, and wiggly legs may be reactions to energy toxins.

3. **Pulse.** A normal pulse is about 80; a racing pulse is 100-110 and may be linked to energy toxins.

4. **Handwriting.** Handwriting that is less legible may be related to energy toxins. Alterations in writing are signs that the nervous system and brain has been affected.

5. **Breathing.** With the presence of energy toxins, breathing may become constricted.

WAYS TO ADDRESS ENERGY TOXINS

As you can see, this is a complex subject that deserves exploration by anyone interested in vibrant well-being. With the relatively recent addition of so many new influences, any holistic approach needs to recognize that there is bound to be an effect on an intricate organism like the human body.

As a starting point, Gary Craig recommends trying the following three steps for using EFT when you suspect that energy toxins may be interfering with your success:

1. **Change your location.** There may be something in the immediate environment that is causing a problem, like a computer, TV, toxic substances in the carpet or fabrics, residues of toxic cleaning products, fragrances in the room, and so on. For this reason, we try to be aware of the environment we are working in when we use EFT

and other healing methods on ourselves and our clients.

If in doubt, it is easy to go someplace else and try the tapping techniques again. If EFT works, you know that something in the original location is interfering. If you are still not having success, Craig recommends going on to Item 2. We also use kinesiology to pinpoint energy toxins. Before proceeding to Item 2, you could also muscle test for energy toxins. We describe ways to do this later in this chapter.

2. **Clean yourself thoroughly.** Remove your clothing and take a bath without soap, cleaning all areas of your body and your hair thoroughly. Something on your clothing may be affecting you, like dry cleaning fluid or laundry detergent. Clothes may have chemicals on them, fabrics may cause sensitivity, and laundry detergents may leave residues. Constricting clothing, jewelry, metal bra underwires, belts, and other items on the body can also block the flow of energy through the body.

Something you are using on your body could also cause a problem, like hair spray, shampoo, or perfume. Once you are clean, try the tapping techniques again before putting on any clothing. This may be awkward if you are helping another person with EFT, but he or she could go home and clean up, then try the tapping techniques again with you over the phone. If EFT works, then you know that something on the body was interfering. If you are still not having success, Craig recommends trying Item 3.

To avoid encountering energy toxins, many holistic practitioners recommend that their clients wear loose natural clothing and no perfumes to their sessions. Starting out this way maximizes the potential for healing.

3. **Wait a day or two.** You may have eaten something that caused a reaction in your body. If this is the case, the

tapping techniques will work once the substance has moved completely through your system. To increase your chances for success, be careful what you eat and drink during this waiting period. Your results will not change if you continue to consume the offending substance. In this regard, Craig suggests including as much variety in your diet as possible, as even healthy foods may become toxic when consumed too frequently. Here is a sampling of foods and substances that have commonly been found to be harmful:

- Herbs
- Corn
- Soy
- Caffeine
- Nicotine
- Perfume

- Wheat
- Refined sugar
- Coffee
- Alcohol
- Pepper
- Medications

Once the toxin is identified, avoid it. Even if the affect of eating something like an ear of corn seems insignificant, a holistic approach looks at the whole picture. If you truly want to be vibrantly healthy physically, emotionally, mentally, and spiritually, placing stress on the body is ludicrous.

Interestingly, most people think that it is normal to feel tired after they eat, or at a specific time of day. This is not true. At a time when we were eating a primarily vegetarian diet, Phillip used to consistently experience extreme fatigue in the middle of the afternoon. After many years on this diet, noticing that we were feeling worse and worse, we changed. Now, Phillip feels fine throughout the day.

ENERGY TOXINS AND KINESIOLOGY

Virtually any substance can trigger a symptom. Fortunately, with muscle testing, you can pinpoint toxins in:

- Foods you eat
- Substances you put on your body
- Environmental influences, which are numerous

Figure 9.1 provides a general list of energy toxins that could be affecting you in a negative way. This is a sample list of statements you can test to determine if energy toxins are affecting you. For generalized items like most of those on this checklist, just focus on the statement and test. A strong response indicates that the test statement is in harmony with your well-being. A weak response means that it is disharmonious.

Once you have identified a general category, you will want to go into specifics and we will discuss how to do this here. When testing specific items, try one of the following:

- Hold a sample of the substance close to the body, preferably in the area where it is used or near the area that is affected by it and test.

- In the case of environmental toxins, like electronic equipment, fluorescent lights, go into their environment and test.

- With food or supplements, you can hold them near the stomach and test. If possible, you can put some in your mouth and test.

- Write the name of the substance or environmental toxin on a piece of paper and hold it close to the body, again close to the area where it is used or the area that is affected by it, and test.

- Think about the substance or environmental toxin and the area of the body that is affected by it and test.

The preferential order would be from the most tangible and concrete (holding the substance) to least tangible (thinking about it). Actually they all can have the same impact, as

---

FIGURE 9.1
TOXICITY CHECKLIST

To determine if energy toxins are affecting you, start each of the following items with the phrase: "Think about your health and well-being in relation to _____," filling in the blank with the phrases on the list below.

STATEMENT	STRONG	WEAK
"Think about your health and well-being in relation to ...		
... the foods you eat generally."	_____	_____
... the foods you ate today."	_____	_____
... the water you drink."	_____	_____
... perfumes in your environment."	_____	_____
... soaps, shampoos and similar products."	_____	_____
... medications or other drugs you are taking."	_____	_____
... cleaning products you use."	_____	_____
... aluminum cookware and foil you use."	_____	_____
... x-rays you have had."	_____	_____
... the air you breathe."	_____	_____
... the materials in your home."	_____	_____
... the materials in your office."	_____	_____
... the lights in your office."	_____	_____
... the emotional environment in your home."	_____	_____
... the emotional environment in your office."	_____	_____
... your computer."	_____	_____
... your TV."	_____	_____

thinking about something recreates the response. When holding a substance, put it by the area of the body that seems most affected, if known. Otherwise just hold it in front of you.

There is some disagreement among experts regarding the relative effectiveness of one method compared with another. If you are new to this approach, using the offending substance and/or accessing the offending environment may be the most convincing, if this is possible. Yet there are so many possible culprits, you can't have samples of everything and go everywhere you would like. In those cases, just write the name of the potential offender on a piece of paper or think about it.

Testing Foods

You can test the effect of any food you ingest with kinesiology. As an example, we have found that most people respond poorly to white sugar, a fact they are often reluctant to hear. This is not always true, but most people muscle test weak when holding a sugar cube. To try this, hold some white sugar next to your stomach and test. The one-hand method comes in handy here, since you can test with one hand and hold the test substance in the other hand. The strength or weakness of the muscle shows how eating sugar affects your body. If you test weak, it means that white sugar is reducing your physical well-being.

If you suspect that energy toxins are affecting your results with EFT, you may want to test the foods in Figure 9.2, Food and Substance Checklist. There are innumerable substances we ingest and inhale daily. Though this checklist is extensive, it is by no means complete.

Testing Other Substances

You can also test the substances you put on your body. Here are some examples:

- Place a bottle of lotion next to your skin and test.

FIGURE 9.2
FOOD AND SUBSTANCE CHECKLIST

____ Canned Foods

____ Baked Foods

____ Broiled Foods

____ Fried Foods

BEVERAGES

____ Milk Products

____ Coffee

____ BlackTea

____ GreenTea

____ Soft Drinks

____ Alcohol

GRAINS

____ Barley

____ Buckwheat

____ Cornmeal

____ Rice

____ Rye

____ Whole Wheat

____ White Flour

____ Oats

____ Soy

CONDIMENTS

____ Black Pepper

____ Sage

____ Salt

____ Catsup

____ Mustard

____ Other

FATS

____ Butter

____ Margarine

____ Canola Oil

____ Corn Oil

____ Flax Oil

____ Olive Oil

____ Peanut Oil

____ Safflower Oil

____ Soy Oil

____ Sunflower Oil

SEA FOOD

____ All Fish

____ Fresh Water Fish

____ Salt Water Fish

____ Shell Fish

MEAT

____ Beef

____ Chicken

____ Duck

____ Goat

____ Goose

____ Lamb

____ Pork

____ Rabbit

____ Turkey

____ Veal

____ Egg

____ Bison

FRUITS

____ Apple

____ Apricot

____ Avocado

____ Banana

____ Blackberry

____ Blueberry

____ Cantaloupe

____ Cherry

____ Cranberry

____ Date

____ Fig

____ Grape

____ Grapefruit

____ Lemon

____ Orange

____ Peach

____ Pear

____ Pineapple

____ Kiwi

____ Plum

____ Pomegranate

____ Raspberry

____ Strawberry

____ Nectarine

____ Persimmon

____ Honeydew

____ Mango

____ Papaya

____ Watermelon

FIGURE 9.2
CONTINUED

VEGETABLES	NUTS	MISCELLANEOUS
___ Artichoke	___ Almond	___ Olive
___ Asparagus	___ Brazil	___ Pickle
___ Dry Beans	___ Coconut	___ Sauerkraut
___ Green Beans	___ Hazelnut	___ Chocolate
___ Beets	___ Macadamia	___ Acidophilus
___ Cabbage	___ Peanut	___ Yeast
___ Carrot	___ Pecan	___ Yeast Products
___ Cauliflower	___ Cashew	___ Yogurt
___ Celery	___ Chestnut	___ Mint
___ Corn	___ Walnut	___ MSG
___ Cucumber	___ Other	
___ Eggplant		ENVIRONMENT
___ Garlic	SUGARS	___ Cotton
___ Lentil	___ Brown Sugar	___ Leather
___ Lettuce	___ Honey	___ Nylon
___ Mushroom	___ Maple Syrup	___ Rubber
___ Okra	___ Molasses	___ Wool
___ Onion	___ Nutra Sweet	___ Animal Fur
___ Peas	___ Saccharin	___ Cat Fur
___ Green Pepper	___ Slimsweet	___ Dog Fur
___ Radish	___ Splenda	___ Dust
___ Spinach	___ Stevia	___ Feathers
___ Squash	___ Sweet n' Low	___ Flaxseed
___ Cooked Greens	___ White Sugar	___ Pollen
___ Tomato	___ Other	___ Hay
___ Turnip		___ Gold
___ White Potato		___ Silver
___ Sweet Potato		___ Platinum
___ Broccoli		___ Turpentine
___ Other		___ Formaldehyde

- Place a perfume bottle next to your neck and test.

- Place a cosmetic bottle where you apply it and test.

- Place a bottle of shampoo, conditioner, or hair coloring next to your head and test.

As you perform each test, focus on how the product is influencing you. A product that is in harmony with your well-being will test strong. If you test weak, the product is harmful in some way. You will not want to use a product regularly if it is producing a negative reaction or weakening the energy system.

Testing Influences in Your Environment

We are always interacting energetically with our surroundings. It is most beneficial for us to be in a place that is harmonious with our frequency. Being in a supportive environment is like floating calmly on a river of water that is leading us to where we want to go in our lives. The temperature is perfect, and the water gently nurtures us as we move forward. In a disharmonious environment, life is more like trying to swim upstream on a raging river. It may take a lot of effort just to stay even, and if we stop swimming, we may find ourselves being swept away from our goals.

In a disharmonious environment, you can easily become overwhelmed, which may create stress or physical illness. A common culprit is the home or office computer. Jane is a sensitive person and she can feel the energy radiating off of a computer if she is anywhere near one. In a similar way, she can feel the pressure that the concentration of electricity places on us, especially in large cities. Whether we are aware of it or not, we are all being influenced by these subtle energies, along with car emissions, and so on.

You can use a technique that is similar to the sugar test for testing the influence of your home or office computer, television, cellular phone, or anything else in your environment. Let us use a computer as an example. First, test yourself while you stand or sit in an area that is away from your computer and similar concentrations of energy. As you perform the test, focus your intent on how the environment is affecting you. If the environment is neutral, you should test strong. If you test strong for the base test, sit down in front of the computer and test yourself again, focusing your intent on how the computer is influencing you.

A strong response to this test indicates that the computer is not interfering with you energetically; a weak response indicates that it is. If you test weak, you may wish to invest in a protective device. Similarly, if you test weak for any of the items in Figure 9.1, you may want to make the changes needed to support your health and well-being. If you test weak for statements like the materials in your home or materials in your office, you will need to do some detective work to identify precisely where there is a problem. We next ask about specific rooms, then items in the rooms until we pinpoint the culprit.

Testing Emotional Toxins

We all know that a harmonious emotional environment is important to our well-being, but, as with other toxins, with repeated exposure, we may become numb to the profound effects of exposure to "bad vibes." Or we may not know what to do and try to ignore them. At the very least, we need to be aware of this potential stressor to the energy system, and, in some cases, we may need to make appropriate changes in our lives to relieve ourselves of the emotional, mental, and/or spiritual stress. We deserve to live in environments that promote well-being, where all are treated fairly and honored.

If you test weak for the emotional environment in your home or office, you may know right away where the problem lies. If not, you may have to do some detective work to identify the exact source. The culprit may be a person, thing, or activity. We once had a client whose wife was into hard metal music and the art that accompanies it. Both are negative energies that could affect the energy system. Similarly, watching too many news programs has a negative affect on some individuals. In some cases, even holidays like Thanksgiving and Christmas can produce negative energies, because of the stress and/or family ties. Dr. Alexander R. Lees describes addressing holiday stress in the next part of this book.

To locate the source, you start by asking is it a person, thing, activity, or event, to narrow down the field. Then ask more questions until you identify the source. It can even be amusing in some cases, like recognizing that avoiding the evening news is a requirement for creating vibrant well-being and a joyful life. Whatever the culprit, the change may produce surprisingly positive results.

Negative Associations

Foods and substances become "anchors" when we associate them with external events. As EFT Practitioners, we need to recognize that reactions to substances may be linked to traumatic experiences. A person who was attacked in a rose garden may unconsciously associate the scent of a rose with being abused. The innocent rose, then, is perceived as a threat, creating a physical reaction, and the victim has no conscious recognition of the association. In such cases, the holistic process can help to link the physical reaction to the emotional, mental, and spiritual associations.

In addition to using the checklists provided in this chapter, remember to ask about the foods and substances the person was exposed to before and during a conflict if EFT is not working. Foods people eat frequently, including their favorite ones, can be culprits.

Doing the Detective Work

Exploring energy toxins may seem complex, but the results are worth the effort. You can also minimize the potential of being affected by energy toxins by eating fresh, whole, organic foods, using chemical-free products on your body, and being aware of your physical and emotional environment. We have found that we feel much more balanced, happy, and stress-free when we follow these steps to nurture and honor ourselves.

In addition, you can use your intuition to pinpoint a disturbing substance or substances. If you are drawn to this approach, use a centering process, still your mind, and ask what's causing the problem.

USING ENERGY TECHNIQUES ON TOXINS

With the prevalence of energy toxins, there may be some substances that disturb your system that you cannot easily avoid, like common foods, dust, computers, car exhaust, and vaccinations. Here, neutralizing the response may be easier than avoiding the offender.

Energy techniques designed to neutralize the body's response to disturbing substances are worth trying. The body seeks balance, and energy techniques provide a way to reprogram the body. If the body feels safe, its response to an energy toxin may be neutralized. After you identify an offender, here are some options for addressing it:

1. **Use EFT:** While holding the substance, say "Even though I have a bad reaction to _____ [substance], I deeply and completely accept myself." Then tap, using the long sequence to include more points.

2. **Use BodyTalk Tapping:** BodyTalk is a modality created by Dr. John Veltheim, which he describes in his book The BodyTalk System. Hold the substance and fo-

cus your attention on it. Stretch out your hand so your fingers extend across the top of the head. Tap lightly and continuously on the head while inhaling deeply. Then tap lightly and continuously on the center of the chest while exhaling fully. Repeat several times.

3. **Use the Spinal Release (S.R.) Procedure:** This one, which requires two people, comes from Sandi Radomski's book *Allergy Antidotes*. Use your fingers or knuckles to tap on either side of the spine, right next to it, but not on the bone, from the neck down to the tailbone. While tapping, have the recipient:

   a) Breathe in, then holding the breath briefly

   b) Breathe out, then holding the breath briefly

   c) Hyperventilate briefly

   d) Relax with normal breathing briefly

   e) Circle the eyes clockwise

   f) Circle the eyes counterclockwise

   g) Close the eyes

   h) With the eyes closed, circle them clockwise

   i) With eyes closed, circle them counterclockwise

Once you are done, if the muscle test is strong, the process is complete. If not, redo the entire sequence. Then ask if the recipient needs to hold the substance, and if so for how long (1 minute, 2 minutes, etc). Have him or her hold it for the designated time. Then ask if he or she needs to stay away from substance. If so, for how long (1hour, 2 hours, etc.)

4. **Massage the Lymph Points:** This process, which Donna Eden recommends in her book *Energy Medicine*,

involves massaging two areas on the body. She cautions that, on occasion, you may feel worse before you feel better as part of the detoxification:

A. The central meridian neurolymphatic points are on the outer rim of your chest. Start deeply massaging the collarbone points (K-27). Continue moving out to the sides below the clavicle, which is the indentation by the shoulder bone.

B. The large intestine neurolymphatic points are on the sides of your legs above the knees. Massaging these points moves the lymph and helps the large intestine move toxins. These points form a straight line from the top side of your leg (the femur) down to the side of the knee. Massage along both sides of your leg slowly and with a strong pressure.

Sandi Radomski, one of the authors in the EFT Experts part of this book, is an energy psychology practitioner who specializes in this area. In her work, Radomski treats energy toxins as allergies. EFT, BodyTalk, and spinal release techniques and their relevance to allergy work are discussed extensively in her *Allergy Antidotes* manuals. Here is what she reports about working with energy toxins:

Allergy Antidotes uses energy psychology techniques to reprogram the body to no longer react negatively to the reactive substances. The reprogrammed body no longer views the substance as a poison. All treatments are done with the patient's focus on the reactive substance. …. By stimulating acupuncture points, we eliminate the energy imbalance in relation to that substance, thereby ending the body's negative reaction.

Radomski suggests the following affirmation if you're not sure what is causing the problem: "Whatever it is that's causing the problem/sneeze/itchy eyes etc., I deeply and completely accept myself."

As you can see, energy toxins are a study in themselves that goes beyond EFT and can greatly enhance all of our lives. You may be surprised how different you can feel if you are more intentional with what you put in and on your body, along with what you surround yourself with energetically and emotionally. We all deserve to have the best possible foods and environments to support ourselves in the creation of more joy, love, and freedom.

Although diet is technically beyond the scope of this book, everything is connected holistically. A person who is affected by poor nutrition is going to suffer on all levels. Nutrient-empty foods like soft drinks, candy, and other sugary foods, refined flour, potato chips, and so on replace the nutrient-rich foods that are the building blocks for a healthy body. If nutritionally deprived, the body's immune system, hormones, brain chemistry, and organ systems suffer, affecting one's ability to heal. Beyond the physical body, a poor diet also affects emotional, mental, and spiritual well-being. A healthy diet, along with regular exercise, can enhance all kinds of healing.

It is worth examining your priorities. Rather than having a consciousness of asking, "How little do I have to do to be healthy and happy?" we prefer to ask, "What more can I do to create vibrant health and well-being?"

CHAPTER TEN

Optimizing Your Effectiveness

Our life is what our thoughts make it.

– UNKNOWN

Exploring the intricacies of the body, the mind, and the energy system raises fundamental questions about the nature of life and the healing journey. In this regard, we still have a few more ideas that can help you to understand yourself and others, and optimize your effectiveness with EFT.

Before we go into specifics, here are a few points:

- **You cannot heal anyone.** Even doctors do not heal their patients; they simply aim to optimize conditions for their patients' bodies to heal themselves. If you are helping others, it is important to recognize that responsibility for healing ultimately lies within each individual.

- **You will not be able to help everyone.** Sometimes personalities conflict. Possible reasons for the difficulties might be because you have similar issues to the person you are helping, or the other person is not open to your approach. Don't take such cases as a personal rejection or failure. If you are in the process of healing yourself, maybe you need more familiarity with the techniques, or could benefit from outside assistance. Addressing deep core issues can be challenging.

- **Timing is a factor.** Each person heals and awakens to new possibilities in his or her own time. Sometimes the wounded ego has the upper hand and the individual is just not ready or fully committed to doing what it takes to overcome an obstacle. A person will quit smoking only if he or she is fully committed to it, and only the individual can provide that commitment. EFT is a big help, but not a substitute for taking personal responsibility.

  If you are helping others, an affirmation to use is "Everything has its own timing. I respect each person and attract those who are the right people for my journey of awakening." Using EFT, you can tap in this affirmation, or one of your choosing.

For helping others, you can find more information on maintaining a healthy perspective in Appendix A, which focuses on fostering healthy therapeutic relationships.

COMPARTMENTALIZING

As the Levels of PR and the Holistic Process showed, you can usually pinpoint unconscious aspects of issues that need to be addressed for EFT to be effective. Both methods also show that you never know where the healing journey is going to lead when you set out on an exploration of the deeper recesses of the mind. One time, Jane worked with a woman we will call Eva who had two issues she wanted to address: her negative reaction to her husband's messiness and her sexuality. By the end of their session, Eva and Jane realized that these issues were connected, though they never would have guessed it when they started.

Many issues are like this, seemingly unrelated, while underneath it all, they may be one and the same. Uncovering these connections and releasing related limitations is exciting, like piecing together a cosmic puzzle. It also shows why using a holistic approach that recognizes the myriad of connections within our energetic makeup is so important.

Connections like Eva's defy logic and can, in some cases, create barriers to healing that are difficult to identify, particularly when a person is compartmentalizing. An individual who is compartmentalizing prevents the organic healing process from occurring by setting areas off limits. This is usually done unconsciously or with the assumption that doing so will not affect the potential for healing in other areas. From our experience, it is generally unwise to impose such limits.

Here are some common examples of compartmentalizing:

- A person may avoid talking about something seemingly unrelated to the issue at hand that is upsetting, like a sister with whom there is conflict and emotional pain. Thoughts go through the mind so quickly that the subject of the sister may just go through and be unwittingly edited out in a second.

- An individual who is working with a marriage counselor to address disagreements with her husband and an EFT practitioner to address other challenges may avoid discussing anything related to her marriage with the EFT Practitioner, thinking that the issues are separate, and her marriage is already being addressed.

- A person who has an intestinal condition that is being treated by a physician may similarly edit out mentioning the abdominal pain that flares up when he starts to talk about his job in an EFT Session.

- A person who is dealing with growing anger related to driving in rush hour traffic may not think it is relevant and edit out mentioning it.

- A woman seeking help with losing weight who is embarrassed by her childish behavior when someone took the last package of her favorite candies at the grocery store may edit out speaking about it.

Any of these edited symptoms may be keys to resolving a seemingly unrelated problem. The situation that first brought compartmentalizing to our attention was one time when Jane was working with a client we will call Paul. Paul was seeing a marriage counselor for problems with his wife. At the same time, he was seeing Jane to address issues related to his self-esteem. During one of their first sessions, Paul experienced a tremendous awakening of the realization that he was perfect just as he was. His awareness of the shift was profound and he headed home in a state of elated amazement.

Jane was pleased that he was feeling so good about himself, knowing that we all need to recognize how special we are. She was equally surprised that the next time he came for a session, Paul had completely forgotten what had transpired the last time they met. He was back at the beginning again. After repeating the same pattern several more times, Jane realized that Paul was clearing his problem when he came for a session, then recreating it when he went home. His self-esteem was deeply tied in to his relationship with his wife. One could not be addressed without the other.

So if, for instance, a person wants to address fears related to money, but is unwilling to address discomfort related to spiritual beliefs, in some cases, healing may be limited, if not impossible. The issues may seem to be completely unrelated, but there is no way of knowing ahead of time.

Take the example of a person we will call Georgia. She comes to you because she feels stuck in her spiritual development and isn't enjoying her life. Georgia is having problems with her sister, but she doesn't want to discuss these issues.

After several sessions dealing unsuccessfully with Georgia's feeling of being stuck, it becomes obvious that she is not making any progress. Something else must be happening, and you have no way of knowing what it is. You have tested the Levels of PR and done the Holistic Process, with little result. While you are trying to figure out what is happening, Georgia is still not talking about her sister, hoping the problem will work itself out somehow and not realizing that the issues overlap.

Though we feel that it is always the client's right not to reveal anything that he or she doesn't want to, holding back can block the healing process. We explain to our clients that their stuff is not real, meaning that they are just misunderstandings, rather than representations of their true identities, so they don't have to take them seriously or feel bad about them in any way. We also ask them to open to whatever comes into their awareness in our discussion, because for optimal success, all relevant information needs to be addressed.

In some cases, a person may be compartmentalizing without being aware of it. A person who is ashamed or embarrassed by a habit or behavior may be reluctant to mention it and simply edit it from his or her thinking. Or a person who has done inner work before may think that a certain issue has been cleared when it hasn't.

Other instances of compartmentalizing can include:

- Splits between one's health issues and one's lifestyle

- Dividing family and friends, or work and family

- Compartmentalizing religious/spiritual teachings with the rest of one's life

- Dealing with addictions (such as food, alcohol, drugs) as isolated issues and avoiding how they affect other areas of one's life

In such cases, the person's conscious mind might not easily make the connections needed for healing. To a degree, compartmentalizing is unavoidable, but it can help to be aware of it. Sometimes, if you sense that a piece of the puzzle is missing, you can speak openly about it, or if you are addressing an issue of your own, open your mind to making new connections.

THE SEVEN DEFENSE PATTERNS

In the 1970's, we (Phillip and Jane) met as members of an organization that studies the works of the Russian philosophers George Gurdjieff and Peter Ouspensky. These teachings, which are known as the Fourth Way, focused on different aspects of the human condition and characteristics people have that are instrumental to the way they relate to their environments. One group of characteristics, which could also be seen as archetypal patterns, is called chief feature, chief weakness, or chief defense. Since we first encountered this concept, we have also found it in the Michael Teachings.

According to these teachings, each of us has a number of different archetypal characteristics relating to the roles we are playing in our lives, our spiritual goals, our mental perspectives, and the ways we approach our goals. These characteristics, which are called "overleaves" in the Michael Teachings, identify soulful qualities and unique strengths. They also include our chief defense or weakness, which is the way we react when we are under pressure.

Spiritually, one's chief defense could be seen as the largest barrier to one's personal and spiritual development. This mechanism, which is generally unconscious, may also be one of the main reasons our efforts to heal and progress don't bear fruit. As with many ineffective coping mechanisms, each of us learned to resort to one of these weaknesses as our primary means of defending ourselves from perceived threats during childhood. We also have some amount of all of the others.

The seven fear-based patterns are: self-deprecation, arrogance, self-destruction, greed, martyrdom, impatience, and stubbornness. Each of us also has a secondary feature, which we also may gravitate to frequently. On an unconscious level, these defenses allow us to feel secure in an unpredictable world, but they are limiting, because they are based on fear. As we mature, they become a source of alienation and negativity.

You may find that exploring this subject is uncomfortable. This is because the wounded ego, which already feels bad about itself, does not like to be exposed for its shortcomings. Viewed from a more soulful perspective, we can see that we have done the best we could with the resources available to us. Nonetheless, it would be silly for us to allow these limiting patterns to continue to rule our lives.

Spiritually, these defenses are meant to be eliminated by conscious awareness, healing of the wounded ego, and strengthening of the soul's presence. We progress by lovingly observing the mechanics of the defenses and choosing more resourceful approaches. A certain amount of clearing will occur just by assimilating this information and observing ourselves to see how these patterns control our lives. As we clear these fear-based parts of ourselves, we open to more soulful, joyous, loving ways of being, free of the need to be defensive.

The Chief Defenses and EFT

In most cases, these aspects of the wounded ego do not prevent EFT from succeeding, but for the rare individuals on whom they have a particularly strong hold, they can completely block making progress with EFT or any other method. With such people, these defenses become deeply entwined with their sense of self and their insecurities. Their positions are so strongly defended that it can be difficult to get by them. In each case, the defense is seeking proof of its position in whatever is happening.

In EFT terms, they could be seen as forms of Massive PR that need to be addressed directly for progress to be possible. This can be difficult, because these individuals are insecure. They need to recognize that the defenses are aspects of the wounded ego that need to be healed so they can love themselves. The defenses are not real; the soul, which can love unconditionally and experience wholeness, is one's true identity.

Here is the basic fear behind each weakness, along with a description of the way it defends itself:

- **Self-Deprecation:** Fear of being inadequate. These people tend to put themselves down and avoid taking opportunities to challenge themselves and try something new out of fear of failure.

- **Arrogance:** Fear of being judged. Beneath their confident exteriors, these people are often self-conscious, insecure, and afraid to admit making mistakes. In some cases, they may not be open to honest self-evaluation, because they cannot admit having any shortcomings.

- **Self-destruction:** Fear of feeling life is not worth living. For these people, nothing ever seems to work out. People with strong addictive tendencies are generally acting from this feature, and, as anyone who has worked with such people knows, they often vehemently deny that they are addicted and vehemently defend their actions.

- **Greed:** Fear of not having enough. This fear results in a voracious appetite, hoarding, and overindulgence. It grabs whatever it can now, for fear that there will not be enough tomorrow. This is often related to being overweight, having credit card debt, an inability to let go of things, and a general lack of self-control, so people on whom it has a strong hold may lack the discipline they need for their goals to come to fruition.

- **Martyrdom:** Fear of being a victim. These people feel that their efforts do not receive adequate appreciation and often want everyone to know about it. They can find ways to see themselves as victims in any situation, including a healing session.

- **Impatience:** Fear of missing out. Such people are constantly rushing on to the next thing, which leads to mistakes and an inability to pay attention to what they are doing in the present moment. They may find it difficult to make time for healing or sitting still during a healing session. This defense may be connected to attention deficit disorder.

- **Stubbornness:** Fear of change. These people tend to present an opposing position. When this tendency is strong, it can present a barrier, because they are busy opposing whatever is being suggested. Because of their insecurity, they may also feel a strong need for these opposing opinions to be heard, so having a constructive conversation can be difficult.

Jane once had a session with Martha, who was deep in the throes of martyrdom, so her sense of victimization was particularly strong. In the session, they addressed several issues with EFT. Each time, Martha's SUDs would go down from around a tearful ten to close to zero, but, just as she completed taking a deep, calming breath at the end of the process, another related problem would arise and the tears would return, taking Martha back to a ten with both issues. As the session progressed, more and more problems appeared. And, beyond experiencing a second or two of relief at the end of the tapping, none of them had improved after nearly an hour.

Jane recognized the martyr pattern. She stopped using EFT and gently told Martha what she was observing. For those with such strong defenses, even the healing session can become a way of supporting their fears and limiting beliefs. With

Martha, a failed session would unconsciously provide another validation of her victimhood. To overcome it, Martha needed to lovingly recognize the pattern, turn back to loving herself, and learn to not allow it to occupy space in her consciousness.

Similarly, Phillip once worked with a woman with strong stubbornness. Every time he tried to help her and repeat back the way she described a problem, she would become oppositional, so they could never pinpoint anything to address. If she said she felt hurt by something a person said at work, Phillip would ask if she wanted to tap on the feelings of being hurt and she would say that she was not actually hurt. Then, if she said that she was actually angry and Phillip asked if she wanted to tap on the anger, she said that anger was not really a problem. After a time, Phillip lovingly changed the direction of the session to address her oppositional perspective.

When we discuss these patterns with clients, we also balance the focus on weaknesses with discussions of their unique strengths. The people who are most affected by these patterns also have a strong need to learn to love themselves.

Remember everyone has all of the defense patterns to some degree, with one or two favorites. They come to the foreground under stress and in recurring situations where we respond defensively. These fear-based patterns can be defused and eliminated by simply becoming aware of them, along with the help of EFT and the other methods described in this book.

Identifying Your Chief Defense

As mentioned earlier, reading about these patterns may make you feel uncomfortable and identifying the ones that apply the most to you may take a bit of time. This is common. Remember they are not your true identity; they are imaginary limitations that need to be released to be totally free. In fact, understanding the workings of these defenses can be tremendously helpful for healing and self-development. When you educate yourself and those you help about these features, everyone becomes more aware.

By knowing the seven weaknesses, we become more confident in our ability to heal ourselves. We come to realize that the defenses are illusory, like when Dorothy pulled back the curtain to see the Wizard of Oz. Then these emotional patterns lose their power over us. It is a matter of seeing how they created habitual limiting thoughts and negative emotions, and dis-identifying with the patterns.

Although initially it may be hard to tell which are your chief feature and back-up defense, they are usually the ones that feel particularly uncomfortable when examining them. Muscle testing, intuition, self-observation, and asking friends can help in exposing them.

OTHER SOUL QUALITIES

We have focused on the chief defense patterns here because of the therapeutic value of recognizing them and reducing their impact. As mentioned earlier, the overleaves also include positive archetypal traits we embody to help us fulfill our purpose in this life. They include our essential way of being or role, our goal, our mental perspective or attitude, and our mode or way of reaching our goal. Recognizing these profound traits can help us to understand ourselves and those around us at a much deeper level and accelerate our progress on the journey.

The overleaves provide invaluable keys for identifying our essential nature, for fully appreciating ourselves, and for progressing on our evolutionary paths. Though addressing these patterns is beyond the scope of this book, we recommend exploring them to better understand your journey and true divine purpose. You can find more information on the seven defenses, the overleaves, the Fourth Way, and the Michael Teachings in our *Awaken to Your True Purpose* audio program, which is described in Appendix C.

CONCLUSION

To recap, here are the special challenges to EFT covered in this part of the book:

- neurological disorganization
- energy toxins
- compartmentalizing
- chief defenses

EFT is magical, transformational, and very practical. Sometimes problems are resolved remarkably quickly in what Gary Craig calls the "one-minute wonders." Other issues can be complex, with many aspects. Dealing with the special challenges to EFT may seem like a large task at first. If you are new to these methods, just take one step at a time. One of the exciting and fulfilling parts of exploring holistic healing is that there are always new depths to explore. Over time, you can add a variety of methods to your toolbox and experience tremendous growth.

CHAPTER ELEVEN

Stepping into the Future

All life is an experiment,
the more experiments you make the better.

– RALPH WALDO EMERSON

The path to your future lies before you. With the tools you have gathered here and the ones you will find in the next part of this book, where you will meet eleven more EFT Experts, you have the possibility of making transformational changes, as thousands of others have done with these methods.

Before turning you over to these experts, we want to share some thoughts about realizing your full potential.

LEAVING THE PAST BEHIND

Creating the future of our dreams means leaving the past behind. Most of us use the burdens of the past as gauges of our potential in the future. Unfortunately, the weight of these burdens can stop us cold on the path to freedom.

Jane once dreamed that she was carrying a heavy backpack up a slippery, ice-covered slope. With this burden, she kept slipping back down to the bottom of the hill, unable to make it to the top. Reflecting on the experience, she removed the backpack and, opening it up, she was shocked to discover that it was filled with dark, slimy worms and other squirmy creatures. Realizing that she didn't need it, Jane quickly cast is aside, scaled the slippery slope with ease and reached a breathtakingly beautiful valley on the other side.

Carrying the limitations of the past with us is like lugging a heavy backpack filled with worthless trash, and many people carry a lot of trash around with them. Each piece of trash takes energy to maintain, vital life force energy we could otherwise be using to create a positive, fulfilling future. EFT allows us to quickly and easily unload ourselves of these burdens and move briskly forward.

With this in mind, it is somewhat surprising and even comical to think that we often resist opportunities to pull out the trash in the knapsack and discard it once and for all. But, as in the dream, many of us continue steadfastly and unsuccessfully trying to move forward lugging heavy burdens.

Opening the Backpack

There is no time like the present to take a look and start making changes. We are intimately familiar with the thoughts so many of us have about waiting until there is more time or when life is easier to do the things we really want to do with our lives. We have been there and finally recognized that the easier time never comes. The time to change is always now.

To start, you may want to close your eyes for a moment now, take a couple of relaxing breaths, notice if you are carrying a backpack or any other unnecessary weight, around with you. If so, open it up and look inside. You may also want to write down what you find there. The contents provide clues about how you can relieve yourself of unnecessary burdens with the methods in this book, so you set your course and step lightly into the future.

SETTING YOUR COURSE

This may also be a good time for goalsetting. Putting your dreams and goals concretely down on paper is a powerful first step toward creating them in your life. To build a bright future, here are some questions you can ask yourself:

- If you had no limitations in place, time, or money, where would you want to be, what would you want to do, and what would you want to have? Just write down whatever comes to mind. To begin, the more ideas the better; just let them come out on paper. You can go through and refine them when you are done.

- If you want to have a lot of money, what does it represent to you? Again, write down whatever comes to mind. When you are done, separate the soulful heartfelt desires from the insecurities that need to be cleared with EFT. Clearing issues related to money will help you to clear the way to realizing your goals.

- If your life ended today, which of the things on your list would be most meaningful to you? Answering this question may help you to refine your list.

When you have completed all of the questions, you may want to organize your thoughts into a final list, which you can review and revise over time.

FUTURE PACING

To realize your full potential and create a wondrous future, we suggest returning to the Future-Pacing Process presented in Chapter Four. Once you have defined your goals, this visualization can help you to bring them into reality. We often use it ourselves, imagining being on a path with the past withdrawing behind us and the future extending out before us as far as we can see. What you see is what you get; whatever you consistently see for your future in any area of your life is what you are in the process of creating. Using future pacing with EFT to strengthen the positive results of any process provides an image to focus on as you step forward.

Lessons on the Path

It is also important as we progress on the path to value our experiences and the lessons they provide. Returning to a holistic perspective, everything is connected and everything has meaning. All of our burdens can also be seen as synchronous opportunities to evolve, connect more with our soul's essential nature, and discover ourselves.

Each roadblock on the path to the future, then, relates to a lesson we need to learn on the journey to wholeness. Our limitations are really just misunderstandings about our true identities as vast spiritual beings with infinite potentials. By learning life's lessons, we can discard the misunderstandings and recognize more about who we really are. We gain wisdom and lightness as we release the burdens that have held us back. By clearing such blockages with EFT, we are participating in the evolutionary journey and preparing ourselves to realize our full potential.

The following questions, which relate to the four levels of healing presented in the Holistic Process and a fifth category that covers higher spiritual levels, provide some aspects of the future to explore. You can ask yourself each of the questions and measure the level of strength of the quality from one to ten or visualize how it is playing out in your future. To visualize, focus on one of the questions, close your eyes for a moment, take a couple of nice, deep breaths to turn your attention inward, imagine yourself on a path with the past behind you and the future extending out before you, and look forward at how this aspect of your well-being is playing out in your future. If you want to be specific, you can imagine going forward a month into the future, then six months, five years, and so on, at whatever increments you wish.

1. **Physical Level:** As you gaze into the future, ...

   - How does your level of physical strength and vitality look?
   - What do you see related to your sense of physical well-being?

2. **Emotional Level:** As you gaze into the future, ...

   - What do you see in relation to having a positive emotional outlook?
   - How much joy is there in your future?
   - How do you see your ability to nurture and be nurtured?

3. **Mental Level:** As you gaze into the future, ...

   - How powerful do you appear to be?
   - How well can you rely on yourself to meet your needs?
   - How do you see your possibilities in relation to your gender?
   - How do you see yourself in relation to being able to create the life of your dreams?

4. **Spiritual Level:** As you gaze into the future, ...

   - How deserving are you of being loved and honored?

- How capable are you of loving others?
- How able are you to forgive yourself and others, and leave the past behind?

5. **Higher Spiritual:** As you gaze into the future, ...

- How able are you to express yourself and your uniqueness with friends, colleagues, and larger groups of people?
- How clear do you feel about your vision and purpose?
- How aligned do you feel with your sense knowing what is true for you?

Having explored personal and spiritual development for nearly three decades now, we recognize that just about all of us need to intentionally focus on having a positive outlook of ourselves and our possibilities to successfully create the life of our dreams. We have done clearing on all of the trash we have found in each of these areas and affirm our potential on all of these levels on a regular basis. The results have exceeded our expectations.

It is our greatest wish that you have the same experience with the methods described in this book and that you create a life filled with joy, love, and freedom.

Part 4

THE EFT EXPERTS

CHAPTER TWELVE

Meet the EFT Experts

*If you do not change direction, you
may end up where you are heading.*

– LAO TZU

EFT is a wonderful healing tool that is used by both lay people and healing practitioners alike. Not surprisingly, a growing number of therapists are using EFT in their practices.

In this chapter, you will hear from eleven practitioners who have profoundly expanded the knowledge about EFT by using it in their practice. These gifted healers have taken the essence of EFT and added their unique experience and perspective on energy psychology. It's exciting that experts are pooling their knowledge so the results can ripple out and so many people can benefit.

Articles in this chapter include the following:

- **Using EFT Creatively**
  by Patricia Carrington

- **Reaching Your Goals**
  by Carol Look

- **Why I Use and Teach EFT**
  by Alexander R. Lees

- **EFT and Hypnotherapy**
  by Marilyn Gordon

- **Using EFT to Eliminate Substance Sensitivities**
  by Sandra Radomski

- **EFT and Peak Performance**
  by Steve Wells

- **Using EFT for Trauma and Physical Pain**
  by Loretta Sparks

- **EFT for Physical Issues**
  by Betty Moore-Hafter

- **Friendship in Relationship: Tapping with Each Other Using Provocative Energy Techniques (P.E.T.)**
  by David Lake

- **Everyday EFT**
  by Carol Tuttle

- **Pressure Point Therapy**
  by Philip H. Friedman

All of the articles in this chapter are copyrighted by the authors and used here with the authors' permissions.

PATRICIA CARRINGTON, PH.D.

Since 1984, Patricia Carrington has been a Clinical Professor of the Department of Psychiatry at Robert Wood Johnson Medical School in Piscataway, NJ. She is the originator of Clinically Standardized Meditation (CSM), a training method used in medical institutions and other organizations. Dr. Carrington is a Contributing Editor to Gary Craig's EFT Email

List and has her e-newsletter, *EFT News & Innovations*. She is the author of *How to Create Positive Choices in Energy Psychology: The Choices Training Manual*.

USING EFT CREATIVELY

EFT has been a major influence in my professional life and for me personally. It is now the central focus of my work. Here is the interesting story of how I came to use this technique.

During the eleven years I was teaching at Princeton University and conducting research on stress management methods, I had always remained interested in new methods, new approaches, the cutting edge of research in stress management ... yet I almost missed out on using EFT when I first encountered it!

I had read an article that insisted that this method could "cure" a phobia (persistent irrational fear) in "just five minutes". As a psychologist and researcher, I was certain this was impossible, so I dismissed the whole concept...

A year later Dr. Milton Shumsky, a respected colleague, phoned me to say, "Pat, I've just come across a stress reduction method you'll want to check out because...It *works*."

I realized that he was talking about the tapping technique I had read about in the article and had hastily dismissed...and I knew that this time I had to pay attention. So, I did. I found out about the tapping method, learned it, and started using it.

I tried it first on myself, then with my clients, and I soon found that the diagnostic muscle-testing that had been recommended was entirely unnecessary in order to get excellent (actually unheard of) results with it. So I created a version of the tapping method that involved only one single algorithm, repeated each round.. It worked superbly, every bit as well as the more elaborate version I had learned, and this "Acutap" technique was what I used for eight years with individual clients and groups – always trying to convince colleagues that there was something wonderful and special here, but never succeeding in interesting them in it at all.

In fact, I felt incredibly alone with Acutap when facing the professional community because absolutely no one wanted to listen to what I had to say about it. Then, in 1997, to my surprise and delight I discovered Gary Craig's EFT method. It was essentially the same as my Acutap — a single algorithm method – except that I thought it improved on my version and so immediately adopted it. It felt wonderful to belong at last to a "family" of people devoted to this technique! I have been a staunch supporter of EFT ever since. It has revolutionized my approach to psychotherapy, and my life.

Three Suggestions for Applying EFT Successfully

1. I consistently tell my clients that they should use the standard EFT protocol in a flexible and creative manner and I will suggest that you do so too. I strongly encourage you to experiment to find ways that can make it more suitable for your own personality and needs. No two people approach EFT in exactly the same way. Some prefer to repeat their Reminder phrase twice at each acupoints instead of the "recommended" once, others like to say their complete set-up phrase rather than just the Reminder Phrase at each acupoints, some benefit most from EFT by doing exactly the steps they learned without deviating from the protocol.

    Gary Craig often reminds us that EFT is a very "forgiving" technique, meaning that you don't have to be exact with it; you need not tap precisely on the spot you are supposed to or never miss a tapping spot, or say the exact words you may have read in a manual. Most people make "mistakes" while tapping, but this does not take way from the beneficial effect of EFT. So I ask you to be kind to yourself when doing your tapping routine. Say to yourself, "Even though I missed a step of the process (or whatever you did), I choose to have a wonderful result from this EFT session."

2. I strongly recommend carrying the effect of EFT into your daily life with the use of reminders. EFT Reminder Cards are excellent for this purpose. Using these cards can assist you in consolidating and making permanent the beneficial changes brought about by EFT. It helps your EFT-generated changes generalize to many aspects of your life. When that happens, you will see true transformation. Here is the procedure I recommend for the Reminder Cards:

   • After completing a session of tapping, write down the EFT Statement you used to effectively bring down your Intensity Level (e.g. "Even though I'm worried about that upcoming interview, I choose to be calm and confident." and copy it onto a 3' by 5' index card.

   • Read over your EFT statement at home, out loud, twice a day (at a minimum), doing this when first waking in the morning, and before going to sleep at night.

   • Carry the cards with you if you wish and read them aloud when you find yourself with spare moments during the day – such as in the car waiting for a traffic light to change, etc.

   Don't bother to think about what is on the card between times, but just read aloud each card once, and then let it slip out of your mind to enter your subconscious mind, which will do the work *for* you.

   You will be amazed at how using EFT Reminder Cards regularly, along with your EFT tapping, can achieve profound positive change in your life.

3. Build a Library of EFT Statements that are meaningful to you. I use a method known as "EFT Choices" to do so – these are a special type of positive affirmation created spe-

cifically to counteract your negative Reminder Phrase (the "Even though.." part of the EFT Set-Up statement). I've written much about these "EFT Choices", given many workshops using them etc. and won't repeat here that information, but I do want to emphasize how valuable it is to introduce the POSITIVE into EFT by means of Choices that are tailor-made for you. EFT can not only be used to rid us of troubling feelings or symptoms, it can also instill in us positive, life-affirming attitudes and feelings. I am deeply impressed by this positive potential of EFT.

There are many ways to create positive Choices in EFT (my *Choices Manual* gives the basic rules for doing so) but one way that I particularly like is to first write out the negative "even though..." portion of your set-up phrase (e.g. "Even though I am hurt by what (so and so) said to me") and then intentionally write down the *opposite* feeling — how you would LIKE to feel about this or have happen – (e.g. "I'd like to find an entirely different way of viewing what happened."

You make this positive statement into an EFT Choice by inserting the words "I choose..." in front of the positive phrase, so that, for example, that phrase would read, "I choose to find an entirely different way of looking at what happened." A CHOICE is very empowering and when you incorporate Choices into your EFT practice, the value of this technique for you grows enormously.

I urge you to keep enhancing your EFT experience. It can be a true adventure.

CONTACT INFORMATION

Patricia Carrington, Ph.D.
P.O. Box 2016, East Millstone, NJ 08875
908-904-9300
support@eftupdate.com
http://www.eftupdate.com

CAROL LOOK, LCSW, DCH

Carol works in private practice in Manhattan and teaches workshops around the country on EFT for anxiety relief, weight loss, smoking cessation, and attracting abundance. Carol's publishing credits include articles in The Enneagram Monthly, The Thought Field, and Hypnotherapy Today. She is the author of two training manuals: *How to Lose Weight with Energy Therapy* and *Quit Smoking Now with Energy Therapy*, and the e-book *Attracting Abundance with EFT*. Carol is also a contributing editor to Gary Craig's EFT web site support list.

REACHING YOUR GOALS WITH EFT

When I discovered EFT, my entire private practice changed for the better. While I was trained as a traditional Social Worker, using EFT for anxiety, addictions, and overall blocks to success made a huge difference in my life as well as the lives of my clients.

After I earned my Doctorate in Clinical Hypnotherapy, I was flooded with referrals for weight-loss clients. I had extensive experience working with addictions, and transferred my substance abuse skills immediately to my weight-loss clients who suffered from uncontrollable cravings, compulsive overeating, and repeated failures at long-term weight loss.

One thing all addictions have in common: people use food, alcohol, drugs or cigarettes to *tranquilize* their anxiety, whether it is from daily stress, past traumas, childhood abandonment, or low self-esteem. I started using EFT as my primary method of treatment for people with compulsive overeating issues. After considerable successes with applying EFT for clearing the conflicts and the emotions underlying overeating, I wrote the training manual *How to Lose Weight with Energy Therapy*.

Weight Loss and EFT

Consider "Gail" who contacted me because she was sick and tired of the extra pounds and the emotional baggage. She described herself as a yo-yo dieter and had tried absolutely everything for weight loss including hypnosis, ear stapling, hair analysis, supplements, weight loss pills, and of course every diet book on the market, with no long-term success. She felt like a huge failure.

After using EFT, Gail was able to unlock the keys to her overeating: (1) self-hatred, (2) fear of abandonment, (3) need to be the family patient, (4) people pleasing, and (5) extreme anxiety that she needed to sedate with food. She just couldn't manage her anxiety and other emotions without overeating.

We used some of the following EFT setup phrases:

- "Even though I am afraid of losing weight because I will feel disloyal to my family, I deeply and completely accept myself anyway."

- "Even though they need me to be sick, and I want to fit in, I deeply and completely..."

- "Even though I'm afraid to lose weight because I don't know who I would be..."

- "Even though the thought of losing weight makes me feel threatened..."

- "Even though I feel unlovable at the core, and don't feel valued unless I am DOING something, I choose to accept all of me."

- "Even though I feel undervalued and under appreciated..."

- "Even though I know I can't protect myself without the weight...

Less than one year later, Gail had dropped 110 pounds. And she reminded me that we never once tapped on her specific food cravings!

Attracting Abundance With EFT

Comfort Zones: I also use EFT to neutralize emotional blocks to success and abundance. When you have comfort zones–ceilings to what you believe you can achieve–you will *always* stay within them. After using EFT for my own comfort zones, I increased my income by over 20% the first year. I had not raised my fee or invested in advertising, and the country's economic situation had in fact worsened. I used phrases such as:

- "Even though I don't dare raise my income, I deeply and completely accept myself…

- "Even though I obviously have a block to earning more than $ XXX, I deeply and completely love and accept myself with this conflict."

- "Even though I don't feel safe making more than $ XXX because they'll be jealous, I deeply and completely accept and love who I am."

Limiting Beliefs: Dozens of clients in my abundance classes have told me that they had siblings who were seen as either "slow learners" or having some form of "difficulty" in school. Some of these siblings turned out to be brilliant while some are still struggling to this day. The point is that my clients learned from their families "I'm not supposed to shine" and that if they *did* shine, they were taking attention away from their struggling sibling. It didn't seem to matter if the sibling was older, younger, the same sex or not. What mattered was that the parents compared the two, and scolded the "fast learner" for looking good, or "showing off." The message was "don't succeed or you'll hurt someone else." I typically use the following phrases for this common conflict:

- "Even though I'm not supposed to shine because it will hurt my sister, I deeply and completely accept my brilliance."

- "Even though I will lose their approval if I do well, I deeply and completely accept my talents."

- "Even though it's not safe to succeed, I choose to feel safe when I am doing what I love."

- "Even though they don't feel comfortable when I succeed, I deeply and completely accept myself anyway."

- "Even though I'll never forget his scolding me when I succeeded, I deeply and completely forgive myself for being so fast."

- "Even though I'm afraid I'll be rejected if I succeed..."

Deserving Issues: I have many individual clients who feel guilty when they have desires to do well financially. Consider "Jeff" who said "Why should I take more away from other people?" (1) The belief that his success would hurt someone else is a mistake. (2) The belief that there is a *limited supply* of abundance is also, in my opinion, off base. (3) As long as he thinks he has had "his share" he will sabotage progress or inadvertently reject opportunities. Jeff didn't feel deserving of financial success, and was finally able to see a pattern of rejecting terrific opportunities for advancement in his job.

- "Even though I don't deserve any more, I've had enough, I deeply and completely accept myself anyway."

- "Even though my mother said we were lucky to have what we had, I deeply...

- "Even though I don't want to be selfish and take more than my share, I accept and love myself for having desires."

- "Even though my father scolded me for wanting more, I deeply and completely..."

Prosperity Consciousness: Whether you believe you don't have enough time, money, love or success, the consciousness behind your belief will block you from receiving financial abundance. Your level of belief exudes a particular *vibration*. In energetic terms, the theory states that your consciousness about abundance has a certain capacity; you will receive exactly what your consciousness is capable of handling. The good news is that your consciousness can be expanded to believe there is enough to go around.

- "Even though she told me there was never enough, I deeply and completely accept my fears."

- "Even though I remember the fights my parents had about money, and I think money is bad, I deeply..."

- "Even though I'm afraid there won't be enough, so I need to hold on to be safe, I deeply and completely accept who I am."

CONTACT INFORMATION

Carol Look, LCSW, DCH
P.O. Box 1953. Madison Square Station, New York, NY 10159
212-477-8645
Carol@CarolLook.com
www.CarolLook.com

ALEXANDER R. LEES, RCC, DCH

Alex Lees has been in private practice since 1987, and presents seminars and workshops in Canada, USA and Europe. He is a member of the EFT Advisory Board, a Contributing Editor to EFT Insights, and he is the author of *Emotional Freedom Techniques – What Is It and How Does It Work?* Alex has also been involved with NLP (Neurolinguistic Programming) for 24 years and is a Certified International Trainer of NLP.

WHY I USE AND TEACH EFT

Having been trained in conventional psychotherapeutic disciplines, I was certainly sceptical when I first watched an EFT demonstration. At the same time, I had been searching for a more direct approach to addressing the emotional aspect of presented problems, as I was convinced that if this aspect could be dealt with more affectively, then the client could heal their pains and discomforts far more easily.

As I began to introduce EFT into my practice, usually explaining it as an experimental concept, I was both surprised and delighted to learn how much more quickly and easily the clients responded to treatment. It was because of these experiences, regardless of the name of the problem presented, that I first ordered the complete set of Gary Craig's training DVDs, and began to study EFT in earnest. This allowed me to more completely separate, in my mind, the presented issue into two components: What had happened in the person's life (content, or the story), and how it made them feel (emotional component).

Thanks to Gary's audios and some additional training in the application of EFT, I gradually incorporated the use of EFT into my practice more and more, and found less need to fall back on the more acceptable mainstream training I had become so familiar with.

The benefits to the clients were obvious: Less expenditure of time and money to achieve relief. As time went by, more and more of them began to request training in the use and application of EFT. This led to me presenting seminars, which befits another philosophy of mine quite nicely: Empowered people contribute positively to the workings of the world, making it a much more pleasant journey for all.

Christmas and EFT

Christmas comes but once a year. It is a time of great anticipation, excitement, joy and good times for many. For some, it is not. There are high expectations, hope and determination that this year, things will be different. Maybe this year everything will work out as planned and everyone will have a wonderful holiday season. Then something happens.

Aunt Matilda once again, offends everyone. Uncle George does a half gainer into the punch bowl, the dog destroys the tree, or the overloaded circuit supplying power to all those lights finally decides to protect the humans by expiring.

Now, all the effort and work, the shopping, the wrapping presents, the baking, cooking the turkey, the planning was supposed to culminate in a wonderful Christmas. Well, before EFT, when the glitches happened, and they always seemed to, the resulting negativity tended to generalize out, and contaminated part, or all, of the festive season. Another Christmas ruined, or not so good.

This year can be different. Here's what you can do to make this Christmas be the joyous occasion you hope and plan for. Turn your attention inwards, and notice your reaction to an event or circumstance. Put what you are feeling into words. Once you have put into words what you are feeling, you are clear on your response, decide if you want to feel that way. If you would prefer "X" never happened, if you would prefer not to feel that way, then now is the time to change it.

Start with tapping the P.R. point, and as you continue to tap, describe to yourself what happened, or how you feel, and place "Even though" in front of it. When you have repeated it three times, tapping the P.R. point the whole time, then tap the rest of the points using a reminder phrase as you do so.

Here's an example. While tapping the P.R. point say,

- "Even though Uncle George is drunk again, and has now dumped the punch bowl's contents all over Aunt Mary, none the less, I deeply and completely accept myself."

Repeat three times, with emphasis. Then tap the rest of the points, using a reminder phrase, such as *"Uncle George."*

Alternatively, you may be more aware of your anger towards Uncle George. Tapping the P.R. point you would say,

- "Even though I'm angry at Uncle George, I deeply and completely accept myself."

Repeat three times, with emphasis. Then tap the rest of the points using the reminder phrase, *"This anger."*

This protocol will work equally well for feelings of disappointment, sadness, loneliness, frustration, etc. The idea is to pay attention to the glitch(s), acknowledge it, frame it into words, and tap it. You will accomplish several things.

You will feel better sooner, thus allowing yourself to enjoy the holidays more.

You will prevent the incident from generalizing out, and thus stop your memory remembering "just another bad Christmas."

By doing so, maybe, just maybe, you will give yourself a Happy Christmas.

And, wouldn't it be a precious gift to give a loved one, the gift of EFT...

CONTACT INFORMATION

Dr. Alexander R. Lees
17265-2 Avenue, Surrey, BC V3S 9P9 Canada
604-542-6277
lees@dralexlees.com
www.DrAlexLees.com

MARILYN GORDON, PHD, DCH, CHT

Marilyn Gordon is a certified hypnotherapist, teacher, speaker, healer, school director and author with over twenty five years of experience both teaching and healing. She was given the Hypnosis Achievement Award for 1997 by the National Guild of Hypnotists. Her books include *Extraordinary Healing, Healing is Remembering Who You Are, Energy Therapy* and three hypnotherapy manuals: *The Manual for Transformational Healing with Hypnotherapy, The Mind-Body Healing Manual* and *Stopping Smoking*, as well as a number of audios.

EFT AND HYPNOTHERAPY

Years ago, a man came to one of our courses, and he told me he'd learned a new technique and that it was miraculous. He began to tap on his body and talk about what he was experiencing, and he asked me if I'd like to give it a try. I too found it miraculous, as it immediately either reduced or totally alleviated symptoms and issues in the body and mind.

I found a way to incorporate this technique called EFT, the Emotional Freedom Techniques, into our work with hypnotherapy. The work with this combination began to evolve into what we now call "The Transformational Healing Method". We do EFT before we do hypnotherapy, and then we do it again during hypnotherapy itself. When EFT is done during hypnotherapy, it's used as a release technique when emotions and other deep experiences come up.

A year or so after I learned EFT, I went to an advanced workshop given by Gary Craig, the founder of EFT. At one of the breaks, I did a demonstration of EFT combined with hypnotherapy, and it now appears on one of Gary Craig's advanced DVD/video presentations. Many people have called or emailed with interest about this combination after they saw the demonstration session on the video.

The great advantage of combining the two modalities is that not only are you able to do the tapping process, which is so powerful and effective, but you can combine it with profound relaxation and the discovery and healing of deep inner issues. This combination is truly a wonder. I've written about it in detail in my book, *Extraordinary Healing*. In this book are many stories and examples, as well as instructions on ways of doing the work. I continue to use the techniques, and I find that they evolve and shift. We've changed some of the points and some of the words, and we get consistently excellent results with all kinds of issues.

I marvel at how so many people have created their own forms of EFT. It's a fluid kind of modality, and it allows for creative interpretation. I sometimes even joke about it, saying that you can create your own EFT modality by giving your interpretation some initials and creating your own web site about it. Still, there is an important truth here, that clients and practitioners of all persuasions and in all walks of life can find ways of doing the tapping techniques that create results in anything they do.

Here are some tips that you might find useful:

- You can tap with your fingers or with your mind, as both are effective.

- You can tap yourself or have someone tap on you. Both work well.

- You can tap on the negative phrase that describes your issue, and you can also shift to include tapping on the positive phrase.

- You can use the tapping for pure relaxation if there are no issues present at any given moment.

- You can use the "Choices" phrasing that Patricia Carrington contributed. Instead of saying, "I deeply, completely accept myself" as the setup phrase, you can say, "I choose to...(here you include that you'd choose to do or experience instead of your current situation.) This is very powerful.

- You can make certain that your phrasing of the issue is as specific as possible

- You can make sure that you're having some kind of experience of your issue at the moment – either in real time or in a remembrance of your experience.

- You can experiment with EFT on all the issues that come up for you, as its applications are infinite.

Thank you very much,
Marilyn Gordon

CONTACT INFORMATION

Marilyn Gordon, PhD, DCH, CHT
401 Grand Avenue
Oakland CA 94610
(800)398-0034
(510)839-4800
mgordon@hypnotherapycenter.com
http://www.hypnotherapycenter.com

SANDRA RADOMSKI

Sandi Radomski is board certified in Social Work, a Psychotherapist and a Naturopathic Doctor. Currently specializing in allergy work, Sandi has written the basic training manual *Allergy Antidotes – The Energy Psychology Treatment of Allergy-Like Reactions*, and the *Advanced Procedures Manual of Allergy Antidotes*.

USING EFT TO ELIMINATE SUBSTANCE SENSITIVITIES

My use of EFT for treating allergy-like reactions began as a matter of family necessity. For many years I had treated allergies with NAET (Nambudripad's Allergy Elimination Treatment) in which the person holds the substance in their energy field while I tap on acupuncture points along their spine. Then in 1998, my mother developed a persistent cough that was caused by her required blood pressure medication. She was about to have cataract surgery and had been told that coughing afterward could be very dangerous.

Mom was 600 miles away and I could not physically treat her along her spine. However, with necessity being the mother of invention, plus Gary Craig's encouragement to try EFT for anything, I considered EFT as the only – and best – treatment I could do over the phone.

I asked Mom to get her blood pressure medicine and had her rub the sore spots on her chest and say 3 times, "Even though I have a bad reaction to my blood pressure medicine, I deeply and profoundly accept myself." Then I led her through the EFT tapping sequence using the reminder phrase "bad reaction to my blood pressure medicine" at each point. She wrote down the procedure and I told her to do it several times a day.

After several days of tapping – and prior to her surgery – her cough was completely eliminated.

As psychotherapists, we need to know that *any* emotional or physical problem can actually be symptomatic of an allergic reaction. Allergic symptoms run the gamut from anxiety, depression, brain fog, fatigue, and learning disabilities, to digestive disorders, aches and pains, and weight gain.

I often find that reactions to an offending substance are actually the presenting complaints. For example, a panic attack is often a reaction to detergents and laundry products. The effectiveness of EFT for this type of allergic reaction was made clear at my two day conference in Oxford, England in 2001.

Catherine approached me during the first morning break in an agitated and tearful state and announced she was leaving because she was having a panic attack. I asked if I could muscle test her and found she was weak on the detergent on her t-shirt. I treated her for the t-shirt and brought her a new one to wear for class. Catherine said she had been plagued by panic attacks recently and had tried many treatments to no avail. She said the problem seemed to be "following her around." Even her bed, once a refuge, was no longer a comfortable environment.

It turned out that Catherine was carrying one of the causes of her reactions on her clothes and sheets! Treating her panic symptoms as an allergic reaction to her t-shirt was successful. She was then able to stay for the full, two day class, and benefited as much from the seminar as she would have from a therapy session.

Suzie is a classic example of sensitivity reactions causing emotional symptoms. A vibrant, bubbly woman in her early 20s, her normally energetic demeanor disappeared during part of her monthly menstrual cycle. Sadly, from day 15 until the onset of her period, Suzie could not stop crying. She lost several days of work each month and spent other days crying while at her computer. Doctors wanted to put her on an antidepressant.

She came to me instead. At our second session, I began to test her on foods she ate and found she was very reactive to wheat. She chose to avoid wheat during the following week. When she returned for her next session, Suzie was all smiles. Day 15 of her period had come and gone with no crying bouts.

Tips for using EFT to treat allergy-like reactions:

1. Treat for the 7 most common reactive foods: dairy products, wheat, corn, eggs, sugar, soy, and peanuts.

2. Treat for any foods you "have to have" or choose to eat frequently.

3. At the first sign of cold or flu, treat your saliva (put on a tissue to treat for whatever infection is in your body) every hour.

4. Treat for all of your medication. (Adverse reactions to prescription medications are now the third leading cause of death in the U.S.)

5. Treat for any medications you had problems with in the past. (Remnants may still be stored in your tissues.)

6. If outside air is a problem, take an air sample and treat. (Wave a wet paper towel in the outside air to get a sample of the particles in the air.)

7. Treat for "whatever is causing my symptoms."

It has been personally and professionally gratifying to me to see how EFT can positively affect people at both their physical and emotional levels.

CONTACT INFORMATION

Sandra Radomski
1051 Township Line Road, Jenkintown, PA 19046
215-885-7917
sandiradom@aol.com
www.allergyantidotes.com

STEVE WELLS

Steve Wells is a psychologist, professional speaker, and peak performance consultant based in Perth, Western Australia. Steve regularly teaches and consults worldwide with elite athletes and corporate personnel to improve their performance and enhance the performance of their teams. Together with David Lake, he also conducts personal development seminars and professional training workshops in Advanced EFT and Provocative Energy Techniques throughout Australia, USA and Europe. He is co-author with Dr David Lake of *New Energy Therapies* and *Pocket Guide to Emotional Freedom*.

EFT AND PEAK PERFORMANCE

I use EFT to assist people to achieve peak performance in any field. EFT is an excellent tool for removing blocks and barriers to performance, in particular dealing with doubts and fears, including fear of failure and fear of success. It can also be used to develop greater clarity of focus and commitment towards your goals iron out values conflicts, overcome belief challenges, release negative effects of past failures, reconnect with success, and allow your peak performance states to emerge.

Typically, I aim to identify a specific area of performance that can be addressed immediately, and apply EFT to this. For a golfer this might be chipping onto the green, for a businessperson it might be team meetings or presentations, for a singer it might be the moment they walk up to the microphone in front of a large audience.

We identify the negative emotional associations and start applying EFT to these. This typically brings success in a very short period of time, which can be built on in subsequent sessions. From this beginning I will then start to explore the person's ultimate goals, underlying belief challenges, potential goal-value conflicts, identity issues, and other larger issues.

In the first session, I teach them EFT so that they can use it in the "challenging" situation, however I believe EFT can offer much more than simply assisting us to improve our handling of one or two performance situations. I am more interested in using it to achieve larger life and performance goals.

At some point, I will ask my clients: "Where do you want to go *ultimately* with this?" and "What prevents you from being there *now?*" Then we start work on applying EFT to:

1. The belief challenges that are preventing them from being able to comfortably see themselves achieving that now (e.g., "I am not good enough.")

2. Any conflicts in values that are causing their energy to be divided (for example, "I want to achieve great things but if I do it will take me away from my family.")

3. Any other negative associations they have to either being successful or the process they believe would be required in order to achieve success

I also work on beliefs and am particularly interested in their self-image or identify beliefs, since this defines their level of achievement. We work on how they see themselves and how they would like to see themselves, using EFT. We use EFT to clear out negative self-perceptions as well as for building and reinforcing positive self-belief. For example, tapping whilst holding the image of yourself "as" the person you would like to be and become can be very productive.

I find EFT works very well with visualization and affirmation strategies, and use a technique I call Connecting With Success, which is essentially holding the success image in mind and tapping on the EFT points whilst holding the intention to associate into the image and connect with the feeling of success. This has been very productive for my clients.

Some tips on using EFT for Peak Performance:

1. Identify a specific area of your performance that causes you problems. Visualize the challenging situation and apply EFT to any anxiety or negative emotion that arises. Persist with EFT through all the aspects. A typical issue for many people is anger at themselves for having the problem, particularly if there have been past failure experiences. It is important to work through these past failures and clear their effects so that you can be free to move forward to success. Do this using the "Tell the Story" technique or "Run the Movie" Technique identified by Gary Craig – The details are available on his website at www.emofree.com/tutorial/tutorltwelve.htm.

2. Identify your ultimate goals. Then identify the objections that come up in your mind when you think about achieving them. Apply EFT to these objections by putting the objection into the set-up and focusing on it as you tap on each of the points. For example, if the thought arises that you won't be disciplined enough to follow through on your goal, insert this thought into the set-up and repeat it through each of the tapping points. As you tap, be open to any other thoughts, feelings and associations that arise, and continue tapping through all of these aspects until the original thought is replaced by more positive thoughts and feelings.

3. Identify any negative beliefs about yourself that are preventing you from having the success you desire and identify what you would like to believe about yourself. Conduct rounds of EFT where you simply insert these negative belief statements into the set-up and repeat the belief statements (and related ideas) at each tapping point. For example, if you believe you aren't intelligent enough to succeed, you would conduct rounds of EFT on this belief "Even though I am not smart enough to

do this I fully and completely accept myself."

4. Go further in your work on beliefs by identifying where you learned those beliefs in the past, and treat those past experiences using the Tell the Story Technique discussed above. This in-depth treatment of past specific events can be very productive.

5. Identify how you would like to see yourself – the ultimate, successful you – and conduct some tapping on the idea of "being" that person now. Step into the future picture of success, where you are being that person, successfully performing and achieving (or having achieved) your goal, and tap continually while you seek to access the feeling of success. As you do so, the barriers will start to come down and you will start to feel more and more comfortable with this identity. Any objections that arise can be treated as described above, but ensure that you spend some time focusing on success whilst holding the intention to access the success feelings and tapping continually on the EFT points at the same time.

Initially, even a small glimpse of success, or a sliver of the success feeling can have an incredible outcome on your system. In the moment that you connect with success, in that moment you *are* successful.

To your success,
Steve Wells

CONTACT INFORMATION

Steve Wells
PO Box 54, Inglewood Western Australia 6052
61 8 9271 9271
info@eftdownunder.com
www.eftdownunder.com

LORETTA SPARKS, LMFT

Loretta Sparks is the Director of the Center for Energy Psychotherapy and TAAP Training Institute. Trained extensively with the developers of a number of energy psychotherapies, she has trained professionals nationally and internationally in EFT and Thought Field Therapy (TFT). A licensed Marriage and Family Therapist in private practice for over 20 years, Ms. Sparks has specialized in the treatment of addiction for 20 of those years and has a particular interest in the application of energy therapies to addiction.

USING EFT FOR TRAUMA AND PHYSICAL PAIN

The profound emotional pain of the woman sitting across from me was eased–visibly eased for the first time in the year we had been working together. The introduction of Emotional Freedom Techniques (EFT) to our psychotherapy session had made the difference. During Joanie's life time she had tried many things to relieve the intrusive memories and pain of a childhood filled with betrayal and horror. Cutting, drinking, suicide attempts all failed to make any of them go away and only made her feel worse. But, now we had EFT to address years of trauma and start the deep healing that was necessary for her to have a life free of the emotional distortions these past traumas caused.

Like Joanie, so many of the people I have treated as a psychotherapist get stuck in past negative experiences or negative beliefs often rooted in childhood and are disabling in adulthood. EFT, unlike so many therapeutic models, allows the negative issues to be treated without retraumatizing the already suffering individual, but for Joanie some of her experiences were still impossibly painful.

There were specific traumatic experiences Joanie didn't want to talk about or focus on due to her vivid and painful recall. Since EFT is 'thought focused' and Joanie couldn't even think about these experiences without suffering, we had our first of many challenges. The Tearless Trauma Technique (www.emofree.com) was not known to me at that time, so we were left to our own creativity to prevent 'treatment trauma.'

Joanie was able to make a list of some of her worst experiences and color code them. Trusting the unconscious mind to remember the specific traumas, we went forward. Trauma number 1 was green, 2 was blue and so on. We would rate the intensity of the color and use the color in the setup phrase, e.g., "Even thought I have this problem with green, I deeply and profoundly accept myself." We would stay focused and tap on the intensity of the color until she reported she could not see the color any longer. Then she would try to bring up the actual experience to test our work. Usually it was no longer emotionally charged; if it still had some charge we would tap it to zero in 1 or 2 tapping sequences.

Sometimes, Joanie couldn't identify a feeling, but had an almost photographic memory of an event. We would rate the intensity of the picture in her mind and tap on it until she could no longer see it. Joanie and I continued working together until she was symptom free and able to get on with her life.

While the work I did with Joanie was focused on emotional pain, I have found EFT extremely helpful with physical pain, as well. The following is my basic approach to working with pain including migraines.

1. I ask the client to rate the intensity [0-10 scale] of the pain and to tell me exactly where the pain is located.

2. The Set Up: My Set Up is focused on my 'intention', not the client's possible psychological reversal. I muscle test (MT) myself asking if my intention is in service of the client. If it is, I proceed with the client's treatment. If not, I treat myself for PR: "Even though my intention is not in service of this client, I accept myself deeply and

profoundly" (I do this 3x while tapping the Karate Chop (KC) point or rubbing the Sore Spot). I MT again making sure the PR has been fixed. Then, I open myself to whatever healing energy I may be in service of by holding that thought consciously. Note: If you do not know how to muscle test yourself, just assume PR and treat yourself for it.

3. Client's Participation: I ask the client to imagine their point of pain glowing a bright red (if there is more than one point, I ask them to pick the one that hurts the most to start with).

4. I then tap the KC point 5-10 x; then tap the gamut spot rapidly and firmly for one minute or approximately 100 x; then have client tap collarbone point, both sides 5x. Rate pain. Continue until pain is rated at 0. Then go to the secondary point of pain and treat the same way.

   This method of tapping on the collar bone point and the gamut point for pain is taught by Dr. Roger Callahan as part of his Thought Field Therapy pain algorithm. Full rounds of EFT are equally effective, but I tend to use the first method more when the client has a migraine.

5. If the pain doesn't respond or stops responding to treatment, then I inquire about trauma, including physical, emotional (including witness trauma) and spiritual trauma (e.g., feeling forsaken or betrayed by God). I find that people with migraines often feel or felt at one time in their lives stuck in an intolerable and impossible situation.

   This feeling of being "stuck" then becomes the focus of a new Setup. Here are examples:

   • "Even though I'm unable to make positive changes in my life, etc."

- "Even though my marriage is intolerable, etc."

- "Even though my job is impossible, etc."

It is frequently the case that the more intractable the migraine/pain, the more aspects have to be addressed. Engage your client in a dialogue seeking possible aspects. Brainstorm using your knowledge of human nature and your client's situation or life story. Don't be concerned if your brainstorming is not 100% correct. An incorrect 'guess' does no harm and it might bring to mind an aspect that is key to effective treatment.

6. Treat traumas and aspects as needed. While focusing on trauma or aspects do the usual Setup (even though I have this problem with_____, I accept myself deeply and profoundly). Then do the full EFT sequence (including the 9 gamut) followed by the sequence again. When the trauma/aspect is cleared, treat the migraine/pain (Steps 1 through 4).

7. Be persistent.

CONTACT INFORMATION

Loretta Sparks LMFT
PO Box 475, Manhattan Beach, CA 90267
Phone/fax 310-374-0440
lsparksma@aol.com
www.energypsychotherapy.com

BETTY MOORE-HAFTER

Trained in more than 600 hours hypnotherapy and related healing arts, Betty Moore-Hafter's background includes certifications in Past Life Regression, Medical Hypnotherapy, Emergency Hypnosis, Reiki, Psychosynthesis and Spirit Releasement as well as personally training in EFT from Gary Craig. She is the author of *Tapping Your Amazing Potential with EFT* and is the Moderator for the *Rising Sun EFT Group, A Forum for Sharing EFT Information*. Betty is a workshop leader and individual consultant.

EFT FOR PHYSICAL ISSUES

I am grateful every day for the gift that EFT is to me both personally and professionally. Personally, I use EFT daily, and it's like maintaining mental and emotional hygiene. There is no reason to let anything negative build up in my system since I can bring myself relief and healing with EFT. Professionally, EFT is the "therapist's dream," a simple tool that can help almost every client feel better fast. My work combines EFT and hypnotherapy and we often get excellent results.

Among the many applications of EFT, I'd like to focus on EFT for physical issues. EFT is almost like a first-aid kit that you can pull out and use effectively with most physical problems. I had a first-hand experience of this recently. We were on vacation and visiting a museum 2 hours from our "home base" of my dad's house. Suddenly my 17-year old daughter started getting the "aura" or vision distortion that warns her of a migraine. We didn't have her migraine medication and she was really worried, knowing that if a migraine set in, it would be excruciating to make that trip back to my dad's since car travel makes the headaches worse.

I was able to take her into a darkened room and have her lie down. Then I spent half an hour tapping and talking. Her occasional migraines had never seemed to respond to EFT before when we had done just a few rounds of tapping. But this time EFT and some hypnotherapy language were all we had, so I pulled out all the stops.

I did a lot of traditional tapping for "this vision distortion," "this discomfort" and "this headache." But I also talked to the body and to the subconscious mind while I tapped. It occurred to me that one of the possible "stuck places" in her energy system was the belief or pattern that whenever she got the aura, a migraine was sure to follow. So I tapped with this message:

"Even though in the past, the aura has led to a migraine, things are different this time.

The aura just signaled an imbalance and we are releasing that imbalance. You'll remain free of discomfort as the aura fades away..."

I also used everything I knew about migraines to tell the body what we wanted it to do.

"Even though the blood vessels in the brain got constricted... they can relax now... calming, relaxing, releasing... an easy blood flow through the brain... nerves and muscles all soothed and calmed and open..."

At one point, I tapped the Karate Chop spot continuously and used some imagery: "just imagine a cooling blue liquid that's flowing in through the top of your head...refreshing and soothing all the tissues... and now see and feel it flowing down through your shoulders and down both arms into your hands... just direct the flow of any excess warmth down into your hands..." (a biofeedback technique that can relieve migraines is to send the blood down into the hands).

I just tapped and talked to her constantly for nearly half an hour. She continued to feel better and better. Finally she sat up and said, "The aura's completely gone and my head doesn't hurt!" That was the first time she has ever gotten the aura without a migraine immediately setting in! We were still holding our breath for the trip home, and though she still felt sensitive, she made the two hour car ride and even her plane trip home the next day without a migraine developing. She thought it was miraculous because she'd never been able to turn this around before. And what a blessing for me, as her mother, to be able to offer her that relief.

In this case, I believe that tapping helped on a number of levels. EFT helped to release the physical energy and stuck pattern of the migraine. It also relieved the fear and dread my daughter had, as well as her expectation that the migraine would follow the aura. And EFT allowed for communication with the subconscious mind, which controls all the body functions. When people close their eyes and focus on the body and the emotions during EFT, they are automatically in a light altered state, and hypnotic language is very well received.

Generally speaking, I find that the best results with physical issues are achieved when the underlying emotions are addressed. It's as if the body is holding the emotion in the affected area, which exacerbates the physical symptoms.

For example, I once worked with a man who had shoulder pain due to a fall suffered while ice skating. He experienced only minor relief when we tapped for "this shoulder pain. "So I asked him how he felt about falling down. He felt "embarrassed" and "like a klutz." When we tapped for those issues, the shoulder pain reduced drastically. It seemed that his shoulder had been holding the embarrassment and self-judgment and finally could release it. I sometimes use creative variations such as, "even though my shoulder is holding this embarrassment, I love and accept my shoulder."

A favorite question is, "if there were any emotion in that part of the body (or, in that pain, stiffness, etc.), what would it be?" The body is also highly metaphorical, as our language indicates. A person with neck pain can be asked, "is there anything or anyone who is a pain in the neck for you?" Amazingly, core issue is often then revealed and tapping on that core issue may resolve most of the discomfort.

I do believe that we can communicate with parts of the body using EFT. I've even tapped to enhance the immune system, with such language as, "even though I have this small symptom (sneeze, cough), I know this symptom is just a signal that my powerful immune system is completely protecting me.... I deeply love and accept my body and deeply appreciate my immune system..."As EFT balances our energy system, it is also enhancing our physical health and well-being, especially if we choose language which affirms and encourages the body.

Tips

1. **Bridging to newcomers:** I've found several ways to present EFT that are non-threatening and make sense to people. I often call EFT "a body-centered stress-relief technique." I say, "We all know that stress accumulates in the body. People get stress-related illnesses. EFT works through the body to relieve stress." Another useful idea is to compare the use of EFT to the rebooting of the computer. "When your computer gets stuck, you have to reboot–you interrupt the process and let the computer rebalance itself. That's a lot like what happens when we use EFT. Tapping releases the stuck places and 'reboots' our system."

2. **Use the Client's Words.** I take lots of notes when a client is describing a problem and then use the client's own words to create set-up phrases for EFT. Clients are the experts on themselves and using their own words is the best way to "tune in" to the way their minds are working.

3. **Locate the Emotion in the Body.** One of my favorite EFT questions is... "So where do you feel that in your body?" I may help by asking, "Is any part of you tight or tense or heavy? Where do you think the emotion is being held?" When we work on the body level, we usually have measurable results and it is easier for people to determine what has changed.

4. **Brainstorm Personal Imagery.** I may ask, "If you could give me an image for that feeling, what would it be?" For instance, if a person "feels trapped," I may help with suggestions such as, "So... is it more like being stuck in quicksand... or locked in a prison cell... or buried somehow?... what is it like for you?" Once we use EFT for the personal imagery, it often changes. One person felt that her leg was "trapped in a bear trap" but once we tapped the trap loosened and she escaped without injury. These images are vehicles for profound internal change.

5. **Brainstorm Affirmations and "Choice" Statements:** Once again, the client's words are the most powerful to her or to him. Ask... "So what would you choose to have instead of this [negativity]? How would you like to feel? What's your highest vision for yourself?" Then incorporate the client's own words into the tapping process–very powerful!

CONTACT INFORMATION

Betty Moore-Hafter
Rising Sun Healing Center
35 King Street, Suite 7, Burlington, VT 05401
802-860-7286
betty@risingsunhealing.com
www.risingsunhealing.com

DAVID LAKE

David Lake is a medical practitioner and psychotherapist who has been in private practice since 1977. He is currently in full-time counseling and psychotherapy from his practice in Sydney, Australia. He is the author of Strategies for Stress, She'll be Right, and co-author of *New Energy Therapies: Rapid Change*

Techniques to Emotional Healing. Together with Steve Wells, he also travels the globe teaching seminars in Advanced EFT and Provocative Energy Techniques (PET).

FRIENDSHIP IN RELATIONSHIP:
Tapping With Each Other Using Provocative Energy Techniques (P.E.T.)

My Approach

I work with couples and I work using EFT. when I can. I choose to work with couples who have a degree of goodwill and friendship, and who don't regularly abuse each other; in the face of cruelty and severe dysfunction I tend to avoid any therapeutic "heavy lifting" to save the relationship.

I also use "Provocative Style" (a derivative of Provocative Therapy) in the relational aspects of "holding" both partners in the session, and work with whatever issues arise. Techniques that address issues quickly and effectively must be tempered with good rapport and personal connection, especially when there are two people to relate to, if you are the therapist. When you have this rapport then the framework of the session is likely to be strong–sufficiently strong to "hold" the couple while they experience their issues in the room with you. The combination of the two approaches is *Provocative Energy Techniques (P.E.T)*.

On the one hand, the Provocative approach uses humorous and paradoxical communication styles and techniques drawn from Provocative Therapy and Brief Strategic Therapy. The approach addresses the multi-level nature of problems through warmth, liberating laughter, and spontaneity – elegantly addressing both mind and body in therapy. It's a powerful combination which allows you to cut through resistance, negative beliefs and other emotional barriers to get right to the heart of problems. On the other hand, the meridian stimulation of EFT helps desensitize and harmonize any aroused negative feelings. When "Provocative style" is used to stimulate the client's problem, the meridian therapy relieves it disproportionately, in our experience. Thus it represents leverage in the use of meridian healing.

The essence of Provocative Therapy is in being able to play the "devil's advocate while being firmly on the side of the angels" (Frank Farrelly). The hallmarks of this therapy or approach are excellent rapport, respect for the person, validating *all* aspects of the client's life, and a lighthearted, humorous style of "playing" with the problems and associated behaviors. Validating someone's dark side compassionately, paradoxically and humorously typically ensures that the problem and its patterns rarely settle back to their original state.

Provocative Energy Techniques interrupt the repeating cognitive, emotional and behavioral sequences behind problems, enabling people to break through these limitations and develop new ways of seeing. Here, the client's own self-defeating experiences are used in the *service* of change. EFT involves meridian stimulation—tapping the points—and I have found from much experience that the more actual tapping done in the presence of the problem, the more likely a "deeper" and better result. Thus I am content to do a lot of tapping—without stopping. I call this *continual tapping*. Any points may be used as long as you vary them (I use half a dozen, mostly on the hand and arm)

With or without "Provocative Style", I find that using EFT. in a compassionate and thoughtful therapeutic approach adds dramatically to the quality of the emotional work that is done.

Relationship

My definition is a devotional friendship, where the wounds from the poison of criticism are healed by compassionate acceptance.

The key to expanding the good things in a relationship is to use the goodwill and friendship that lives within it for productive purposes. Since "relationship" is much too hard for most people to understand I am quite happy for those wanting insight to practice being friendly towards each other. It is only our own negativity and bad habits that stand in the way of deepening connection with the one you have chosen to love and be with.

Criticism is the end-result of the noxious habit of pretending that another's problems are more fascinating and important than your own. As a result, you feel that it's necessary to remind the one you love that they are not perfect because of their bad behavior or actions (and when so often you are oblivious to how much your own behavior is utterly frustrating to them...).

My own take on this noxious habit is that it is completely unnecessary. The only time you are entitled to do it is when you have cleaned up your own act to the complete satisfaction of your partner—and you hear this from them. Mutual help is far more rewarding and satisfying.

One opposite of criticism is *admiration.* The feelings that are brought up in each partner, by contemplating the good that is the original intention of each, are life-affirming. I would like more partners to feel some of the feelings of success more often, when their good work bears fruit. This is the role of admiration and acceptance. I facilitate this every chance I get.

The final common pathway of the personal work that EFT. helps you to do on yourself is *acceptance.* According to Eckhart Tolle in *The Power of Now* it is the great catalyst for change in relationship—when you can accept your partner as he or she is, without wanting to change him or her in any way. Then the door opens to many possibilities.

You accept that these problems are here and that they may not change. You are going to work on your own reactions (upset, hurt, disappointment, sadness) first, and see what happens afterwards. Accept that you don't accept all of your partner (nor yourself for that matter) but work on it. Neither of us is perfect but I am only in charge of one of us—me. I call this whole process *being stretched*. In this context EFT is the balancing and healing agent.

How to Work Together Using EFT

Commonly for a therapist there is not a couple present in most cases but only a partner seeking help. If you do have a couple ready, then obviously each partner needs to learn how to do EFT — ideally on a neutral subject first (such as body tension). Then you can progress to using EFT together because each knows the points and is comfortable with that concept. I find it is too much to assess a couple and teach EFT. and start couple therapy all in the first session; it takes a few meetings to have all the elements in place.

If the couple problems were amenable to logic and reason and intellect, then most would be ameliorated by discussion and agreement. Obviously the emotional hurts are the main blocks to being able to bear with the unacceptable behaviors or habits. Thus a third person is often the necessary mirror for a couple to move forward. EFT. is the ideal technique in my opinion since it is so easy to use and extremely effective.

The simplest way to move forward in couple work is to graft the habit of *continual tapping* on to the problems and the discussions just as they are. This is rudimentary acceptance of the fact that they exist and this is the way things are now. The tapping becomes a pattern interruption, and a facilitating process, by virtue of its relaxation and inherent stress-management. As well, each partner is able to gain some benefits most of the time.

I think it is very useful for each partner to use individual continual tapping for personal blocks or objections while doing whatever works best in their dialogue. This is *preparing*.

Later it's possible for one partner to tap on the other's hand points while the other talks (the tapper is silent here while looking into the talker's eyes). Then you switch for equal time. This is *engaging* with a supercharged version of "active listening". If all is well and sufficient tapping and listening has been done, then at the end of enough time spent in dealing with the mundane issues of right and wrong, you could progress to 5-10 minutes of tapping on each other's face points simultaneously — in silence, looking into each other's eyes, while each recalls something to *admire* in your mate (from the present or the past). Something that they have done just for you, or efforts that have been appreciated by you. This promotes *intimacy*.

Obviously the conditions must be right for this mutual tapping as I have found it to be quite powerful as a reconnecting force. It cannot be rushed (the 'positive bypass') or done without working on the dark misperceptions that caused the troubles in the first place. Mutual tapping is where I have found a great deal of the "magic" of EFT.

In many cases it is more important to get "leverage" on a problem than to decide the fine points of where and how to tap. This is akin to working on a blocking belief when treating a personal issue — the effect on the issue is strong because the belief drives much of the negative feelings. I find that the more tapping you can do while in the 'hot' part of the problem, the greater the positive effect, as long as you have good support and connection with a person or therapist, as an emotional safety net. The relational aspects of a treatment are as important as any technique.

In Summary

Attend to your friendship and give up all criticism. Tap for the hurts that do come even when they are not intended. Work on accepting your partner the way he or she is, and more to the point, accept yourself with all your faults. Use EFT —

particularly *continual tapping* — for all this effort, and for gaining and keeping clarity.

Conclusion

The work of dealing with our own problems and reactions in relationship never ends. The negative problems must be balanced with some hope and faith (for this I specifically focus on friendship and goodwill). If not, there is an imbalance created in the solution too.

These are the essential elements in a session of couple work that I find work well together to produce a shift in *being* together. If this EFT-facilitated approach brings an interruption of a habitual pattern of negativity, and allows some heartfelt mutual understanding with more acceptance, then I am satisfied.

Note: P.E.T. is the therapeutic approach originated by Steve Wells and David Lake

CONTACT INFORMATION

David Lake
PO Box 738, Newport, New Australia 2106
61-2 9997-3848
dlake@optusnet.com.au
www.eftdownunder.com

CAROL TUTTLE, MRET

Carol Tuttle is an Energy Psychologist and Certified Master Level Rapid Eye Therapist, best-selling author, and very successful speaker. She has appeared on hundreds of radio shows and many television appearances. She and her husband Jon reside in Salt Lake City, UT and utilize these energy clearing techniques in their everyday lives with their family. Carol is the author of *Remembering Wholeness* and many articles and audios on healing and personal growth. In addition, she has an Energy Healing Learning Center, an interactive website that utilizes these techniques for clearing issues.

EVERYDAY EFT

As a Certified Energy Psychologist, I have worked with EFT for several years in my practice, family, and personal life.

Every client I work with is taught how to use EFT. I teach them that with EFT you are able to release energy blocks that are created by limiting beliefs, fear, doubt, anger, and a myriad other thoughts and emotions.

By using EFT to clear these energy blocks you are freeing your life force energy to have more radiance and a clearer vibration, so you are free to attract into your life more of what you desire. When your life force energy is flowing vibrantly you are a powerful creator to manifest more of your dreams and life purpose.

My husband and I have taught our five teenage and young adult children how to clear their energy blocks using EFT. My children know they are accountable for what they attract into their lives. They have learned to "tap" out the negative and "tap" in the positive.

When my now sixteen year-old son was eight years-old, he was being crumpy and complaining to me. He was going out to play and I said to him, "Come here for a minute." He replied, trying to stay crumpy, but with a smirk on his face, "No, you are only going to starting tapping me or something!" "Well, of course!" I responded, "I want you to feel the best you can feel!"

My children now come to me to ask for assistance in clearing their issues that are keeping their energy blocked. We tap until they feel a shift, and then tap in a lot of positive "I am" statements to anchor in a new fresh vibrant feeling.

I like to teach my clients and my family how to use EFT with the most common of life's problems and struggles. I know that if I can help my client, or child to shift their energy, they will shift their life. When we change our energy of thought and feeling about our life experience, our life experience can start to change for us.

EFT and Making Money

One of the most common issues of our time for many people is the experience of not having or making enough money. Most people are creating lack and struggle with money. Most people are having a negative experience with money.

If you're not making as much money as you'd like, then you're holding onto some negative beliefs about yourself and how much money you're capable of flowing.

Money is a resource with a neutral energy that we project our beliefs onto. Money takes on that energy and that is the experience we get with it. When you change your beliefs about money, money changes for you.

When you choose wealth, and start to believe that wealth is spiritual and abundant, wealth finds you.

Using EFT is a glorious way to help you begin to flow money and grow money. What better work can you do on this planet than to help yourself and others come into alignment with your God-given truth, free to create lives of wellness, prosperity, and joy.

Wealthy people who are humble, generous, and wanting to do the right thing are some of the most powerful people who have the most choices to make a difference in the world in which we live.

Tap out these old limiting beliefs about money, and then tap in the new beliefs to reframe and re-pattern your energy with money. While tapping all the points repeat the following set-up phrase to release your destructive beliefs about money.

Even though I am still believing, I now choose to release:

1. Money is not spiritual.

2. I will never have enough money.

3. I'll probably just fail anyway.

4. But we can't afford that.

5. Rich people are greedy and dishonest.

6. If I'm successful, my friends will be jealous and stop liking me.

7. I'm no better than my parents, so I shouldn't make more then they did.

8. I might forget what's truly important and not like the person I've become.

9. Money is the root of all evil.

10. I'm not worthy.

(Did you realize that most people have an issue with low self-esteem? It's the No. 1 thing that holds people back and prevents them from living their dreams).

Next, while tapping all the points, repeat this set-up statement with each of the following reframes.

I am now believing and radiating these truths about money:

1. I am grateful and I am free to create whatever I want with money. I now choose to experience money as a spiritual resource in my life.

2. I am grateful that there is enough money for everyone and it is everyone's birthright to create wealth. I choose to create mine now.

3. I am successful, I am safe making mistakes and learning better ways to do business, I am ready.   Success is my God-given natural right.

4. I am always flowing more in than is going out, I am wise in my purchases and a good steward of my money.

5. I am grateful that I am an honest and generously rich person.

6. I am a great example to my friends and associates, as I choose my birthright of wealth, others are more free to choose this as well.

7. I am knowing my parents did the best they knew how, and I am free and it is appropriate to create more than what they chose to experience.

8. I am safe to create wealth. I am always following my spiritual guidance, it does not matter how much money I have, I always choose this.

9. Money is a God-given resource that I am choosing to use to bless my life and others

10. I am worthy and I am ready, I choose wealth now.

A good addition to the above process is to recall any significant childhood events around money that influenced your current beliefs and perceptions. Use EFT to release any energy you still have from these formative experiences with money.

When you are triggered by money and start running your limiting beliefs and heavy emotions about money, use EFT to release yourself immediately. The more vibrant energy you radiate about money and the more gratitude you hold for money, the more money can flow to you.

People in debt and who do not make enough money think about their money problems every day of their lives. Wealthy, spiritual people are free to engage in their life purpose allowing the money to flow free of any worries.

Use EFT to create this balance with money.

CONTACT INFORMATION

Carol Tuttle
PO Box 900546, Sandy, Utah 84094
801-523-0982
carol@caroltuttle.com
www.caroltuttle.com
Interactive /Learning Center:
www.caroltuttlelearningcenter.com

PHILIP H. FRIEDMAN, PH.D.

Director of the Foundation for Well-Being, Dr. Philip Friedman is a licensed clinical psychologist and psychotherapist, certified life coach, and certified intuitive healer. He has been practicing psychotherapy and healing for 30 plus years. He is the author of the book *Creating Well Being*, the *Creating Well-Being Audio Course*, the *Integrative Healing Manual* and the Friedman Assessment Scales on Well-Being, Beliefs, Quality of Life, Affect and Personal/Spiritual Growth. He is also one of the founders of Integrative Psychotherapy and Integrative Healing, which he first developed around 1980.

PRESSURE POINT THERAPY (PPT)

Pressure Point Therapy, levels 1 to 3, is a variant of both the Emotional Freedom Technique (EFT) and Touch and Breathe (TAB) and also an expansion of the Miracle Acupressure Tapping Technique (MATT).

Level 1 of the Pressure Point Technique

Clients select one area of emotional distress, such as anger, guilt, sadness or fear and rate it on a 10 point scale with 10 being very distressed and 1 being not distressed at all. They then engage in the Psychological Uplifter with distressing emotion.

Psychological Uplifter:

"Even though I have some of this problem or negative emotion (fill in the emotion/problem) e.g. fear, anxiety, hurt, anger, depression, sadness, guilt, shame, low self-esteem, work, marital, relationship and family problems _____etc.) I accept myself deeply and profoundly and I am a good person".

Repeat 3 times while rubbing on the sore point i.e. the neurolymphatic point. Then say "I love myself unconditionally despite my problems, limitations and challenges." 3 times while rubbing on the sore point, i.e., the neurolymphatic point.

Then say "I am entitled to miracles" 3 times while rubbing on the sore point, i.e., the neurolymphatic point.

(Do 10-20 times per day or as often as you can)

1. Clients are asked to attune to the emotional distress, e.g. guilt or sadness, and then taught a series of 8 points to tap on, in 2 groups of 4 with a SUDs rating in between. Clients are taught to do this in level one of the PPT, 15-20 times without using any affirmations.

2. The 8 points are: center of the forehead; inside corner of the eye; outside the eye; under the eye; above the lip; below the lip; behind the neck and the collarbone points. Clients are encouraged to do this with 2 fingers of both hands for most of the points bilaterally and with all the fingers of both hands behind the neck. They are told to tap up, down and all around on the back of the neck points 20-25 times as this area is especially beneficial. I demonstrate the technique while explaining it to them. The reader will notice that 6 of these points correspond to EFT points and there are 2 new ones.

3. Whether or not the SUDS level has dropped to 1, (which it often does) after the tapping sequence, clients are taught in round 2 to hold each of the 8 points with 2 fingers (usually the 2nd and 3rd finger next to the thumb) and take 2 to 3 slow deep breaths after briefly attuning to the remaining emotional distress area. By the time clients have completed this sequence they almost always have dropped their SUDS level to 1.

4. Clients are then given a handout with pictures of the 8 Pressure Points, the sore (neurolymphatic) point and some additional points we may use in future sessions.

5. Clients are told this is called the Pressure Point Technique (PPT) because it works with acupressure points that are similar to points used in acupuncture on the body except we don't use needles. They are also told that it has its roots in 3 related techniques (EFT, TAB and MATT).

6. Clients are told that there are three frames of reference, analogies, or metaphors that clients need to be aware of to make the technique work for them most effectively.

    A. **Trees and the Forest:** All the clients problems are like a forest with an unknown number of trees in the forest. Each problem is like a tree and each time a client uses the PPT he/she cuts down one tree in the forest. After so many trees are cut down (and we don't know how many trees there are in advance) the trees cut down will fall over and knock down the rest of the forest. (In other words, generalization will occur and all the clients problems will be solved)

    B. **River and the Ocean:** Under ordinary circumstances water will flow smoothly down a river to the ocean unless the flow of water in the ocean is dammed up or blocked by trees, debris, garbage, etc. In this case, there is a blockage in the flow of the water to the ocean. In the same way, people have lines of energy that flow through and around the body. In Chinese medicine, these are called meridians and vessels. (There are 12 major meridians and 2 major vessels).

When energy is blocked from flowing freely along these lines of energy, emotional distress occurs. By tapping on the pressure points and/or breathing deeply while holding the pressure points (while attuned to the distressing emotion) the energy begins to flow freely (the water flows back to the Source, the ocean) and the emotional distress is released. This brings about peace and healing.

C. **Stacked Cafeteria Plates:** In this analogy, client's distress is compared to a series of plates stacked one above another in a cafeteria. Each problem represents one plate. When one problem is resolved using PPT a plate is removed from the pile of stacked plates. Underneath the first plate (problem) is another one that the client can't see/feel until the first stacked plate/problem is removed. It is important for clients to be aware of this analogy/example because sometimes when one problem is being released another one pops up and unless clients realize this is natural they may mistakenly think the technique is not working when in fact it is working perfectly.

Clients are encouraged to practice level one of the PPT 10-20 times a day or as often as they can before the next session and to experiment with using it on all kinds of distress.

Level 2 of the Pressure Point Technique

After receiving feedback about their experience with PPT-L1, I introduce the second level of the Pressure Point Technique.

This gradual approach is especially good with skeptical clients. Level 2 is similar to level one except I introduce affirmations to the clients. The client again gives him/herself a SUDs rating from 1 to 10, again does the Psychological Uplifter, again attunes to the problem, and uses the same 8 pressure points. However, the client is taught when tapping on each pressure point to use the generic formula:

- I release X, I choose to be at Y

- I release X, I am Y.

Repeat 2 to 3 times. (usually 3 at first)

More specifically, "I release anger, I choose to be at peace" and "I release anger, I am at peace" or "I release guilt, I choose to be at peace" and "I release guilt I am at peace." This set of affirmations both focuses on empowerment (I choose) and acknowledgment/remembrance of one's true nature (peace). It reinforces what clients have been learning in other ways, i.e., releasing darkness and choosing/acknowledging light.

Clients are then taught to practice the hold and breath process on each pressure point, with the idea that they are breathing in peace on the inbreath and breathing out whatever distress they are attuned to on the outbreath. For example, they are breathing in peace and breathing out anger or guilt.

During this process, the therapist/healer has the opportunity to use his/her intuition by sensing if there are deeper emotions behind the one the client has selected and to introduce that into the tapping affirmations. For example, the therapist/healer (who is modeling the process for the client) might suggest the client say "releasing anger, hurt and disappointment" instead of releasing just anger after 2 or 3 pressure points have already been tapped because he/she senses there is hurt and disappointment behind the anger.

He might also suggest the client say releasing guilt and sadness, instead of just releasing guilt after 2 or 3 pressure points are tapped if he/she senses that sadness is behind the guilt. Also the therapist/healer might sense that instead of saying "I choose to be at peace" it would be stronger if the client said "I choose to be calm, relaxed and at peace" or "I choose to be calm, confident and at peace" and then "I am calm, relaxed and at peace" or "I am calm, confident and at peace".

Clients are asked to write down the generic and specific affirmation formulas and then to practice the technique 10-20 times a day or as often as they can. In the next session (usually the 4th), clients are taught:

Level 3 of the Pressure Point Technique

Level 3 is exactly like level 2 except "forgiveness affirmations" are introduced after the client has worked with the basic 8 pressure points and while the client is tapping under the arm continuously, first under the right arm and then under the left arm. (There is no a priori reason that the forgiveness affirmations can't be used while tapping other pressure points). Finally the client taps on the center of the chest.

The forgiveness affirmations are used to further emphasize that forgiveness is a key to happiness, to strengthen the client's connection with the Path of Light and to further connect the person with his or her true identity.

Forgiveness Affirmations

Repeat while tapping under the right arm:

- I forgive myself for my contribution to the problem.

- I forgive myself I am doing the best that I can.

- I forgive myself, I release all judgments against myself.

- I forgive myself I release all criticisms against myself.

- I forgive myself I release all grievances against myself.

- I forgive myself I release all attack thoughts against myself. Forgiveness is the key to happiness.

Repeat while tapping under the left arm:

- I forgive him/her (use the person's name) for his/her contribution to the problem.

- I forgive him/her (use the person's name) he/she is doing the best that he/she can.

- I forgive him/her, I release all judgments against him/her.

- I forgive him/her I release all criticisms against him/her.

- I forgive him/her I release all grievances against him/her.

- I forgive him/her, I release all attack thoughts against him/her. Forgiveness is the key to happiness.

Repeat while tapping in the center of the chest:

- Forgiveness is the key to happiness (2 times).

- There is forgiveness in my heart for myself and for him/her (2 times-usually use the person's name).

- There is love in my heart for myself and for him/her (use their name) (2 times)

- Deep down I am the Presence of Love (2 times)

- I thank God or the universe (choose one) that all my problems have been solved and I am at peace.

- I thank God or the universe (choose one) that I am healed and at peace.

- I thank God or the universe (choose one) that I am out of darkness and experiencing light.

- I am at peace (2 times); I am calm, relaxed and at peace (2 times)

Close your eyes and take 3 slow deep breaths.

Troubleshooting Methods

When a person gets stuck, I use any of the following approaches:

1. Access an earlier or deeper upset/affect
2. Tap the 9 gamut
3. Tap the karate-chop point
4. Dialogue to elicit limiting beliefs
5. Use Floor-to-Ceiling Eyeroll.

In summary, the Pressure Point Technique (PPT) is a variant of and extension of EFT, TAB and MATT and developed to release emotional distress, enhance well-being and facilitate a client's journey on the path of light.

CONTACT INFORMATION

Philip H. Friedman, Ph.D.
P.O. Box 627, Plymouth Meeting, PA 19462
610-828-4674
integrativehelp@aol.com
http://www.integrativegrativehelp.com
http://www.philipfriedman.com

Following Up
and Following Thru

The future belongs to those
who believe in the beauty of their dreams.

– *ELEANOR ROOSEVELT*

You have covered a lot of territory since you first opened this book. Having come this far, how can you digest and assimilate what you have read? And where can it take you?

We hope that this will be a book that enhances your life. This, of course, is up to you. We realize our readers have a wide range of backgrounds, from healing novices to professional healers, along with an equally wide range of dreams and goals. Your unique perspective will determine how you apply EFT and the other methods presented here. If you have a solid foundation in these or other holistic modalities, you may already be well on your way. This book may provide some new gems to add to your toolbox.

If you are new, we want you to know that you have all of the gifts you need to succeed. As an example of humble beginnings, we want to share a little about our first experiences in the areas of holistic and energetic healing.

A COMPLETE BEGINNER

When we embarked on our journey into healing years ago, we took a Reiki (hands-on healing) class. We were both fascinated with the human energy system and the possibility of making powerful changes energetically.

Phillip had some experience in this area, and he felt comfortable with his ability to learn more. Jane, on the other hand, lacked this confidence. At that time, she was practicing as an architect, so concepts of holistic and energetic healing were new and foreign to her well-developed logical mind. She felt inept, not ever believing she could feel energy or play a positive role in anyone's healing. But with an avid interest in the subject, she wanted to give it a try. Unknown to herself, Jane was following her soul's heartfelt joy.

At the first Reiki class, Jane regarded herself as one of the least gifted participants. She was enjoying herself so much, though, that she didn't really care. She was happy to learn the methods and practice with the group. Afterwards, she had more opportunities to practice and continued with more Reiki classes. Each new technique opened more doors in her mind and added more methods to her toolbox.

Over the next year or two, we continued taking different classes, learning methods related to spiritual healing, hypnotherapy, and more. Jane continued to enjoy each new skill and received powerful healings, still focusing more on her interest in the subject than on her personal performance.

A year or two after taking the first Reiki class, she suddenly noticed that many positive things had occurred. She recognized that she could now feel subtle energy as tangibly as she could solid materials. She also had an understanding of the energy system and its relationship to different qualities of awareness we have in our bodies, emotions, minds, and spirits, along with ways to clear blockages on all levels.

In a way, Jane's abilities crept up on her almost without notice. Embarking on this new direction provided a fundamental shift that has transformed both of our lives and opened new doors to a beautiful future.

FOLLOWING YOUR HEARTFELT JOY

We share this story with the wish that this book will encourage you to follow your heartfelt joy and excitement wherever they may lead you. You probably have already been experimenting with some of the methods in this book. To follow your heartfelt joy, we suggest you focus on the ones that interest you most. If all of this is new, don't focus on every detail of the techniques or on doing everything right. They are, after all, simply means to an end, and it is the healing journey that is most important. Just keep exploring the methods and have fun with them.

The theory and knowledge in this book provide food for thought, but the magic comes with the actual application of the tools. The most important element to anyone's success with holistic and energetic healing is practice, practice, practice. Over time, as Jane discovered, the techniques become secondary, as you learn to simply flow with the healing experience and appreciate the profound nature of the human soul. While setting some goals, preferably in writing, on how to proceed with learning, also let your intuition guide you. You may want to practice a certain technique regularly for a specific period, say for a week or a month, and then move on to another area.

The levels of healing and soulful insights you can experience with these techniques are virtually limitless. The opportunity is great; you just have to provide the commitment. With application will come wisdom. If we or any of the EFT experts in this volume can be of assistance, feel free to contact us.

Remember you are not only helping yourself and those

around you. You are contributing to making the world a more peaceful and harmonious place.

We leave you with the dream that guides us with the organization we founded, the Awakenings Institute:

Imagine a world where love is the guiding force, where the unique gifts that each individual brings receive honor and respect, where all are nurtured in allowing their gifts to blossom, to manifest the joy of living in each moment...

Imagine a world where all of nature is also honored, so all may live in harmony and share an increasingly vibrant and beautiful environment...

What we imagine we can create, starting in this moment. This vibrant world will come into being as each of us empowers ourselves to live the dream now and share it with others. Playing a part in the creation of this dream is the mission of Awakenings.

You can find more information about the organization and its offerings at the end of this book.

Fostering Therapeutic Relationships

In our e-book *The Heart and Soul of Being Therapeutic*, we discuss the how-to's of fostering healthy, productive therapeutic relationships. Because of its importance, we wanted to share some of that information here.

The details of establishing appropriate healing relationships needs to be carefully taken into account when you are helping others. EFT is an extraordinary technique, yet, as you may detect or know from first hand experience, addressing deeper issues involves a certain art and skill. This includes helping others to discover wondrous parts of themselves, and assisting them to release whatever is preventing them from joyfully living their lives fully.

Exploring deeper issues can be a profound and enlightening experience for both the client and the practitioner. By bringing out the best in both the healer and the person being helped, everyone experiences a profound sense of fulfillment.

The following ten elements can help optimize healing sessions with others:

1. **Build a firm foundation** with your presence.

2. **Be free of agendas.** The best results come when the healing practitioner can be compassionate and neutral. Having theories to "prove," such as a certain behavior links to a certain causes, will bias your results.

3. **Establish rapport** at the beginning of the session and bring the person into a state that is appropriate for healing. Starting with a bit of light conversation and helping the person to unwind generally puts him or her at ease. This is particularly important for new clients, who are generally facing some fear of the unknown.

4. **With a repeat client, review what has transpired since the last session,** including the results of any action plans that were made.

5. **Let the client know that he or she is in control.** If the person is not comfortable with a particular technique or subject, he or she just has to let you know, then move on to something else. As a note, continue to be aware of the person's comfort level throughout the session.

6. **Establish desired goals and set priorities for the session.** Remember that you are responsible for setting the direction for the session and staying on course. This often involves coming up with a list of things the person wants to address, helping the person to set priorities, and suggesting how much the person might be able to address in this session.

7. **Clear the blockages that stand in the way,** focusing on the client's lead modality, whether it be visual, auditory, or sensorial. Remember, it is not necessary to

dwell on the negative. With powerful healing techniques, you can generally clear them quickly and shift your focus to the new awareness that is emerging.

8. **End on a positive note.** Summarize the key areas covered during the session, along with ideas for how the person can further integrate them in the following days and weeks. The summary can include reviewing the person's insights and revelations during the session, sharing ideas related to the persons purpose, and practical follow-up strategies. To help summarize and for future reference, it is a good idea to take notes during the session.

9. **Let the person know that the integration process will continue** for a period of days or weeks and to be aware of his or her needs for rest, water, exercise, and nurturing. Be sure he or she is grounded before leaving. If necessary, grounding can be achieved by having the person do some deep breathing, taking a walk, or imagining being grounded to the center of the earth.

10. **Honor the changes that have occurred.** Often people are transformed by deep healing sessions. The most important point is to embrace the experience and bring the higher awareness of the soul to it.

To study the above points in depth and other important considerations, we refer you to our e-book, *The Heart and Soul of Being Therapeutic*, described in the Resources section.

Glossary

Acupuncture Point: A term derived from traditional Chinese medicine referring to points on the body located along the energy meridians. Stimulating these points balances the flow of energy through the meridians and restores normal function to various parts of the body, along with balancing the emotions.

Anchoring: Anchoring is a term derived from Neurolinguistic Programming (NLP) that refers to how a memory in one the senses stimulates a response in one or more of the other senses.

Apex Problem: An EFT term referring to a form of denial that some people experience in relation to subtle energy techniques. Their limited belief systems do not include the possibility that these techniques could produce rapid and profound changes. When the changes occur, these people block out their memories of the former problems.

Aspect: An EFT term referring to a specific part of a problem. An emotional pattern may have one or more aspects.

Chief Defense: One of seven possible defense mechanisms, largely fear-based and unconscious, that can be identified and eliminated by awareness and clearing processes.

Compartmentalizing: A kind of split off thinking that creates barriers to healing. When we divide certain areas of our lives, making it becomes forbidden to examine them, then healing cannot occur.

EFT: Emotional Freedom Techniques. A series of meridian-based healing processes developed by Gary Craig and Adrienne Fowlie, based on the discoveries of Dr. Roger Callahan.

Energy Toxins: An EFT term referring to energies and substances that irritate the energy system. Energy toxins include substances that are ingested or in contact with the body, along with negative energies in the environment.

Future Pacing: By focusing on a positive state, you can then imagine extending it out into the future. Often used after clearing an issue.

Gamut Point: A point located on the back of the hand, which is also known as the brain balancing point. It is used for the Nine Gamut Process and the Floor-to-Ceiling Eye Roll.

Generalization Effect: An EFT term that describes how clearing achieved with one aspect of an emotional pattern generalizes over the entire emotional pattern after neutralizing some of the aspects.

Getting Thru Techniques: A group of processes that are designed to help individuals to bring greater awareness to what is happening in their unconscious minds, to clear any blockages they encounter, and to integrate the changes into their conscious awareness. These processes help individuals to progress in their personal and spiritual growth, with the ultimate goal of achieving joy, love, and freedom in all aspects of life.

Grounding: Connecting the body with the earth to balance energy.

GTT: Getting Thru Techniques.

Holistic: Related to or concerned with integrated whole or complete systems rather than with analyzing or treating separate parts. In relation to healing, this term commonly refers to dealing with the body, emotions, mind, and spirit as parts of an integrated whole.

Holistic Hypnotherapy: A state-of-the-art approach to hypnotherapy that includes the body, emotions, mind, and spirit. It provides ways to tap into the vast resources each person has in the unconscious mind that can lead to an expanded sense of fulfillment and wholeness.

Intermittent: When used in reference to a physical disorder, pertains to a condition that alternates between periods of activity and inactivity. This may include symptoms like headaches, asthma attacks, and other disorders that come and go.

Kinesiology: The use of muscle testing to access information from the unconscious mind and the body's innate intelligence. It works by testing how the strength of a muscle is affected by focusing on an external stimulus or a part of the body.

Levels of Psychological Reversal (PR): An EFT term referring to specific forms of PR, involving judgments and limiting beliefs that need to be released to achieve success with the EFT tapping sequences.

Massive Psychological Reversal: An EFT term referring to people who experience psychological reversal in most areas of their lives. With these people, the energy flow through the body is disturbed in a way that makes both physical and emotional healing difficult.

Meridian System: A term derived from traditional Chinese medicine referring to a continuous series of energy channels running throughout the body. Each meridian is associated with a particular emotion and organ system. Life force energy, sometimes called "chi," flows through the meridians.

Muscle Testing: The practical use of Kinesiology. By isolating a specific muscle, you can test its response to access conscious and unconscious information.

Neurolinguistic Programming (NLP): A group of techniques and skills that some call the art and science of excellence. NLP includes communication skills that can help anyone to understand how different people experience life, thereby improving both personal and professional relationships. It also includes techniques that are similar to hypnotherapy, which can help with overcoming difficulties and with achieving excellence in all aspects of one's life.

Neurological Disorganization: An EFT term referring to a form of energy blockage that thwarts the effectiveness of the tapping sequences. Neurological Disorganization must be addressed to achieve success with the tapping sequences.

NLP: Neurolinguistic Programming

PR: Psychological Reversal.

Psychological Reversal (PR): An EFT term referring to the

presence of unconscious beliefs and judgments that may prevent an individual from achieving positive results with the
EFT tapping sequences. In such cases, the PR must be addressed directly for the tapping sequences to be effective.

Reframing: An NLP technique that clears blockages by replacing an unbalanced pattern with a balanced one.

Reiki: A hands-on healing approach that involves the trans-
mission of life force energy to the body and the surrounding
energy field. Reiki includes techniques to use for the physical,
emotional, mental, and spiritual levels of healing, along with
long distance healing.

Soul Centering: By focusing on your soul's energy, either by a
visualization, sensing or knowingness, you can use this energy
for guidance and healing.

SUDs Level: A psychology term that stands for "subjective
unit of distress or disturbance." The SUDs level measure the
intensity of a problem. With EFT, this intensity of emotions
and other symptoms is measured on a scale of one to ten,
where one is the least intense and ten is the most intense.

Surrogate Muscle Testing: The use of Kinesiology to test responses in another individual. This method is commonly used
when an individual is not in a suitable condition to test directly and for testing an individual long distance.

Switched Circuit: Refer to "Massive Psychological Reversal."

Thought Field Therapy (TFT): A group of meridian-based
processes developed by Dr. Roger Callahan. These techniques
form the basis of the Emotional Freedom Techniques, which
are the subject of this book.

Resources

ADDITIONAL EFT RESOURCES FROM HOLISTIC COMMUNICATIONS

Getting Thru to Your Emotions with EFT
Two DVDs or Video Tapes with Phillip and Jane Mountrose

These professionally produced DVDs/tapes present the processes described in the book through real examples, demonstrations, and commentary. Seeing the techniques in action will
help with your timing, precision, and presentation.

- **DVD or Video One** presents the EFT processes.
- **DVD or Video Two** presents the GTT (Getting Thru
  Techniques) processes to address deeper issues.

Getting Thru to Your Emotions with EFT
Two-CD set with Phillip and Jane Mountrose

This audio set provides guided versions of the deeper GTT
Processes presented in the book, with background music. The

CDs allow you to relax, while you are guided through each of the processes. There is also a section describing how to do EFT and some tips for success. Great for self-healing!

Getting Thru to Your Emotions with EFT
Paperback Book by Phillip and Jane Mountrose
The book includes parts of this book: the basic EFT information plus some of the information about the impediments to EFT. In addition, it details four other Getting Thru Techniques besides the Holistic Process.

The paperback version also describes a variety of ways to apply EFT to common problems. Individual chapters include eliminating stress, overcoming insomnia, relieving pain, creating physical well-being, stopping smoking and other habits, reaching your ideal weight increasing physical activity and performance, and achieving genuine freedom. As one reviewer said, the book contains "a goldmine of information that I keep handy as a database of information."

RECOMMENDED BOOKS

Bishop, Jacqui and Grunte, Mary. *How to Forgive When You Don't Know How*. Barrytown, New York: Station Hill Press, 1993.

Callahan, Roger J. *Tapping the Healer Within*. Chicago, Illinois: Contemporary Books, 2001.

Dennison, Paul and Dennison, Gail. *Brain Gym*. Ventura, California: Edu-Kinesthetics, 1992.

Dennison, Paul and Dennison, Gail. *Brain Gym Teacher's Edition*. Ventura, California: Edu-Kinesthetics, 1989.

Diamond, John. *Life Energy*. New York: Paragon House, 1990.

Durlacher, James. *Freedom From Fear Forever*. Tempe, Arizona: Van Ness Publishing, 1995.

Eden, Donna. *Energy Medicine*. New York: Jeremy P. Tarcher/Putnam, 1998.

Friedman, Philip H. *Creating Well-Being*. Saratoga, California: R & E Publishers, 1989.

Gruder, David. *The Energy Psychology Desktop Companion*. Del Mar, California. Willingness Works, 2000. www.willingness.com.

Luskin, Fred. *Forgive for Good*. San Francisco, California: Harper/San Francisco, 2003.

Radomski, Sandi. *Allergy Antidotes Manual*. www.allergyantidotes.com.

Temple-Thurston Leslie and Yates Brad. *The Marriage of Spirit*. Santa Fe, New Mexico: CoreLight Publications, 2000.

Also refer to the EFT Experts part of this book in Chapter Twelve for more resource information.

WEB SITES

Gettingthru.org: This is the Mountroses' website, which has a wealth of information on EFT and other healing modalities; EFT, Spiritual Kinesiology (SK), and Spiritual Counseling Certification Courses; BA, MA and PhD Degree Programs offering degrees in EFT and other holistic subjects; free *Soul News* email newsletters; and ordering for their publications at www.gettingthru.org.

Emotional Freedom Techniques: Gary Craig, the originator of EFT, has developed this site. It contains extensive information and support for EFT users at www.emofree.com.

MORE FROM HOLISTIC COMMUNICATIONS
Getting Thru to Your Soul Books, CDs, DVDs/Tapes

Getting Thru to Your Soul
Book by Phillip and Jane Mountrose
Learn the four keys to living your divine purpose and Spiritual Kinesiology, a healing tool developed by the Mountroses that is as powerful as EFT and may be used along with EFT to clear issues that stand between you and the fulfillment of your true purpose. *Getting Thru to Your Soul* is a follow-up to *Getting Thru to Your Emotions with EFT* and includes effective ways to use both EFT and Spiritual Kinesiology to help with your spiritual development.

Getting Thru to Your Soul
DVDs or Video Tapes with Phillip and Jane Mountrose
These three professionally-produced DVDs/tapes present the Spiritual Kinesiology (SK) processes described in the book through real-life examples, many demonstrations, and insightful commentary. Seeing the techniques in action will help with your timing and precision. The clear visual presentation will help you master these techniques.

- **DVD or Video One** presents an overview of SK and the Basic Techniques.

- **DVD or Video Two** focuses on using SK with inner child issues and relationships.

- **DVD or Video Three** presents SK and GTT techniques with archetypes and subpersonalities.

Getting Thru to Your Soul
Two-CD set with Phillip and Jane Mountrose
This audio set provides guided versions of the SK and GTT processes presented in the book, with background music. The CDs are great for self-healing as you are guided through each of the processes. Also included is a track on how to do SK.

Intuitive Techniques for Getting Thru to Your Soul
Four CDs with a Workbook, by Phillip and Jane Mountrose, Workbook includes extensive information about developing your intuition, descriptions of the techniques, and scripts of the information on the CDs.
This spiritual development program, which is a companion to the *Getting Thru to Your Soul* book, will help you open to your intuition as an integral part of your spiritual journey. The material presents a whole toolbox of techniques that allow you to understand yourself and others in a more profound way. Like learning a new language, it can open you to a new (and enlightening) form of communication.

Awaken to Your True Purpose:
More Pieces to the Puzzle of Getting Thru to Your Soul
Five CDs and Study Guide, narrated by Phillip Mountrose, also available as a workbook
This works draws from the ideas of Gurdjieff and the Michael Teachings, which is invaluable for understanding one's essential nature. The program describes your personality traits (overleaves) that your soul chose, including your role, goal, attitude, body type, center of gravity, as well as your chief weakness. Also detailed are 10 specific obstacles and opportunities for living your purpose.

E-Books

The Heart and Soul of Being Therapeutic:
7 Keys for Getting Thru to Clients in Healing Environments
E-Book by Phillip and Jane Mountrose
downloadable e-book, spiral-bound copy

Learn the keys to becoming a great healing practitioner. A concise guide for anyone in the helping professions, it is based on extensive research combined with the Mountroses decades of working with clients and teaching healing classes. Receive dozens of tips and tools for fostering therapeutic relationships. A unique resource that you will refer to time and again.

The Heart and Soul of Teaching:
5 Keys for Getting Thru to Others in Learning Environments
E-Book by Phillip and Jane Mountrose
downloadable e-book, spiral-bound copy

Learn the keys to becoming a great teacher, presenter, facilitator, and leader, and have fun teaching the classes you've always longed to teach. You will find countless tips and techniques in this unique resource, which comes out of extensive research and the Mountroses' decades of teaching classes. Take your classes and presentations to the next level.

Other Books

The Holistic Approach to Eating
by Jane Mountrose, booklet

Learn the keys to losing extra weight and keeping it off for life. Find out the reasons traditional diets fail and techniques that really work. Make real progress and feel good about yourself.

Holistic Healing Training Manual
by Phillip and Jane Mountrose, in 3-ring binder

This is the manual used in the Mountroses' Holistic Healing Certification Course, which can serve as a comprehensive model for healers in the development of their holistic practices and training programs. If you are interested in developing a program in your area based on this approach, support materials including course outlines are also available, on request.

Getting Thru to Kids: The Five Steps to Problem Solving with Children Ages 6 to 18
Book by Phillip Mountrose
In an easy-to-read format, learn the 5 steps to communicating with kids. Empower yourself and kids with more trust, honesty, and improved relationships and school attitude. A Best Book Award by Sacramento Publishers Association and a Parent Council Selection

To order any of the materials, call toll-free 866-304-4325 or order online at www.gettingthru.org.
You can purchase materials from Awakenings using the order form at the end of this book or by placing a secure internet order at the gettingthru.org website. Your purchase directly supports Awakenings in its mission of helping people fulfill their true purpose.

Index

abundance, 151, 223, 225-227
abuse, 16, 192
acupuncture points, 23, 33,
    36, 42
Allergy Antidotes, 11, 194-195,
    234, 285
anchoring, 131, 133, 257, 277
anger, 13, 23, 38, 39, 41
anxiety, 96
apex problem, 40, 277
aspect, 24- 25, 35, 38, 44, 54
Awaken to your True Purpose,
    3, 149, 207, 287

Be Set Free Fast, 161
beliefs, 41, 88, 112, 117
Bishop, Jacqui and Grunte,
    Mary, 157
BodyTalk System, 193
brain, 52, 96
breath, 43, 136

Callahan, Roger, 9, 16- 17, 23,
    27, 40, 109
Carpenter, Carl, 134
Carrington, Patricia, 10, 63,
    217- 218, 222, 233

centering, 62, 98, 108, 112,
    115, 119, 126, 130, 133, 149,
    163, 175, 281
Christmas, 192, 229, 230
compartmentalizing, 27, 170,
    198-202, 278
Complete Sequence, 25- 26,
    34, 45-53, 85-88
Craig, Gary, 8-10, 16-18, 25,
    33, 35, 86- 87, 112, 115, 144,
    170-172, 177, 182, 208, 218,
    220, 223, 228, 232, 234, 239,
    245, 278, 286
defense patterns, 27,170, 202-
    207
Diamond Approach, 112, 144,
    175
Diamond, John, 144-147, 173
doubt, 105

Eden, Donna, 194, 285
energy field, 132
Energy Medicine, 194
*Energy Psychology Desktop
    Companion*, 107, 173
energy toxins, 27, 100, 178-
    193, 278

Environmental Protection
  Agency, 178

fear
  and kidney meridian, 23
  and Kinesiology, 96
  clearing, 34
  identifying, 39
  phobic, 35
fibromyalgia, 17
Floor-to-Ceiling Eye Roll, 24,
  34, 44, 52
Forgive for Good, 157
forgiveness, 153
Fourth Way, 202, 207
Friedman, Phil, 218, 260, 267,
  285
fulfillment, 279
future pacing, 68, 74, 211, 212

Gamut Point, 48
generalization effect, 36, 278
Getting Thru Techniques,
  1- 2, 28, 278- 279, 283- 284
*Getting Thru to Your Emotions
  with EFT*, 1, 8, 28, 31, 73,
  88, 118, 124, 170, 175, 283-
  284, 286
Getting Thru to Your Soul, 1,
  80, 131, 150, 286, 287, 305

goals
  and anchors, 131
  and being therapeutic, 274

and Diamond Approach,
  147
and dreams, 211, 269
and EFT, 223
and energy toxins, 190
and forgiveness, 158
and future pacing, 212
and massive PR, 110, 113
and Neurological
  Disorganization, 171
and peak performance, 237,
  239
and positive attitude, 152
and PR, 94, 123
and testing statements, 92
archetypal, 202
in writing, 271
soulful, 149
Gordon, Marilyn, 10, 11, 63,
  218, 231, 233
grief, 42
grounding, 98, 115, 129, 130,
  133, 279
Gruder, David, 107, 173, 285
GTT. *See* Getting Thru
  Techniques
Gurdjieff, George, 202

headache, 41, 246
Holistic Process, 15, 35, 85,
  99, 107, 112, 115, 118-125,
  137, 141, 143, 146, 164, 171,
  175, 198, 201, 212, 284
*How to Forgive When You
  Don't Know How*, 157

Huber, Colleen, 178
Hypno-Kinesiology, 134
hypnotherapy, 11, 20, 218,
   223, 231, 245, 279

intent, 42, 101, 191

joy, 8, 117
judgments, 41, 88, 112

kinesiology
   and energy toxins, 27, 183-
      187
   and identifying blocks, 102
   and neurological
      disorganization, 172
   and PR, 88, 89
   before testing with, 96
   definition, 279
   different methods, 96
   Holistic Process as
      alternative, 118
   tips, 102
   with EFT, 26

Lake, David, 11, 63, 218, 237,
   249, 255
Lazaris, 161
Lees, Alexander R., 10, 192,
   218, 231
Life Energy, 144, 150, 284
Look, Carol, 10, 12, 151, 217,
   227
love, 8
Luskin, Fred, 157-160

Magic Question, 45, 53, 55,
   64, 82, 85, 93, 99118
Massive PR. See Massive
   Psychological Reversal
Massive Psychological
   Reversal, 164-165, 173, 204,
   280
medication, 186
Mercola, Joseph, 13
meridian system, 22, 23, 35,
   36
Michael Teachings, 202, 207,
   287
money
   and compartmentalizing,
      200
   and EFT, 229
   and limited beliefs, 80, 122,
      257, 258, 259
   and no limitations, 211
   and prosperity
      consciousness, 227
   and resources, 122
Moore-Hafter, Betty, 11, 34,
   63, 120, 218, 245, 249
muscle testing. See
   kinesiology

Neurolinguistic
   Programming. See NLP
Neurological Disorganization,
   27, 59, 107, 111, 170-177,
   280
neurolymphatic points, 195
Nims, Larry, 107, 161, 162

NLP
  and anchoring, 131, 277
  and eye movements, 106,
    139
  and future pacing, 73
  and reframing, 81, 132, 281
  definition of, 280

peak performance, 11, 63, 237
positive affirmations, 68, 76,
  113
positive attitude, 152, 153
positive installations, 79
PR. *See* Psychological
  Reversal
Psychological Reversal
  and fears, 151, 154
  and low thymus, 146
  and Magic Question, 53, 64
  and reframing and
    anchoring, 131
  and test statements, 88-94,
    102-103
  definition of, 26, 279- 280
  description of, 85, 86
  eliminating, 41, 88
  example of, 65, 242

Radomski, Sandi, 11, 178,
  194, 218, 236
Rapp, Doris, 181-182
Reed, Steve, 139-140
Reframing and Anchoring, 2,
  26, 73, 81, 115, 130-133,
  138, 143

reminder phrase, 34
resentment, 38

sadness, 38
shame, 117
Short Sequence, 24, 25, 34-45,
  47-50, 87
Soul, 21- 22
soulful states, 76
Sparks, Loretta, 11, 39, 218,
  241, 244
Spinal Release, 194
Spiritual Kinesiology, 1- 3, 86,
  130, 137, 150, 285, 286
stress, 190
SUDs
  and apex problem, 40
  and defense pattern, 205
  and Holistic Process, 124
  and installing the positive,
    68
  and low thymus, 146
  and Pressure Point
    Therapy, 261, 264
  and reframing and
    anchoring, 132
  and Short Sequence, 57, 59,
    108
  definition of, 40, 281
Swack, Judith, 106

Temple-Thurston, Leslie, 76
TFT, 16, 17, 40
*The Heart and Soul of Being
  Therapeutic*, 273

The Impossible Child, 181
The Marriage of Spirit, 77
Thought Field Therapy. *See*
    TFT
thymus, 112, 145-153, 173, 175
Tuttle, Carol, 11, 122, 146,
    218, 255, 260

unconscious
    and anchors, 131
    and blockages, 35, 41, 58,
        64, 89, 92, 112, 119, 125,
        132139, 151, 157-158,
        192, 198
    and chief defense, 202, 278
    and Getting Thru
        Techniques, 278
    and hypnotherapy, 20, 279
    and kinesiology, 85-88, 96,
        101, 279
    and Magic Question, 93

and meridian system, 22, 23
and programming, 21
and reminder phrase, 34, 42
and the brain, 54
and trauma, 242
convincing the, 42

Veltheim, John, 193

weight
    and compartmentalizing,
        200
    and EFT, 32, 224
    and energy toxins, 181, 235
    and *Getting Thru to Your*
        Emotions with EFT, 29
    and greed, 204
    and kinesiology, 102
    and PR, 89, 92
Wells, Steve, 11, 12, 63, 218,
    237, 240, 250, 255

About the Authors

Phillip and Jane Mountrose have studied and developed methods for self-help, personal growth, and accelerated spiritual development for nearly thirty years. Together, they lead the Awakenings Institute, a non-profit religious organization located in California.

PHILLIP MOUNTROSE is a co-founder of the Awakenings Institute and continues to co-direct this enlightening organization that unites healing and spirituality. He is a Holistic Hypnotherapist, NLP (Neurolinguistic Programming) Practitioner, Spiritual Counselor, Reiki Master, and Intuitive Counselor serving others as a Minister of Holistic Healing.

In addition to his diverse training in different aspects of holistic healing and spirituality, Phillip has a Masters in Education from University of Massachusetts, a Special Education Certification from Sacramento State College, and a Masters in Fine Arts from UCLA. He is a veteran educator and innovative instructional video creator who taught children of all ages for over twenty years.

Phillip now teaches certification courses in Holistic Healing. He also works with people individually to help them achieve their goals. Phillip enjoys helping to identify and release their blockages, so they can experience more joy, love and freedom in their lives.

JANE MOUNTROSE is a co-founder of the Awakenings Institute. She is a holistic teacher, Holistic Hypnotherapist, Spiritual Life Coach and Counselor, Reiki Master, and Intuitive Counselor, serving others as a Minister of Holistic Healing. In addition to her diversified experience helping people to realize their highest potential, Jane has a Bachelor's Degree from Rhode Island School of Design in Art and more than 25 years of experience as an artist and an architect. She remains actively involved in the arts. Based on her own weight problems, she also wrote the book *The Holistic Approach to Eating*, which presents a program for reaching your ideal weight and maintaining it for life.

Jane's personal consultations and teaching methods include the use of EFT, intuitive reading, hypnotherapy, kinesiology, and energetic healing. This unique combination of techniques helps her clients and students to understand what is holding them back from reaching their full potential and to clear the blockages that are in their way.

You can find more information about the authors on the internet at http://www.gettingthru.org.

Awakenings Institute: Offerings and E-News

Awakenings Institute is a non-profit religious organization founded by Phillip and Jane Mountrose to provide a vehicle for uniting holistic healing and spirituality. This transformational organization offers educational programs, ordination for likeminded spiritually/holistically oriented individuals, and a worldwide spiritual community. You can find out more about Awakenings and becoming a member of its spiritual community by contacting Phillip and Jane Mountrose. Refer to the end of this section for contact information.

HOME-STUDY CERTIFICATION COURSES

Awakenings Institute is pleased to offer an Independent Home-Study Program for those wishing to develop skills in Holistic Healing and Spiritual Counseling. This Spiritual Counseling Certification Program includes four courses, or modules, for certification in the following areas:

- EFT (Emotional Freedom Techniques) Practitioner
- SK (Spiritual Kinesiology) Practitioner
- Intuitive Techniques Practitioner
- Soul Purpose Advisor

Any of the modules may be taken individually or as part of the overall program. Each module qualifies as 36 hours of study toward the 150-hour Spiritual Counselor certification.

Along with studying the materials, this easy-to-follow program emphasizes practicing the techniques in each course. Practice is one of the main keys to your success. It helps you to build confidence, refine your approach and timing, and understand what your client is experiencing under a variety of circumstances.

Benefits of Certification

The core benefit of these courses is the opportunity for focused study as a part of your life-learning process. It helps you to fulfill your purpose and to likewise help others to fulfill theirs. Certification provides confirmation of your experience, which is beneficial for those seeking your services as well as your own development. Successful completion of any of the four certification courses also provides the following:

- Many powerful tools and much practical knowledge for making quantum leaps in personal and spiritual growth for yourself and others you help.

- A Certificate of Completion, suitable for display.

- An opportunity to be listed as a certified practitioner on Awakening's "gettingthru.org" website.

- Hours of credit toward the Spiritual Counselor Certification and/or the Ministerial Program.

BECOMING A MINISTER OF HOLISTIC HEALING

Ordination with Awakenings Institute provides a unique opportunity for holistic/spiritual practitioners who want to use their skills in service to others locally and, potentially, as part of Awakenings' supportive worldwide spiritual community. As an ordained minister, you can realize your spiritual mission with all of the blessings provided to all ordained persons in the United States, including:

- The use of holistic practices that create wholeness and balance

- Serving others through teaching

- Performing weddings and other appropriate ceremonies

- Practicing your spiritual/ religious beliefs with all of the freedoms offered with the separation of church and state

- Conducting as a ministry in a legal non-profit religious organization

DIVINITY DEGREE PROGRAMS

Awakenings Institute offers a unique alternative university that is on the leading edge of higher education. Through Awakenings Institute, you can receive a Bachelor's, Master's, or Doctor of Divinity degree in fields such as Spiritual Counseling, Holistic Hypnotherapy, energetic healing, or another related field of interest. You will be personally guided through every phase of the program by Phillip or Jane Mountrose.

HOLISTIC HEALING CERTIFICATION PROGRAM

Awakenings offers a unique 160-500 program in holistic healing, uniquely blending Holistic Hypnotherapy, EFT, Spiritual Kinesiology, NLP, and more. Classes are held in the San Luis Obispo/Santa Maria and Sacramento, California areas. In addition to this life-transforming program, the Mountroses give seminars around the country.

INDIVIDUAL CONSULTATIONS

Phillip and Jane Mountrose also offer in-person and telephone sessions to help people connect more deeply with their evolutionary journey and true purpose. These consultations can save years of suffering and confusion as well as greatly accelerate your spiritual progress.

FREE EMAIL NEWSLETTER

Soul News – Free Monthly Email Newsletter
People interested in living a soul-based life will enjoy receiving this free monthly newsletter. The *Soul News* includes practical, leading-edge holistic healing information to help you develop your life purpose and your spiritual well being. Specific tips and techniques for soul development are shared.

AWAKENINGS E-CATALOG

More information about Awakenings and its many offerings is available on the website, including an E-Catalog, which you can find at www.gettingthru.org/acatalog.pdf. You can also request an electronic copy by e-mail, along with information packets on the University Degree Programs and the Ordination Program.

For more information about Awakenings' offerings, contact:

Awakenings Institute
Phillip and Jane Mountrose
P.O. Box 279, Arroyo Grande, CA 93421
www.gettingthru.org
E-mail: joy@gettingthru.org
Phone: (805)929-1584

Phillip and Jane also welcome your communication, especially your experiences, insights, challenges, and successes with the interactive tools in this book.

Ordering Information

PRODUCT LIST

The Heart & Soul of EFT and Beyond
- Paperback Book $16.95
- E-Book $16.95 (sent by email or download from website)

The Heart & Soul of Teaching
- E-Book $16.95 (sent by email or download from website)
- Hard Copy, Spiral Bound $ 19.95

The Heart & Soul of Being Therapeutic
- E-Book $16.95 (sent by email or download from website)
- Hard Copy, Spiral Bound $ 19.95

Getting Thru to Your Emotions with EFT
- Paperback Book $13.95
- Two-CD Set $24.95
- DVD or Video Part 1: The EFT Techniques: $21.95
- DVD or Video Part 2: The GTT Techniques: $21.95
- DVD or Videos Part 1 and Part 2 together $39.95

Product List (continued)

Getting Thru to Your Soul
- Paperback Book $14.95
- Two-CD Set $24.95
- DVD or Video Part 1: SK & Basic Techniques $21.95
- DVD or Video Part 2: Inner Child & Relationships $21.95
- DVD or Video Part 3: Archetypes & Subpersonalites $21.95
- DVD or Videos Parts 1, 2, 3 together $59.95

Intuitive Techniques for Getting Thru to Your Soul
- Four-CD Set and Workbook $69.95
- Workbook alone, in 3-ring binder $24.95

Awaken to Your True Purpose:
- Five-CD Set & Study Guide $44.95
- Workbook, in 3-ring binder $24.95

Getting Thru to Kids
- Paperback Book $11.95

Holistic Approach to Eating: Booklet $12.95

Holistic Healing Training Manual:
- Manual, in 3-ring binder $75.00

ORDER FORM

ITEM	QUANTITY	COST
_____	_____	_____
_____	_____	_____
_____	_____	_____
_____	_____	_____
_____	_____	_____
_____	_____	_____
_____	_____	_____
_____	_____	_____
_____	_____	_____
_____	_____	_____
_____	_____	_____
	Subtotal	_____

Free US Domestic Shipping on orders of $50 or more.
US Shipping $4.00 first item, $.75 each extra item   _____
For shipping out of the U.S., add $9 for the first product,
$6 each additional product, except $5 for the first product
and $2 for each additional product to Canada and Mexico. _____

California residents please add 7.25% for sales tax   _____

AMOUNT ENCLOSED   _____

Quantity Discounts are available on bulk purchases of this book for educational training purposes, resale, fund raising, or gift giving. For information contact the publisher.

Order Form (continued)

<u>Free</u> Email Newsletter: *Soul News* (or subscribe at
www.gettingthru.org).
E-mail address: _____

Ship to:

Name: _____

Company: _____

Address: _____

City: _____ State: _____

Zip: _____ Phone:(_____)_____

Email: _____

Payment:

___ Check   ___ Money Order

Credit Card: ___ Visa   ___ Mastercard

Card Number: _____

Name on Card: _____

Expiration Date: _____/_____

Mail To: Holistic Communications
       P.O. 279, Arroyo Grande, CA 93421, USA

Toll-Free 24 Hour Order Line: (866) 304-4325
Fax: 805-929-1594

For more information, visit our Web site: www.gettingthru.org

Money Back Guarantee!